| 중등교원 임용고시 시험대비 |

최시원
전공영어

영어교육학

영어교육학 최고의 선택
명/쾌/한 설명으로 영어교육학이 쉬워진다!

Practical

CONTENTS

Chapter 01   Approaches to Language Acquisition   8

     (A) Three Approaches: Behaviorist / Nativist / Interactionist   8
     (B) Other views   14

Chapter 02   Models of Second Language Acquisition   19

     (A) An Innatist Model: Krashen's Five Hypotheses   19
     (B) Cognitivist Models: Attention-Processing Model, Implicit & Explicit Processing, Noticing Hypothesis, and others   20
     (C) Social Constructivist Models: Long's & Swain's Hypotheses   23

Chapter 03   Language Analyses   36

     (A) Contrastive Analysis   36
     (B) Interlanguage   37
     (C) Stages of Learner Language Development   41
     (D) Error Analysis   44
     (E) Communicative Competence   55
     (F) Discourse Analysis   57
     (G) Conversation Analysis   70
     (H) Types of Nonverbal Communication   82
     (I) Genre Analysis   82

Chapter 04   Learner Variables   86

     (A) Age & Critical Period Hypothesis   86
     (B) Cognitive factors & Learning Styles   87
     (C) Affective factors   91
     (D) Socio-cultural factors   92
     (E) Techniques in teaching culture   92
     (F) World Englishes   94
     (G) Autonomy   99

(H) Strategies ... 100

(I) Strategies-based Instruction ... 112

Chapter 05 Teaching Methodologies ... 116

(A) Traditional Approaches ... 116

(B) Innovative Approaches ... 119

(C) Communicative Approaches ... 120

(D) Roles of the Interactive Teacher ... 148

Chapter 06 Syllabus Design and Material Development ... 150

(A) Curriculum components ... 150

(B) Classification of Syllabus ... 150

(C) Types of Syllabus ... 151

(D) Material Development ... 157

Chapter 07 Teaching Listening ... 162

(A) Types of Spoken Language (L/S) ... 162

(B) Bottom-up vs. Top-down Processing (L/R) ... 163

(C) Features of Authentic Materials in Listening ... 165

(D) Types of Listening Performance ... 167

(E) PWP (Process Listening) ... 168

(F) Listening Exercises ... 176

(G) Listening Techniques and Tasks ... 181

(H) Assessing Listening Comprehension - Dictation ... 183

Chapter 08 Teaching Speaking ... 186

(A) Accuracy vs. Fluency issues & Complexity ... 186

(B) Types of Speaking Performance ... 186

(C) Speaking Techniques and Tasks ... 186

(D) Assessing speaking ... 189

Chapter 09   Teaching Reading   192

(A) Bottom-up vs. Top-down process & Interactive process
(interactive-compensatory model)   192

(B) Schema Theory   197

(C) Comprehension Level: Types of Questions   197

(D) Authenticity vs. Readability issues in choosing texts   204

(E) PWP   206

(F) Reading Techniques and Tasks   206

(G) Assessing reading comprehension−Cloze tests   211

Chapter 10   Teaching Writing   214

(A) Product- vs. Process-oriented Writing   214

(B) Process Writing (Writing Techniques and Tasks)   219

(C) Responding & Correcting   227

(D) Types of writing performance   228

(E) Assessing writing - Portfolios   229

Chapter 11   Teaching Grammar   232

(A) Approaches to Teaching Grammar & FFI   232

(B) Deductive vs. Inductive teaching   238

(C) Techniques and tasks in teaching grammar   243

Chapter 12   Teaching Vocabulary   258

(A) Incidental vs. Intentional learning   258

(B) Corpora   262

(C) Lexis   262

(D) Techniques and Tasks in teaching vocabulary   265

Chapter 13　Teaching Pronunciation　　268

(A) Segments & Suprasegmentals　　268

(B) Teachability issues in pronunciation　　268

(C) Intelligibility issues in pronunciation　　268

(D) Techniques and tasks in teaching pronunciation　　269

Chapter 14　Technology in Language Learning and Teaching　　272

(A) CALL & MALL　　272

(B) CMC (= Computer-mediated Communication)　　275

(C) Types of CALL Activities　　275

(D) Corpora and Concordancers　　275

(E) Computer Adaptive Testing　　277

Chapter 15　Language Assessment　　280

(A) Principles of Language Tests　　280

(B) Types of Testing: in terms of Purposes　　288

(C) Types of Test items　　288

(D) Multiple-choice Tests　　290

(E) Integrative Testing　　293

(F) Alternative Assessments　　295

(G) Holistic vs. Analytic Scoring　　297

최시원 **전공영어 영어교육학 PRACTICAL**

Chapter 01~02 Mind Map

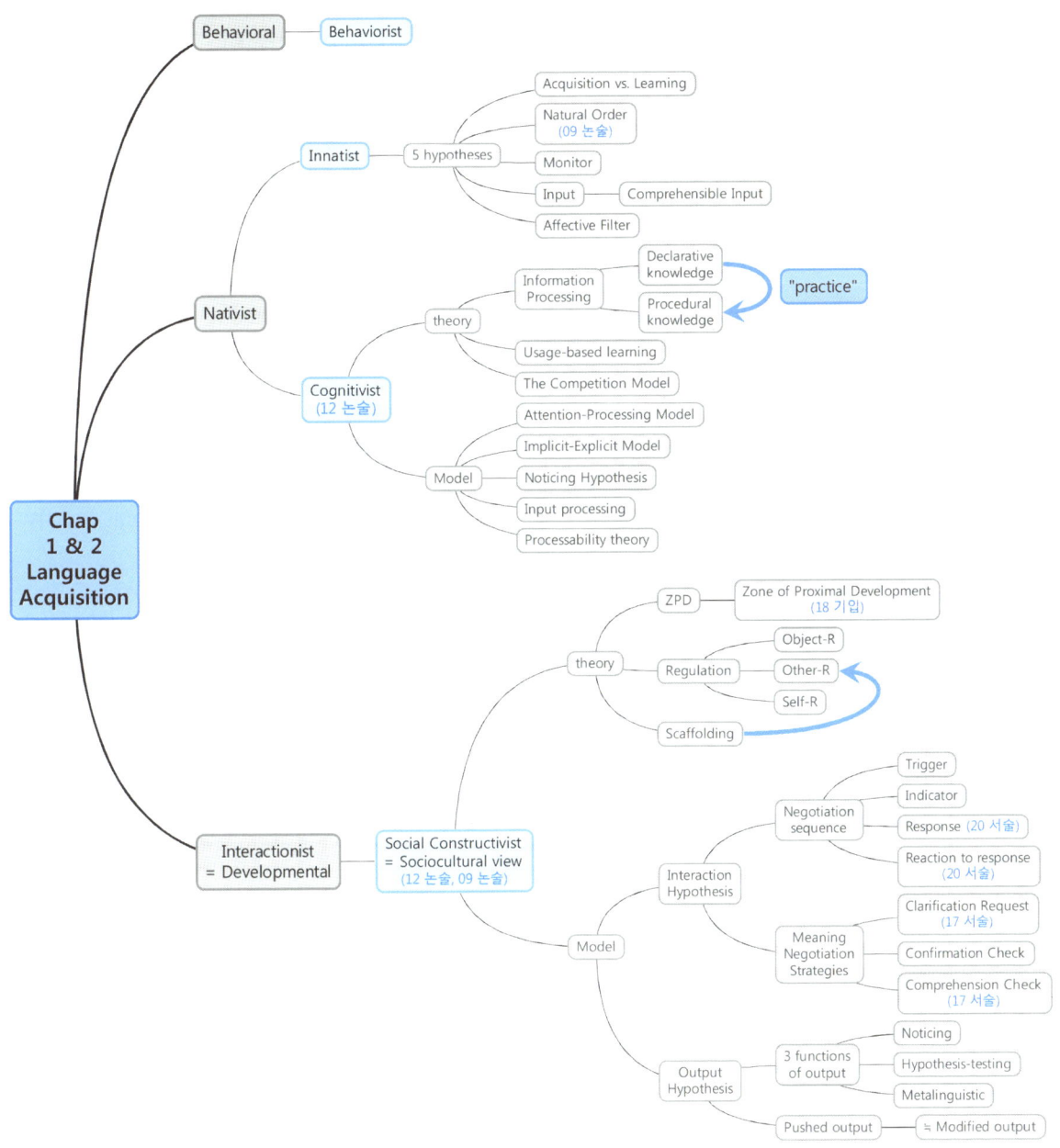

Chapter 01 Approaches to Language Acquisition

(A) Three Approaches: Behaviorist / Nativist / Interactionist

L1 Approach	Behaviorist	Nativist		Interactionist
Psychology	Behaviorism	Cognitivism		Constructivism
Linguistics	Structural	Transformational-generative		
SLA Model	Behaviorist	Innatist	Cognitivist	Social Constructivist
Language Analysis	Contrastive Analysis	Error Analysis		Discourse Analysis, Conversation Analysis
Methodology	ALM	NA / TPR	CLT / TBLT	

There have been at least three theories of language learning that are relevant to the teaching of speaking: behaviourist, cognitivist, and sociocultural theory, and we shall briefly review each in turn.

According to behaviourism, language learning is essentially the formation of good language 'habits' through repeated reinforcement. In its popularized form, audiolingualism, the three stages of learning were called **presentation**, **practice**, and **production** (PPP). The three-step PPP process was aimed at developing automatic habits largely through classroom processes of modelling, repetition, and controlled practice. PPP was applied originally to the teaching of grammar, but, by extension it has been used to structure the teaching of language skills as well, including speaking. A typical teaching sequence might involve listening to, and imitating, a tape dialogue, followed by repetition of features of the dialogue, and then performance of the dialogue in class.

A cognitivist account of language learning rejects the behaviourist view of the learners as empty vessels waiting to be filled, and instead credits them with an information processing capacity, analogous to computers. According to this view, the learning of a complex skill, like speaking, is seen as a movement from controlled to automatic processing. Initially, conscious attention (or awareness-raising) is applied to the learning of the individual stages (or rules) of a procedure that, through repeated activation, are chunked into a single manageable 'program'. This is integrated into existing knowledge, a stage which will involve some restructuring of the user's linguistic system, and is then readily available for use, with minimal attentional control on the part of the user. This is the stage known as **autonomy**.

In teaching terms, cognitivist theory replaced the PPP model with one that progresses from **awareness-raising**, through **proceduralization**, to **autonomy**. In fact, it is only the first stage that is significantly different, in terms of classroom practice. Awareness-raising implies an *explicit* focus on the rules of the system, whereas strict audiolingual practice insisted on simply imitating models without any explicit attention being given to the rules that generated them.

The cognitivist model prioritizes mental functions over social ones. Sociocultural theory, on the other hand, situates the learning process firmly in its social context. According to this view, all learning — including the learning of a first and a second language — is mediated through social and cultural activity. To achieve autonomy in a skill, the learner first needs to experience **other-regulation**, that is, the mediation of a 'better other', whether parent, peer, or teacher. This typically takes the form of assisted performance, whereby the teacher interacts with the learner to provide a supportive framework (or **scaffold**) within which the learners can extend their present competence. Through this shared activity, new knowledge is jointly constructed until the learners are in a position to appropriate it — i.e. to make it their own — at which stage the scaffolding can be gradually dismantled. Learners are now able to function independently in a stage of **self-regulation**. A good example of this is the way an older child will teach a younger one the rules of a game, by both talking and walking it through, until the younger one has got the hang of it.

Learning, according to the sociocultural view, is fundamentally a social phenomenon, requiring both activity and interactivity. In classroom terms, it takes place in cycles of assisted performance, in which learning is collaborative, co-constructed, and scaffolded. For example, learners may set about solving a problem in small groups, during which the teacher intervenes when necessary to provide suggestions or even to model the targeted behavior.

All three theories have elements in common, especially when these are translated into classroom procedures. The following table attempts to display the relation between different elements of each model:

Behaviorist theory	Cognitivist theory	Sociocultural theory
presentation, modelling	awareness-raising	other-regulation
practice	proceduralization, restructuring	appropriation
production	automaticity, autonomy	self-regulation

These surface similarities, however, shouldn't be allowed to disguise the fact that each theory reflects a very different conception of the mind. The behaviourist mind is simply a brain, pushed, pulled, and moulded by forces beyond its control. The cognitivist mind is a computerized black box, busily processing input into output. The sociocultural mind is a network, a joint construct of the discourse community through which it is distributed. Each metaphor for the mind clearly has different implications in terms of learning, and of language learning in particular. Nevertheless, each theory incorporates a stage which roughly equates with awareness, whereby the learner encounters something new. And each theory attempts to explain how this knowledge is integrated, or appropriated, into the learner's existing systems. And finally, each theory accepts that at least some of this new knowledge becomes available for use: it is automated and the learner is autonomous.

‹Constructivist Psychology›

A language-based theory of learning is fundamental to a sociocultural view of learning, as first propounded by Vygotsky (1978), a view that focuses primarily on the social and cultural processes that contribute to the development of higher order cognitive functions. Sociocultural theory rejects both a behaviourist view of learning, i.e. that behaviours are externally modelled and 'conditioned', and an information-processing view, which argues that the mind is a limited-capacity input processing system. Rather, according to the sociocultural view, knowledge — including knowledge of language — arises from activities in particular contexts of use, and learning is essentially a social, rather than an individual, process. The child (or learner) achieves the capacity to function autonomously in a skill by first sharing responsibility for the achievement of tasks with a more competent adult or peer — a process of joint problem-solving, or *other-regulation*. Gradually the child-learner appropriates the regulatory means to perform the task him- or herself, and is able to function independently and without mediation — achieving what is called *self-regulation*.

Mediation by a more competent 'other' is optimal when it takes place in what Vygotsky called 'the zone of proximal development' (ZPD), that is 'the distance between the actual developmental level as determined by independent problem solving and the level of potential development as determined through problem solving under adult guidance or in collaboration with more capable peers'. The notion of 'assisted performance' as a prerequisite for unassisted performance is fundamental to a sociocultural view of learning. Verbal scaffolding is one of the ways in which such assistance is provided and by means of which cognitive structures are inferred. As the structures become internalized, the scaffolds are gradually removed.

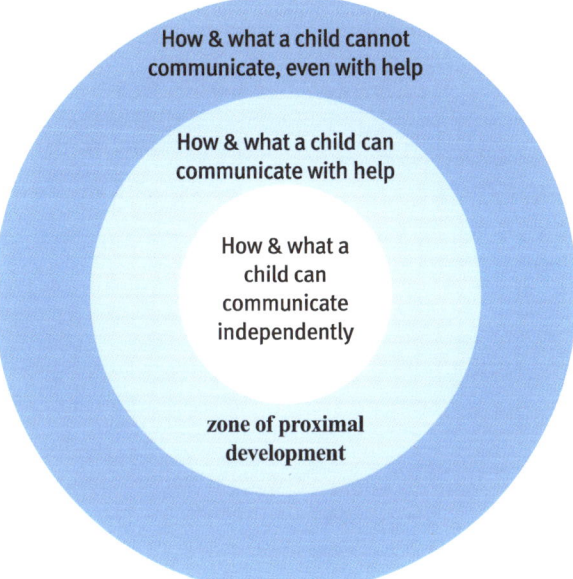

‹Scaffolding›

Scaffolding refers to the way a competent language speaker helps a less competent one to communicate by both encouraging and providing possible elements of the conversation. It is the way a primary-school teacher might help a young child to communicate, or the way a chat-show host might draw out a guest. The listener offers support — like scaffolding round a building — to help the speaker create his own spoken structure.

Scaffolding in class isn't a normal conversation in the sense that the teacher/listener is not aiming to contribute any personal stories or opinions of her own; the aim of her own speaking is solely to help the speaker tell his story.

Here are some notes on techniques that might be appropriate:

> **Scaffolding techniques**
>
> - Showing interest and agreeing: nodding, 'uh-huh', eye contact, 'yes', etc;
> - Concisely asking for clarification of unclear information, eg repeating an unclear word;
> - Encouragement echo: repeating the last word (perhaps with questioning intonation) in order to encourage the speaker to continue;
> - Echoing meaning: picking on a key element of meaning and saying it back to the speaker, eg 'a foreign holiday';
> - Asking conversation-oiling questions (ones that mainly recap already stated information) eg *Is it? Do you? Where was it?* etc;
> - Asking brief questions (or using sentence heads) that encourage the speaker to extend the story, eg *And then ··· He went ··· She wanted ···* etc;
> - Unobtrusively saying the correct form of an incorrect word (but only if having the correct word makes a significant positive contribution to the communication);
> - Giving the correct pronunciation of words in replies without drawing any particular attention to it;
> - Unobtrusively giving a word or phrase that the speaker is looking for.

> **Identifying scaffolding techniques**
>
> Which scaffolding techniques can you identify in this short transcript of a lesson at Elementary level, where a learner wants to tell his teacher about a TV story he saw concerning the rather unlikely sport of 'extreme ironing'?
>
> Student: It is like sport ···
> Teacher: Uh-huh.
> Student: ··· but is with 'eye ron'.
> Teacher: With an iron?
> Student: Yes, is 'eye ron' sport. They ··· er ···
> Teacher: What do they do?
> Student: Er, yes. It is like sport ex ··· ex ···
> Teacher: An extreme sport?
> Student: Yes. They use 'eye rons' in extreme place.
> Teacher: Ha — irons in extreme places? Where?
> Student: Ah, like onto a mountain.
> Teacher: On a mountain!
> Student: Yes (laughs), on a mountain or river.
> Teacher: What do they do?
> Student: They iron and in tree on top.
> Teacher: At the top of trees?
> Student: Yes.

‹Competence vs. Performance & Comprehension vs. Production in L1 acquisition›

For centuries scientists and philosophers have drawn a basic distinction between competence and performance. In reference to language, competence is one's underlying knowledge of the system of a language — its rules of grammar, vocabulary, all the 'pieces' of a language, and how those pieces fit together. Performance is actual production (speaking, writing) or the comprehension (listening, reading) of linguistic events. Chomsky (1965) likened competence to an 'idealized' speaker-hearer who does not display such performance variables as memory limitations, distractions, shifts of attention and interest, errors, and hesitation phenomena (e.g. repeats, false starts, pauses, omissions).

Look at this typical child-adult exchange:

> Three-year-old Lisa: My name is Litha.
> Adult: Litha?
> Lisa: No, Litha.
> Adult: Oh, Lisa.
> Lisa: Yeah, Litha.

Lisa clearly perceives the contrast between English *s* and *th*, even though she cannot produce the contrast herself, a common characteristic of L1 acquisition. Of course, we know that even adults understand more vocabulary and grammatical structure than they produce in speech and writing. How are we to explain this difference, this apparent 'lag' between comprehension and production?

First. let's dispel a myth. **Comprehension** (listening, reading) must not be equated with competence, nor should **production** (speaking, writing) be thought of only as performance. Human beings have the ***competence*** (the internal unobservable mental and physical 'wiring') both to understand and to produce language. We also ***perform*** acts of listening and reading just as surely as we perform acts of speaking and writing.

Second, we can generally concede that for child language, most research evidence points to the superiority of comprehension over production. Children seem to understand 'more' than they actually produce. For instance, a four-year-old child may understand a sentence with a relative clause, such as "Give me the ball that's red," but not be able to produce it word for word, "Okay, Daddy, red ball" (Brown 1970).

(B) Other views

(B1) Information Processing

Declarative knowledge	'knowing that'	Declarative → Procedural
Procedural knowledge	'know how'	through 'practice' (to fluency)

(B1a) Information processing: automaticity, restructuring, & U-shaped learning

McLaughlin (1990) noted two concepts that are fundamental in second language learning and use: automaticity and restructuring. **Automaticity** refers to control over one's linguistic knowledge. In language performance, one must bring together a number of skills from perceptual, cognitive, and social domains. The more each of these skills is routinized, the greater the ease with which they can be put to use. **Restructuring** refers to the changes made to internalized representations as a result of new learning. Changes that reflect restructuring are discontinuous or qualitatively different from a previous stage. Learning means the inclusion of additional information which must be organized and structured. Integrating new information into one's developing second language system necessitates changes to parts of the existing system, thereby restructuring, or reorganizing, the current system and creating a (slightly) new second language system. Mere addition of new elements does not constitute restructuring.

An underlying assumption in looking at SLA from the perspective of these two concepts is that human beings have a limited capacity for processing. Central to the ability to process information is the ability to attend to, deal with, and organize new information. Because of the limited capacity that humans have available for processing, the more that can be handled routinely — that is, automatically — the more attentional resources are available for new information. Processing resources are limited and must be distributed economically if communication is to be efficient.

(1) Automaticity

There are a number of ways that automaticity can be conceptualized, but the most central of these is that there is fast, unconscious, and effortless processing. When there has been a consistent and regular association between a certain kind of input and some output pattern, automatization may result; that is, an associative connection is activated. This can be seen in the relative automaticity of the following exchange between two people walking down the hall toward each other:

> Speaker 1: Hi.
> Speaker 2: Hi, how are you?
> Speaker 1: Fine, and you?
> Speaker 2: Fine.

The conversational routine is so automatic in a language one knows well that most people have had the experience of responding *fine* before the question is even asked and of responding *fine* when it turns out that a different question is being asked, as in the following conversation:

> Speaker 1: Hi, Sue.
> Speaker 2: Good morning, Julie.
> Speaker 1: Fine, and you?

(2) Restructuring

The second concept of import within the framework of information processing is that of **restructuring**, which takes place when qualitative changes occur in a learner's internal representation of the second language or in the change in the use of procedures — generally from inefficient to efficient. In terms of child language acquisition, McLaughlin described restructuring in the following way: "Restructuring is characterized by discontinuous, or qualitative change as the child moves from stage to stage in development. Each new stage constitutes a new internal organization and not merely the addition of new structural elements" (1990). The following table presents data from R. Ellis (1985) to illustrate this.

<Evidence of restructuring>

Time 1	Time 2	Time 3	Time 4
I am no go.	I am no go.	I am no go.	I am no go.
No look.	No look.	Don't look.	Don't go.
I am no run.	I am don't run.	I am don't run.	I am no run.
No run.	Don't run.	Don't run.	Don't run.

At Time 1 only one form, *no*, is used. At Time 2, a new form, *don't*, has entered this learner's system. Now *no* and *don't* are being used in apparent free variation in both indicative and imperative forms. By Time 3, this learner has created a system in which there are the beginnings of a one-to-one correspondence between form and function. **Don't** is now the only form used for imperatives, whereas for indicatives both forms remain. Thus, restructuring takes place at Time 3, when the learner has begun to sort out the form/function relationship. The learner in this case is reorganizing and reshuffling her L2 knowledge until she has appropriately sorted out form/function relations (if that stage is ever reached).

Lightbown (1985) provides the following rationale for restructuring:

[**Restructuring**] occurs because language is a complex hierarchical system whose components interact in nonlinear ways. Seen in these terms, an increase in error rate in one area may reflect an increase in complexity or accuracy in another, followed by overgeneralization of a newly acquired structure, or simply by a sort of overload of complexity which forces a restructuring, or at least a simplification, in another part of the system.

(3) U-shaped learning

Destabilization, as discussed above, is a consequence of restructuring and often results in what are known as **U-shaped patterns**. U-shaped patterns reflect three stages of linguistic use. In the earliest stage, a learner produces some linguistic form that conforms to target-like norms (i.e., is error-free). At Stage 2, a learner appears to lose what he or she knew at Stage 1. The linguistic behavior at Stage 2 deviates from TL norms. Stage 3 looks just like Stage 1 in that there is again correct TL usage. This is illustrated in the following figure.

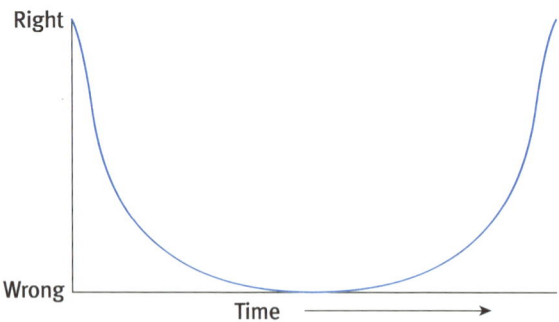

Lightbown (1983) presented data from French learners of English in a classroom context. She examined the use of the *-ing* form in English among sixth, seventh, and eighth grade learners. Sentence (1) was a typical Grade 6 utterance when describing a picture.

(1) He is taking a cake.

By Grade 7, (2) was a typical response to the same picture.

(2) He take a cake.

How can we account for an apparent decrease in knowledge? Lightbown hypothesized that initially these students were presented only with the progressive form. With nothing else in English to compare it to, they equated it with the simple present of French. That is, in the absence of any other verb form, there was no way of determining what the limits were of the present progressive. In fact, with no other comparable verb form in their system, learners overextended the use of the progressive into contexts in which the simple present would have been appropriate. When the simple present was introduced, learners not only had to learn this new form, but they also had to readjust their information about the present progressive, redefining its limits. Evidence of the confusion and subsequent readjustment and restructuring of the progressive was seen in the decline in both use and accuracy. It will take some time before these learners eventually restructure their L2 knowledge appropriately and are able to use both the progressive and the simple present in target-like ways. Thus, given these data, a U-shaped curve results (assuming eventual target-like knowledge), as in the following figure.

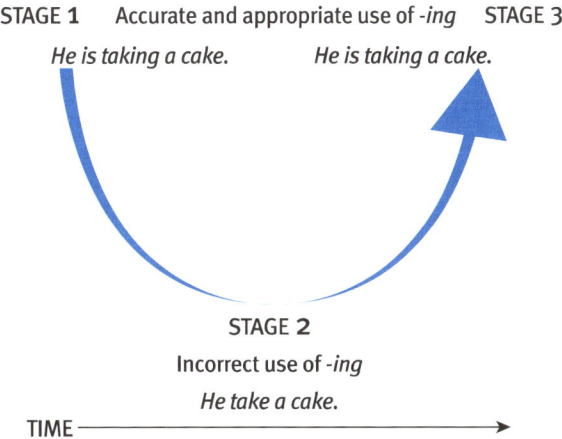

(B2) Usage-based learning (Connectionism)

Usage-based learning	exposure / chunk / frequency

Usage-based approaches hold that we learn linguistic constructions while engaging in communication (Bybee 2010). Psycholinguistic research provides the evidence of usage-based acquisition in its demonstrations that language processing is exquisitely sensitive to usage frequency at all levels of language representation, from phonology, through lexis and syntax, to sentence processing (Ellis, 2002). That language users are sensitive to the input frequencies of these patterns entails that they must have registered their occurrence in processing. These frequency effects are thus compelling evidence for usage-based models of language acquisition that emphasize the role of input.

In explaining language acquisition of a given form, research shows a critical distinction between **type** and **token** frequency. Type refers to the 'class' of linguistic items, while tokens are the individual members of the class. The pragmatic-type 'greetings' can be realized in a number of tokens such as ***hello, what's happening, how's it going***. It has been found that the learning of phonological, morphological, and syntactic rules is a function of type rather than token frequency (Bybee & Hopper 2001). The reason for such a claim is based largely on a psychological principle: The more items that are heard (or read) in a certain linguistic position (type), the less likely it will be that the learner will remember the particular instances (tokens), and the more likely it is that a general category (type) will be internalized (Bybee & Thompson 2000).

(B3) The Competition Model

The Competition Model	exposure

Chapter 02
Models of Second Language Acquisition

(A) An Innatist Model: Krashen's Five Hypotheses

(A1) Acquisition vs. Learning Hypothesis

Krashen claimed that adult second language learners have two means for internalizing the target language.

Acquisition	a subconscious and intuitive process of constructing the system of a language, not unlike the process used by a child to 'pick up' a language
Learning	a conscious process in which learners attend to form, figure out rules, and are generally aware of their own process

Adults should, therefore, do as much acquiring as possible in order to achieve communicative fluency; otherwise, they will get bogged down in rule learning and too much conscious attention to the forms of language and to watching their own process. Moreover, for Krashen, our conscious learning processes and our subconscious acquisition processes are mutually exclusive: learning cannot 'become' acquisition. This claim of 'no interface' between **acquisition** and **learning** is used to strengthen the argument for recommending large doses of acquisition activity in the classroom, with only a very minor role assigned to learning.

(A2) Input Hypothesis

According to Krashen, **comprehensible input** is 'the only true cause of SLA'. The Input Hypothesis claims that an important condition for language acquisition to occur is that the acquirer *understand* (via hearing or reading) input language that contains structure 'a bit beyond' his or her current level of competence. ... If an acquirer is at stage or level i, the input he or she understands should contain $i+1$. In other words, the language that learners are exposed to should be just far enough beyond their current competence that they can understand most of it but still be challenged to make progress.

An important part of the Input Hypothesis is Krashen's recommendation that speaking not be taught directly or very early in the language classroom. Speech will 'emerge' once the acquirer has built up enough comprehensible input ($i+1$).

(A3) Monitor Hypothesis

The '**monitor**' is involved in learning, not in acquisition. It is a device for 'watchdogging' one's output, for editing and making alterations or corrections as they are consciously perceived. Such explicit and intentional learning, according to Krashen, ought to be largely avoided, as it presumed to hinder acquisition. Only once fluency is established should an optimal amount of monitoring, or editing, be employed by the learner.

(A4) Natural Order Hypothesis

Following the earlier morpheme order studies of Dulay and Burt and others, Krashen has claimed that we acquire language rules in a predictable or 'natural' order.

Krashen's morpheme acquisition sequence

Group	Morphemes Included	Example
Group A	Ing / Plural / Is, Are	He sleeping. / Boys, over there. / Maria is happy.
Group B	Auxiliary / Article	I am leaving. / The dog.
Group C	Irregular Past	Chu went home.
Group D	Regular Past / Third-Person Singular / Possessive	The dogs played. / Marcella runs. / Robert's ball.

Krashen's sequence is organized into groups of early- (Group A), mid- (Group B and C), and late-acquired (Group D) morphemes rather than a sequence of individual morphemes. This grouping suggests that learners will acquire all the morphemes in an earlier group before they go on to acquire morphemes in the next group. In addition, learners may acquire the morphemes either one by one or a few at a time.

(A5) Affective Filter Hypothesis

Krashen has further claimed that the best acquisition will occur in environments where anxiety is low and defensiveness absent, or, in Krashen's terms, in contexts where the '**affective filter**' is low.

(B) Cognitivist Models: Attention-Processing Model, Implicit & Explicit Processing, Noticing Hypothesis, and others

(B1) Attention-Processing Model

Focal ⇔ Peripheral	Attention	Processing	Controlled ⇔ Automatic
controlled·focal → controlled·peripheral / automatic·focal → automatic·peripheral			

Processes	Examples of grammar teaching
1. Controlled / Focal	Explaining a specific grammar point / Giving an example of a word usage / Learning prefabricated routines / Repeating after the teacher
2. Controlled / Peripheral	Giving simple greetings / Playing a simple language game / Using memorized routines in new situations / Completing very limited conversations
3. Automatic / Focal	Monitoring output / Giving brief attention to form during conversation / Scanning for specific keywords / Editing writing, including peer editing
4. Automatic / Peripheral	Participating in open-ended group work / Skimming and rapid reading / Freewriting / Engaging in natural unrehearsed conversation

(B2) Implicit and Explicit Model

Explicit knowledge	facts that a learner knows *about* language
Implicit knowledge	information that is automatically and spontaneously used in language tasks

The distinction between implicit and explicit knowledge is not controversial. What is disputed, however, is the relationship between them. According to Bialystok (1991), children begin by acquiring implicit knowledge and then 'analyze' it, thus making it explicit. Implicit knowledge, then, serves as a basis for the development of explicit knowledge. Such a model may also be applicable in some L2 learning situations, for example, when learners begin by picking up an L2 through natural exposure but it is less relevant to classroom situations where the teaching of explicit knowledge is emphasized. The question here is whether explicit knowledge can convert into implicit knowledge. Very different positions have been espoused on this point. Krashen (1981), Zobl (1995), and Hulstijn (2002) adopt a **non-interface** position, i.e. explicit knowledge does not convert into implicit knowledge, Sharwood Smith (1981) and DeKeyser (1998) argue for a strong **interface** position and Rod Ellis (1994) proposed a **weak-interface** position, according to which explicit knowledge facilitates the development of implicit knowledge rather than changes into it. According to this view, explicit knowledge serves to prime attention to form in the input and thereby to activate the process involved in the acquisition of implicit knowledge.

(B3) Noticing Hypothesis

Noticing Hypothesis	noticing the target feature & noticing the gap

(B3a) Awareness-raising

Attention	being on the alert
Noticing	the conscious registering
Understanding	the recognition of general rule

The concept of 'awareness' comes from cognitivist learning theory, which argues that, as a prerequisite for the restructuring of the learner's mental representation of the language, some degree of conscious awareness is necessary. Awareness involves at least three processes: attention, noticing, and understanding.

- **Attention**: Learners need to be paying attention, i.e. they need to be on the alert — interested, involved, and curious — if they are going to notice features of the target skill.

- **Noticing**: This is more than simply paying attention. While someone is driving, they can be paying attention without noticing a great deal until a kangaroo suddenly bounds onto the road. Noticing, then, is the conscious registering of the occurrence of some event or entity. Noticing is more likely if the event or entity is somehow surprising (like the kangaroo) or if it is salient because of its frequency, size, significance, or usefulness, among others. We also notice things if they have been previously pointed out to us. Many learners, having recently been taught a new word, will be familiar with the experience of noticing it everywhere.

  It's also possible to notice the absence of something. For example, a learner might notice a 'hole' in their language proficiency as the result of being incapable of expressing a particular idea. They can notice the difference between their own, novice, performance and the performance of an expert. This is called noticing the gap.

- **Understanding**: Finally, there is no real awareness without understanding. Understanding means the recognition of general rule or principle or pattern. This is more likely if there are several instances of the item that is being targeted for learning, so that the pattern or rule can be more easily perceived.

(B4) Input processing

Input processing	comprehension practice > production practice

(B5) Processability theory

developmental features	learned along a predictable path, when developmentally ready
variational features	learned at different developmental stages, at anytime

(C) Social Constructivist Models: Long's & Swain's Hypotheses

(C1) Long's Interaction Hypothesis

The Interaction Hypothesis proposed that comprehensible input that arises when the less competent speaker provides feedback on his/her lack of comprehension assists acquisition. Pica (1992, 1994) proposes that opportunities to negotiate meaning assist language learners in three principal ways. First, as Long and others have claimed, they help learners to obtain comprehensible input. There is considerable empirical support for the claim that negotiation facilitates comprehension. Pica suggests that one way in which this takes place is when the conversational modifications that arise through negotiation break down or segment the input into units that learners can process more easily. In this way, learners are able to attend to L2 form, a view endorsed by Schmidt (2001) in his account of the role that attention plays in L2 acquisition. Second, Pica suggests that negotiation provides learners with feedback on their own use of the L2. When more competent interlocutors respond to less competent speakers they frequently attempt to reformulate what they think they meant in ways that provide very specific feedback on a problem item. For example, in this exchange from Pica (1994) the L2 learner receive feedback on how to pronounce 'closed', something that was obviously problematic to her:

```
NNS:   the windows are crozed
NS:    the windows have what?
NNS:   closed
NS:    crossed? I'm not sure what you're saying there.
NNS:   windows are closed
NS:    oh the windows are closed oh OK sorry.
```

Finally, Pica argues that negotiation prompts learners to adjust, manipulate, and modify their own output. In this respect, exchanges where the more competent speaker requests clarification of the less competent speaker seem to work best. Learners are pushed into producing output that is more comprehensible and therefore more target-like. Thus, in the example above, the learner is pushed into improving her pronunciation of 'closed'. Swain (1985, 1995) has claimed that such output contributes to language acquisition.

The Interaction Hypothesis, then, suggests a number of ways in which interaction can contribute to language acquisition. In general terms, it posits that the more opportunities for negotiation there are, the more likely acquisition is. More specifically, it suggests: (1) that when interactional modifications lead to comprehensible input via the decomposition and segmenting of input acquisition is facilitated; (2) that when learners receive feedback, acquisition is facilitated; and (3) that when learners are pushed to reformulate their own utterances, acquisition is promoted. These claims provide a basis for investigating tasks. Tasks that stimulate negotiation and through this provide comprehensible input and feedback and push learners to reformulate are the ones that will work best for acquisition. The relevant properties of tasks, then, are those that have these psycholinguistic outcomes.

However, there is a problem. Whereas it is fairly easy to see how interaction can show learners how utterances are segmented into parts thus facilitating the acquisition of syntax, it is less clear how it can contribute to the acquisition of morphological features, particularly when these are redundant. Consider the following exchange:

```
NNS:   I go cinema.
NS:    Uh?
NNS:   I go cinema last night.
NS:    Oh, last night.
```

Here the NNS is pushed into clarifying her initial utterance, which is not marked for time. She responds by adding a lexical marker of past time reference ('last night') and the conversation proceeds. Thus, successful communication takes place without the learner needing to modify her output by incorporating the past tense marker. This example demonstrates the need to distinguish between pushed and modified output, showing that not all pushed output is in fact modified.

Despite some problems like this, the Interaction Hypothesis has assumed a central place in SLA research and has much to offer task-based research. It offers a theoretical basis and a set of clearly defined discourse categories for analyzing the interactions that arise in the performance of a task. While it may be dangerous to evaluate tasks solely in terms of the quantity of meaning negotiation they give rise to, there are solid ground for believing that tasks that afford opportunities for this kind of discourse work will contribute to the acquisition of at least some aspects of language.

(C1a) Negotiation of Meaning

Clarification Request	by Listener	Pardon?
Confirmation Check	by Listener	[repetition] ↗
Comprehension Check	by Speaker	[tag question] ~ right?

Negotiation of meaning is defined as the instances in which interlocutors in a conversation face a problem in understanding and they engage in a reciprocal work to solve the comprehension problem or to stop the flow of the conversation to check whether their interlocutor is following the flow of the conversation through interactional modification including comprehension checks, clarification requests, confirmation checks and recast.

Varonis and Gass (1985) outline the structure of negotiation sequence in terms of the following categories:

1. Trigger (i.e., the utterance that causes the communication problem)
2. Indicator (i.e., the utterance that demonstrates a communicative problem has occurred)
3. Response (i.e., the utterance that attempts to address the communication problem identified in the indicator)
4. Reaction (i.e., the utterance that indicates a speaker's uptake to the response).

To deal with this kind of sequence, Varonis and Gass (1985) point out that reaction is an optional element in negotiation sequence. It means that the speaker's response can stimulate a further trigger and as a result, it is possible for one negotiation sequence to consist of several negotiation exchanges (Ellis & Barkhuizen 2005).

Researchers have tended to focus on a fairly narrow set of strategies used in these sequencing, using counts of these as measures of the extent to which different tasks promote negotiation. Four strategies have been investigated using the data from the present research.

(1) Comprehension checks

They refer to any expressions designed to establish whether what the interlocutor meant has been understood correctly by the addressee.

> A: He has curly hairs.
> B: No. He has soft hair I mean not curly. OK?
> A: OK. In mine is curly.
> B: So, that is one of the differences.
> A: Yes, let's check it.

(2) Clarification requests

They refer to any expressions designed to elicit more information for clarification of the previous utterance. They are mainly formed by yes-no questions and uninvited tag questions.

> A: When you speak do you translate from your mother language to English? → (Trigger)
> B: I didn't get the point. → (Indicator)
> A: You know we have different cultures. We translate sentences in our language and when we want to speak we translate to English. → (Response to the trigger)
> B: Yes, I know it but sometime we need in some situations. → (Reaction)
> A: But most of the students do. If they speak English every day, they can solve the problem.

(3) Confirmation checks

They refer to any expressions designed to confirm whether they understood the previous utterance correctly.

> A: I am sorry there isn't any discount just the yellow one has. → (Trigger)
> B: So, there is any discount yes? → (Indicator)
> A: Yes, only the yellow one. → (Response to the trigger)
> B: OK. → (Reaction)

(4) Recast

It refers to any utterances that are rephrased by changing some parts while the focus is still on the meaning.

> A: Did she wear glass? → (Trigger)
> B: Glasses. → (Indicator)
> A: Yes, glasses. → (Response to the trigger)

Recasts resemble confirmation checks but, as Oliver (2000) has pointed out, they are not identical. Some recasts do not perform the function of confirmation checks (as when one speaker corrects another speaker even though no communication problem has arisen). Also, not all confirmation checks take the form of recasts (as when one speaker paraphrases rather than reformulates what another speaker has said).

(C1b) Negotiation of Form

Lyster & Ranta (1997) identified four interactional moves that teachers use to push learners to improve the accuracy of their nontarget output.

- Clarification request: the teacher indicates to the student, by using phrases such as *"Pardon me"* and *"I don't understand"*, that the message has not been understood or that the utterance is ill-formed in some way, and that a repetition or a reformulation is required.

- Repetition: the teacher repeats the student's erroneous utterance, adjusting the intonation to highlight the error.

- Metalinguistic clues: the teacher provides comments, information, or questions related to the well-formedness of the student's utterance, without explicitly providing the correct form (e.g., *"Do we say, 'goed' in English?"*, *"Is it masculine?"*).

- Elicitation: the teacher directly elicits correct forms from students by asking questions such as *"Comment ça s'appelle?"* or *"How do we say that in French?"*; or by pausing to allow students to complete the teacher's utterance or by asking students to reformulate their utterance (e.g., *"Try again!"*).

Lyster & Ranta (1997) qualified these moves as **negotiation of form**, for two reasons. First, unlike other types of corrective feedback (i.e., recasts and explicit correction), these moves return the floor to students along with cues to draw on their own resources, thus allowing for negotiation to occur bilaterally. Second, in contrast to the conversational function of the negotiation of meaning, the four moves comprising the negotiation of form serve a pedagogical function that draws attention to form and aims for accuracy in addition to mutual comprehension (Lyster 1994). Above all, what distinguishes all four moves from other feedback moves is the way in which they serve as prompts for students to self-repair. That is, these moves do not provide learners with correct rephrasings and instead push learners to retrieve the correct forms from what they already know.

Slimani (1992) gives several examples that were claimed as being noticed. Among these were items that had arisen incidentally during classroom interaction, and some of these resulted from the negotiation of form, as in the following example:

> T: OK. Did you like it?
> L: Yes, yes, I like it.
> T: Yes, I …?
> L: Yes, I liked it.
> T: Yes, I liked it

The teacher simply uses an elicitation move ("Yes, I …?") to elicit the target form, "I liked it." Thus, learners tended to notice forms that they were pushed to self-repair more than forms that were implicitly provided by teachers. Negotiation of form includes not only corrective feedback moves following students' nontarget output, but also moves that provide or elicit information about other relevant form-function relationships in the second language during teacher-student interaction.

(C1c) Positive evidence and Negative evidence in Interaction Hypothesis

The new version of the Interaction Hypothesis affords a much richer view of how negotiation can assist language learning. As in the early version, negotiation is seen as enabling learners to obtain comprehensible input, thereby supplying them with <u>positive evidence</u> (i.e. 'models of what is grammatical and acceptable' — Long 1996). The exchange in (1) illustrates this; student 2 receives a model of the past tense form, 'retired'.

> (1) Student 1: And what is your mmm father's job?
> Student 2: My father is now retire.
> Student 1: Retired?
> Student 2: Yes.
> Student 1: Oh, yes.

Pica's detailed analyses of negotiation sequences (Pica 1992, 1996) have shown how negotiation can give salience to both form-function relationships and also how it helps learners to segment message data into linguistic units. In (2), for example, the native speaker's modification helps the learner to segment a constituent ('above') in the input. Such external segmentation processes can be expected to assist 'noticing' because they help learners to analyze chunks of input into their parts.

> (2) NS: with a small pat of butter on it and above the plate
> NNS: hm hmm what is buvdaplate?
> NS: above
> NNS: above the plate
> NS: yeah

The later version of the IH also posits two other ways in which interaction can contribute to acquisition; through the provision of negative evidence and through opportunities for modified output. Long (1996) defines **negative evidence** as input that provides 'direct or indirect evidence of what is grammatical'. It arises when learners receive feedback on their own attempts to use the L2. One of the major ways in which this takes place is through 'recasts' (i.e. utterances that rephrase a learner's utterance 'by changing one or more sentence components (subject, verb or object) while still referring to its central meanings' (Long). (3) provides an example. Here the learner produces an erroneous utterance ("I don't have a telephones picture.") which the native speaker immediately recasts by modifying the direct object to 'a picture of a telephone'.

> (3) NS: and right next to her a phone rings?
> NNS: forring?
> NS: a phone? Telephone? Is there a telephone next to her?
> NNS: yeah … I don't have a telephones picture.
> NS: you don't have a picture of a telephone?

Research based on the later version of the IH has also focused on the **modified output** that learners produce as a result of meaning negotiation and recasts. Long and Pica have both argued that modified output contributes significantly to acquisition. Long (1996) sees spoken production as 'useful … because it elicits negative input and encourages analysis and grammaticization'; it is 'facilitative, but not necessary'. Pica (1996) argues that modified output helps learners to analyze and break a message into its constituent parts and also to produce forms that may lie at the cutting edge of their linguistic ability.

(C2) Swain's Output Hypothesis

Noticing function	be aware of the gap
Hypothesis-testing function	modify by feedback
Metalinguistic function	learn by internalization

Input alone is not sufficient for acquisition, because when one hears language one can often interpret the meaning without the use of syntax. For example, if one hears only the words **dog, bit, girl**, regardless of the order in which those words occur, it is likely that the meaning **The dog bit the girl** is the one that will be assumed rather than the more unusual **The girl bit the dog**. Similarly, if one hears a sentence such as **This is bad story**, one can easily fill in the missing article. Little knowledge, other than knowing the meanings of the words and knowing something about real-world events, is needed.

This is not the case with language production or output, because one is forced to put the words into some order. Production then 'may force the learner to move from semantic processing to syntactic processing' (Swain 1985). Swain studied children learning French in an immersion context, suggesting that what was lacking in their development as native-like speakers of French was the opportunity to use language productively as opposed to using language merely for comprehension. The lack of proficiency on the part of the immersion children, coupled with their apparent lack of productive use of French, led Swain to suggest the crucial role for output in the development of a second language.

Izumi, Bigelow, Fujiwara, and Fearnow (1999) specifically investigated the noticing function of output, finding partial support for this hypothesis and pointing out the need to balance cognitive and linguistic demands. In particular, participants were exposed to written input and had to underline words that they felt would be essential to their subsequent reproduction of the same passage. The experimental group was then given a production task, whereas the control group was not. This was followed by a second exposure (again with underlining) and a second reproduction by the experimental group. Participants noticed the targeted feature (past hypothetical conditional, such as **If Kevin got up early in the morning, he would eat breakfast**) and incorporated the feature into their output, but this did not carry over into a posttest. In a second phase, both groups produced a written essay on a topic that called for the use of the target form. Despite the fact that the results after the first phase did not show retention on the posttest, there was greater improvement on this written essay by those who had produced output than by those in the control group, who had not been involved in a production task in phase 1, thereby suggesting that output may indeed be important for acquisition.

The notion of hypothesis testing has been central to research in second language acquisition for a number of years. Output, particularly when it occurs as part of a negotiation sequence, is a way of testing a hypothesis. This is not to say that hypotheses are being consciously tested every time a second language speaker produces an utterance. It is to say, however, that through negotiation and through feedback, learners can be made aware of the hypotheses that they are entertaining as they produce language. That is, the activity of using language helps create a degree of analyticity that allows learners to think about language.

Another piece of evidence supporting the fact that learners test hypotheses through production is self-correction. Negotiation sequences produce many instances of corrective feedback to learners, from NSs and NNSs alike. And, importantly, these instances appear to have long-lasting effects on language development in some cases. In the following examples (Gass and Varonis 1989), it appears that Hiroko is 'ready' to accept a correction. Her quick and easy acceptance of Izumi's *at* suggests a tentativeness that bespeaks of hypothesis testing, rather than a conviction of the correctness of her own utterance.

> (1) Hiroko: Ah, the dog is barking to —
> Izumi: At
> Hiroko: At the woman.
>
> (2) Hiroko: A man is uh drinking c-coffee or tea uh with uh the saucer of the uh uh coffee set is uh in his uh knee.
> Izumi: In him knee.
> Hiroko: Uh on his knee.
> Izumi: Yeah.
> Hiroko: On his knee.
> Izumi: So sorry. On his knee.

In this negotiation, it appears that both Hiroko and Izumi are tentative and are in a sense 'fishing' for the right form. This is supported by the frequent hesitation on the part of Hiroko in her initial utterance and by the apology on Izumi's part at the end. Other examples suggest the longer-term retention that results from these negotiations. This can be seen in (3) (Gass and Varonis 1989).

> (3) Atsuko: Uh holding the [kʌp].
>   Toshi: Holding the cup?
>   Atsuko: Hmm hmmm ...
>   (seventeen turns later)
>   Toshi: Holding a cup.
>   Atsuko: Yes.
>   Toshi: Coffee cup?
>   Atsuko: Coffee? Oh yeah, tea, coffee cup, tea cup.
>   Toshi: Hm hm.

In this example, the initial clarification request by Toshi suggests to Atsuko that something is wrong with her pronunciation of the word cup [kʌp]. This indication caused her to notice something in her pronunciation that did not match the expectation of her partner. The remainder of the dialogue was one of hypothesis testing in which she matched her phonetic formulation against that of her partner's.

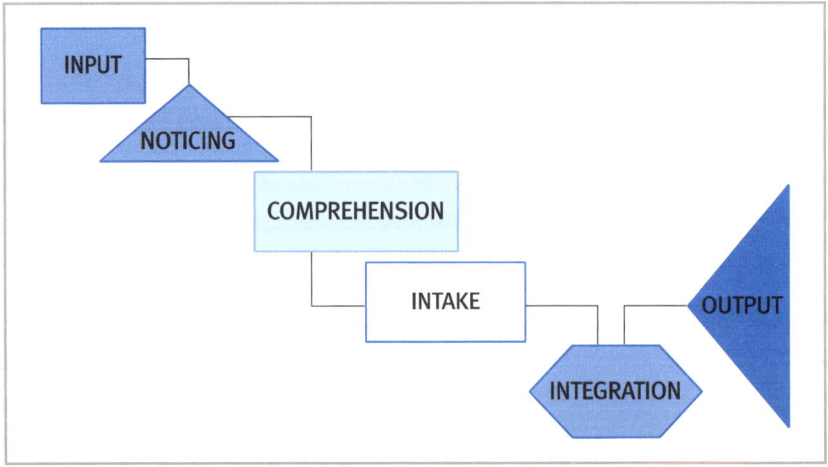

(C2a) Modified Output (vs. Pushed Output)

The current version of the Interaction Hypothesis (Long 1996) draws on Swain's Output Hypothesis (Swain 1985, 1995) in proposing that 'pushing' learners to produce output that is precise, coherent and appropriate can induce learners to engage in the kind of bottom-up processing necessary for extending interlanguage grammar. There are potentially many ways of 'pushing' learners to produce such output but here we will be concerned with just one — the use of clarification requests.

When a learner produces an utterance that is not comprehended the listener may respond with a clarification request, which causes the learner to subsequently reformulate the problematic utterance, as in this example:

> (1) Student: Cinderella change into the beautiful girl.
>   Teacher: Sorry?
>   Student: Cinderella changed into a beautiful girl.

Here, the learner, who is attempting to tell the story of Cinderella, says something that the teacher does not understand. The teacher requests clarification, causing the learner to reformulate his utterance, substituting the target language verb form ('changed') for the non-target-form in the initial utterance ('change'). The result of this negotiation is what Takashima (1995) calls 'enhanced output' (i.e. output that has been 'grammaticalized' as a result of 'pushing').

Pushing learners through clarification requests can have three possible outcomes. First, learners may simply repeat rather than reformulate their utterances, as in this example:

> (2) Student: Cinderella have to go home.
>   Teacher: Cinderella? I beg your pardon?
>   Student: Cinderella have to go home.

In this case, the output is not enhanced. That is, the learner simply repeats the initial utterance without making any grammatical modification. Second, it can lead to reformulation where the learner fails to use the correct target language form but does substitute a more advanced interlanguage form, as in this example:

> (3) Student: The prince fall in love at first glance.
>   Teacher: Sorry?
>   Student: The prince falled in love at first glance.

Here the learner modifies the initial utterance by substituting 'falled' for 'fall'. This is ungrammatical, but it represents a form that typically occurs later in the acquisition of irregular past tense (Doughty and Varela 1998). The third possibility is that the clarification request causes the learner to substitute the correct target language form for an initial incorrect interlanguage form, as in (1) above. Enhanced output arises when learners grammaticalize their output either through the use of more advanced interlanguage forms or of target language forms.

But how does enhanced output contribute to acquisition? In the case of recasts, learners are exposed to grammatical forms that may not yet be part of their L2 competence. Thus recasts can potentially help learners to acquire completely new forms. However, it is self-evident that learners cannot themselves reformulate using grammatical forms that they have not yet acquired. Thus, if a learner modifies output by substituting a correct target language form for an incorrect form, as in (1) above, this must be because (s)he already knows the target language form. What then is acquired from enhanced output? Possibly, reformulating helps the learner to produce grammatical forms that have already entered their interlanguages but which they have difficulty in accessing, particularly in the context of on-line communication. According to this argument, then, enhanced output does not result in the acquisition of ***new*** forms but in greater control of those forms that have already been acquired. This is the most likely way in which pushed output contributes to acquisition. However, pushing learners to reformulate may also motivate the kind of overgeneralization error observed in (3) above. That is, faced with the need to make their output more comprehensible, learners may apply a grammatical rule they have acquired inappropriately, resulting in transitional constructions such as 'falled'. If such interim stages of acquisition are seen as an essential feature of interlanguage development, as suggested by research on developmental sequences (Ellis 1994), it might be claimed that pushing learners to modify their output induces learners to engage in the kind of restructuring that McLaughlin (1990) has claimed to be a key aspect of language acquisition. Finally, it can be hypothesized that clarification requests alert learners to potential gaps in their interlanguage which they seek to fill by paying closer attention to input (Swain 1995).

Chapter 03 Mind Map

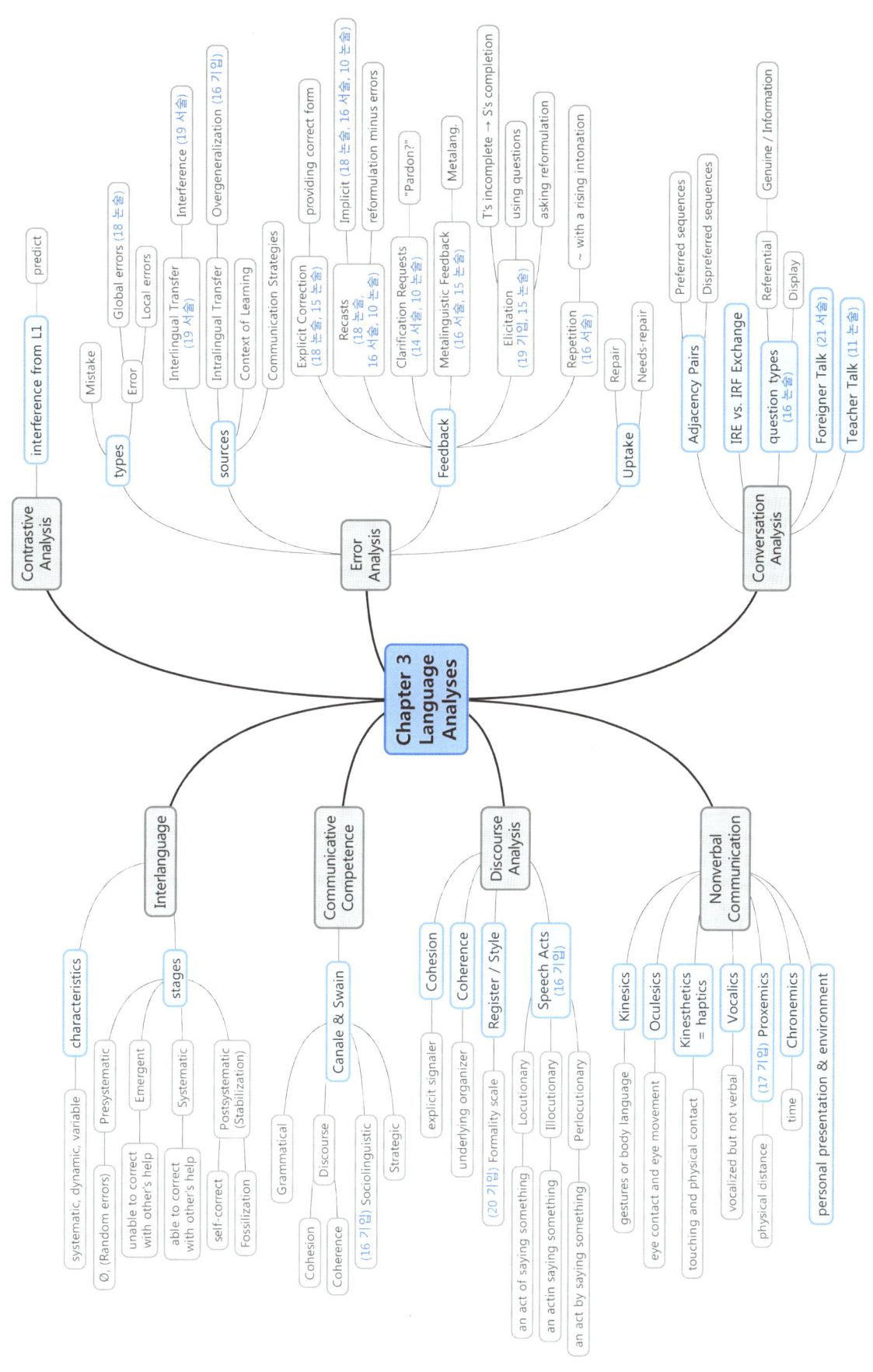

Chapter 03 Language Analyses

(A) Contrastive Analysis

(A1) Hierarchy of Difficulty

A well-known model for Contrastive Analysis Hypothesis was offered by Stockwell, Bowen, and Martin (1965), who posited what they called a **hierarchy of difficulty** by which a teacher could make a prediction of the relative difficulty of a given aspect of the target language. Further, they posited eight possible degrees of difficulty for phonology and 16 degrees for grammar. Clifford Prator (1967) subsequently reduced those numbers to six degrees for both phonology and grammar, using English and Spanish in contrast.

Level 0: <Transfer> No difference or contrast.

Examples: English and Spanish cardinal vowels, word order, and certain words (***mortal, inteligente, arte, americanos***)

Level 1: <Coalescence> Two items in the L1 become coalesced into one item in the L2.

Examples: possessives require gender distinction (***his/her***), and in Spanish they do not (***su***)

Level 2: <Underdifferentiation> An item in the L1 is absent in the L2.

Examples: English learners of Spanish must delete English ***do*** as a tense carrier, possessive forms of ***wh-*** words (***whose***), or the use of ***some*** with mass nouns.

Level 3: <Reinterpretation> An item in the L1 is given a new shape or distribution.

Example: An English speaker learning Spanish must learn new pronunciation for 'j' and 'x' (***baja, Mexico***) and the Spanish cardinal vowels.

Level 4: <Overdifferentiation> A new item bearing little similarity to the L1 item.

Example: An English speaker learning Spanish must include determiners in generalized nominals (Man is mortal / ***El hombre es mortal***).

Level 5: <Split> One item in the L1 becomes two or more in the L2.

Example: An English speaker learning Spanish must learn the distinction between ***ser*** and ***estar*** (to be).

(A2) Cross-Linguistic Influence

The weak version of the CAH remains today under the label cross-linguistic influence (White 2012), suggesting that we all recognize the significant role that prior experience plays in any learning act, and that the influence of the L1 as prior experience must not be overlooked. The difference between today's emphasis on *influence*, rather than prediction, is an important one. Phonology of course remains the most reliable linguistic category for predicting learner performance, but far more variation among learners is found in syntactic, lexical, discourse, and pragmatic interference. With such variation comes the need to take cross-linguistic influence seriously, but hardly predictively.

(B) Interlanguage

(B1) Interlanguage Theory

Interlanguage Theory which originated from investigations into learner errors and L2 developmental patterns was one of the first important attempts to unravel the complexities of SLA. Its importance also lies in the fact that it gave rise to many later developments. The same scientific methods of investigation that had contributed to the creation of a model for native speakers' competence were applied to the study of nonnative competence. L2 learner language became the object of investigation as a logical, rule-governed system, evolving along a sequence of stages, being a dynamic response to the requirements of the context in which it functions and gradually approximating the system used by native speakers of the target language (Ellis 2008). Different terms were used to refer to this phenomenon: Selinker (1972) called it *interlanguage*, stressing its distinctive character, and Brown (2000) offered the following definition: "(…) a structurally intermediate status between the native and target languages". Nemser (1971), in turn, used the term *approximative system* to account for the fact that it gradually approximates the target language, whereas Corder (1971) chose to address it as *idiosyncratic dialect*, thus pointing to the fact that the learner's language belongs to a particular individual and is governed by the rules typical of this individual only. Despite such important differences, the three concepts uniformly assume that the language learners create, distinct from their L1 and L2, is a self-contained linguistic system (Brown 2000).

Having established that learner language was systematic and subject to change, researchers aimed to determine the processes responsible for IL formation and explore the mechanisms accounting for its transformation. Initially, the discussion evolved around a number of learning strategies and cognitive processes such as language transfer, overgeneralization or simplification. The classification proposed by Selinker (1972), although not immune from criticism, is perceived as a valuable attempt to specify the cognitive processes responsible for L2 acquisition (Ellis 1994). It is as follows:

1. Language transfer (although not complete, transfer of data from the learner's L1 is feasible)
2. Transfer of training (interlanguage restructuring may be a result of instruction)
3. Strategies of second language learning (the learner's approach to the material to be learned)
4. Strategies of second language communication (effective communication techniques adopted by learners)
5. Overgeneralization of the target language material (interlanguage restructuring may result from the overgeneralization of target language rules and features)

More generally, however, it was agreed that IL restructuring was driven by the process of hypothesis formation and testing. The proponents of this solution suggested that L2 learners form hypotheses about the ways the target language is structured on the basis of the input they are exposed to, thus formulating a hypothetical grammar which is tested in reception and production. Learners' hypotheses become confirmed and reinforced if the output they produce does not evoke corrections or misunderstanding. On the other hand, if the output triggers corrective reactions or fails to convey the intended meaning, the learner may attempt to test the hypothesis and, consequently, restructure it. It is assumed that IL is systematic because learners build their utterances relying on the rules they have already internalized.

The novel utterances may not be correct from the native-norm perspective, but they are 'grammatical' in the sense that they conform to the rules that learners have already internalized. New forms and rules extracted externally, from the exposure to L2 input, or internally, due to L1 transfer or overgeneralization of an already internalized rule, cause incessant changes to the system, thus making it a continuum rather than a stable phenomenon. IL is said to consist of a series of overlapping grammars where newly coined or revised rules coexist with the old ones.

The operation of competing or concurrent hypotheses might explain systematic variability in learner language (Ellis 1990) when one and the same form is used correctly or incorrectly in different contexts. IL transformations, fed by the incoming data and their interplay with the already acquired knowledge, are characterized by complexification. While the idea of gradual sophistication and growing complexity of successive interim grammars may have been generally approved of, the issue of the starting point for the process has been surrounded by much controversy. No matter where the process starts, its 'final state' never equals the complexity of native competence. The process in the course of which certain nonnative rules and forms become fixed has been referred to as **fossilization** (Ellis 1994).

Fossilized forms persist despite error correction, explicit grammatical explanation or instruction and even if they become eliminated, they are likely to reappear in spontaneous production, a phenomenon known as **backsliding**. An interplay of external factors such as communicative pressure, lack of learning opportunity, type of feedback, and internal factors, such as age or no desire to acculturate, can be blamed for the recurrence of inaccurate forms in learner speech (Ellis 1994).

The tenets of Interlanguage Theory were soon reflected in classroom practices that respected the legitimacy of learner language and, following the assumptions of the Identity Hypothesis, aimed to recreate naturalistic learning conditions. Naturally, teaching revolved around error analysis and remedial work (cf. Ellis 1990).

Most fundamental changes concerned syllabus design: since it was agreed that learners followed their own syllabus, sequencing of the material to be taught became questionable. One of the proposals aiming to reconcile the sequence of teaching content with the internal syllabus of each learner was teaching according to the natural developmental sequences diagnosed by research (Ellis 1990). Another pedagogic recommendation, being a corollary of Interlanguage Theory, was a proposal to create conditions for meaningful interaction minimizing instruction, concerning grammar in particular. It was assumed that communicative practice will not only enable learners to communicate successfully but also equip them with the proper knowledge of the linguistic system. In fact, it is hard to overestimate the tremendous influence that Interlanguage Theory has exerted on foreign language pedagogy since it sparked many important teaching initiatives such as the Natural Approach, the Communicational Teaching Project or immersion programmes.

(B2) Interlanguage pragmatics

Interlanguage pragmatics deals with both the acquisition and use of second language pragmatic knowledge. In learning a second language one must learn more than just the pronunciation, the lexical items, and the appropriate word order; one must also learn the appropriate way to use those words and sentences in the second language. For example, we pointed out that one must learn that, within the context of a telephone conversation, ***Is Josh there?*** is not only a request for information but is also a request to speak with that person. In fact, children are known to respond to this question only on the basis of an information request such that a typical response from a child is ***Yes***, with no further indication that he or she will call the person to the phone. Thus, a child in learning a first language must learn to go beyond the literal meaning of utterances to understand the pragmatic force. The same can be said for second language learning and use. Consider (1), an example of a conversation between a British tourist and a native speaker of Finnish, provided by Maisa Martin (personal communication):

> (1) Tourist: We're trying to find the railway station. Could you help us?
>   NS of Finnish: Yes. (full stop)

In Finnish, the pragmatic force of a request for directions does not coincide with the pragmatic force in English. Thus, despite a native speaker of Finnish's perfectly grammatical English, one often finds what might be interpreted as abrupt responses.

Much of the work in interlanguage pragmatics has been conducted within the framework of ***speech acts***. **Speech acts** can be thought of as functions of language, such as complaining, thanking, apologizing, refusing, requesting, and inviting. Within this view, the minimal unit of communication is the performance of a linguistic act. All languages have a means of performing speech acts, and presumably speech acts themselves are universal, yet the ***form*** used in specific speech acts varies from culture to culture. Thus, the study of second language speech acts is concerned with the linguistic possibilities available in languages for speech act realization and the effect of cross-cultural differences on both second language performance and the interpretation by native speakers of second language speech acts.

It is easy to imagine how miscommunication and misunderstandings occur if the form of a speech act differs from culture to culture. In (1), a native speaker of British English and a native speaker of Finnish were seen to differ in the ways they ask for directions and interpret requests for directions. When breakdowns occur, they are frequently disruptive because native speakers attribute not linguistic causes to the breakdown, but personality (individual or cultural) causes. Thus, in (1), the British tourist is likely to have interpreted the Finnish speaker's response as rude and/or uncooperative. Or, similarly, consider the response to the situation in (2), produced in English by a native speaker of Hebrew (Cohen and Olshtain 1993):

> (2) Context: You promised to return a textbook to your classmate within a day or two, after Xeroxing a chapter. You held onto it for almost two weeks.
> Classmate: I'm really upset about the book because I needed it to prepare for last week's class.
> Response: I have nothing to say.

It is clear that this response sounds rude to an NS of English and suggests a lack of willingness to apologize. However, what was meant was the translation of something equivalent to *I have no excuse*.

(C) Stages of Learner Language Development

Presystematic	∅
Emergent	unable to correct errors when pointed out
Systematic	able to correct errors when pointed out
Postsystematic (Stabilization)	self-correct (but Fossilization)

(C1) Developmental sequences

(C1a) Negation

① **Stage 1**

The negative element (usually 'no' or 'not') is typically placed before the verb or the element being negated. Often, it occurs as the first word in the sentence because the subject is not there.

e.g.) No bicycle. / I no like it. / Not my friend.

② **Stage 2**

At this stage, 'no' and 'not' may alternate with 'don't'. However, 'don't' is not marked for person, number, or tense and it may even be used before modals like 'can' and 'should'.

e.g.) He don't like it. / I don't can sing.

③ **Stage 3**

Learners begin to place the negative element after auxiliary verbs like 'are', 'is', and 'can'. But at this stage, the 'don't' form is still not fully analysed.

e.g.) You can not go there. / He was not happy. / She don't like rice.

④ **Stage 4**

In this stage, 'do' is marked for tense, person, and number, and most interlanguage sentences appear to be just like those of the target language.

e.g.) It doesn't work.

We didn't have supper.

(C1b) Possessive determiners

① **Stage 1 Pre-emergence**

No use of 'his' and 'her'. Definite article or 'your' used for all persons, genders, and numbers.

e.g.) The little boy play with the bicycle.

He have band-aid on the arm, the leg, the stomach.

This boy cry in the arm of your mother.

There is one girl talk with your dad.

② **Stage 2 Emergence**

Emergence of 'his' and/or 'her', with a strong preference to use only one of the forms.

e.g.) The mother is dressing her little boy, and she put her clothes, her pant, her coat, and then she finish.

The girl making hisself beautiful. She put the make-up on his hand, on his head, and his father is surprise.

③ **Stage 3 Post-emergence**

Differentiated use of 'his' and 'her' but not when the object possessed has natural gender.

e.g.) The girl fell on her bicycle. She look his father and cry.

The dad put her little girl on his shoulder, and after, on his back.

(C1c) Relative clauses

Second language learners first acquire relative clauses that refer to nouns in the subject and direct object positions, and only later (and in some cases, never) learn to use them to modify nouns in other sentence roles (e.g., indirect object and object of preposition). A summary of the observed pattern of acquisition for relative clauses is shown in the table below. It is referred to as the 'accessibility hierarchy', and it reflects the apparent ease with which learners have 'access' to certain structures in the target language.

Part of speech	Relative clause
Subject	The girl who was sick went home.
Direct object	The story that I read was long.
Indirect object	The man who(m) Susan gave the present to was happy.
Object of preposition	I found the book that John was talking about.
Possessive	I know the woman whose father is visiting.
Object of comparison	The person that Susan is taller than is Mary.

It came from patterns found in studies of large number of languages by Edward Keenan and Bernard Comrie (1977). They found that those languages which included the structures at the bottom of the list in the table above would also have those at the top, but the opposite was not necessarily true. Subsequently, Susan Gass (1982) and others found that if a second language learner could use one of the structures at the bottom of the list, he or she would probably be able to use any that precede it. On the other hand, a learner who could produce sentences with relative clauses in the subject or direct object positions (at the top of the list) would not necessarily be able to use them in any of the positions further down the list.

Despite the similarity of the general pattern that has been found, several types of first language influence have been observed in the acquisition of relative clauses. First, it has been observed that for learners whose first language does not have a particular clause type (for example, object of comparison), it is more difficult to learn to use that type in English. Second, where learners have a first language with a substantially different way of forming relative clauses (for example, Japanese or Chinese, where the relative clause precedes the noun it modifies), they may avoid using relative clauses even when their interlanguage is fairly advanced. Third, first language influence is seen in the errors learners make. For example, Arabic speakers often produce both the relative marker and the pronoun it replaces (for example, 'The man who I saw him was very angry'), as they would in Arabic.

(D) Error Analysis

(D0) Mistake & Error

Mistake	Performance-related, self-corrected
Error	Competence-related, a noticeable deviation from TL

In order to analyze learner language in an appropriate perspective, it is crucial to make a distinction between two very different phenomena: mistakes and errors. A **mistake** refers to a performance error that is either a random guess or a 'slip', in that it is a failure to utilize a known system correctly. All people make mistakes, in both L1 and L2 situation. Mistakes, when attention is called to them, can usually be self-corrected. An **error** refers to a noticeable deviation from the adult grammar of a native speaker, reflecting the competence of the learner. The errors can be classified as either global or local. **Global errors** impede communication; they are incomprehensible to the hearer (or reader). **Local errors** do not inhibit communication, usually because there is only a minor slip, allowing the hearer/reader to make an accurate guess of the intended meaning.

It is impossible to tell the difference between an error and a mistake always. However, the fact that learners do make errors, and that these errors can be observed, analyzed, and classified to reveal something of the system operating within the learner, led to a surge of study of learners' errors, called **error analysis** (Corder 1971).

(D1) Sources of Error

Interlingual Transfer (Interference)	from generalization between L1 and L2
Intralingual Transfer (Overgeneralization)	from generalization within L2
Context of Learning	from teachers, materials, or social situations
Communication Strategies	from production strategies

(D2) Different Types of Interactional Feedback

Explicit Correction	explicit provision of the correct form
Recasts	reformulation minus the error
Clarification Requests	requiring a repetition / reformulation
Metalinguistic Feedback	using metalanguage w/o E. C.

Elicitation	eliciting S's completion
Repetition	repeating with a rising intonation

Interactional feedback can occur in different ways. In general, two broad categories of such feedback can be distinguished: reformulations and elicitations (Nassaji 2007). **Reformulations** are those feedback strategies that rephrase a learner's erroneous production, providing the learner with the correct form. **Elicitations**, on the other hand, do not provide learners with the correct form. Instead, they push or prompt the learner directly or indirectly to self-correct. These two feedback categories have also been called input providing and output prompting strategies (e.g., R. Ellis 2009).

The aim of interactional feedback can either be conversational, in which the interlocutor attempts to deal with problems of message comprehensibly, or pedagogical when the interlocutor understands the message, but still attempts to correct the learner error or push the learner to produce a more formally correct or appropriate utterance. Conversational feedback involves negotiation of meaning, defined as side sequences to the flow of interaction 'when a listener signals to a speaker that the speaker's message is not clear, and the listener and speaker both work linguistically to resolve the problem' (Pica 1992). Pedagogical feedback involves negotiation of form, defined as more deliberate attempts to draw learners' attention to form (Van den Branden 1997).

In the following section, we will describe the different types and subtypes of interactional feedback along with examples. These strategies have been identified in a number of studies on how teachers react to learner errors during conversational interaction and have been shown to facilitate L2 acquisition.

(1) Recasts

One type of interactional feedback that has received much attention in the field of SLA is the recast. **Recasts** refer to utterances that reformulate the whole or part of the learner's erroneous utterance into a correct form while maintaining the overall focus on meaning (Nicholas, Lightbown, & Spada 2001). The reformulation not only provides the learner with the correct form but may also signal to the learner that his or her utterance is deviant in some way. In other words, the feedback 'draws learners' attention to mismatches between input and output', and hence 'causes them to focus on form' (Long & Robinson 1998). Doughty and Varela (1998) described recasts as 'potentially effective, since the aim is to add attention to form to a primarily communicative task rather than to depart from an already communicative goal in order to discuss a linguistic feature'. The following provides an example of a recast.

> **Example (1)**
> STUDENT: And they found out the one woman run away.
> TEACHER: OK, the woman was running away. [Recast]
> STUDENT: Running away.

In the above example, the recast has been triggered by the learner's utterance that contains an error related to the verb tense. The teacher has provided a recast by reformulating the learner's incorrect form into a correct form without changing the overall meaning. The learner has modified his original utterance by repeating the feedback.

In the SLA literature, the immediate response of the learner to the feedback has been called **uptake** (e.g., Lyster & Ranta 1997). Uptake is an optional move in that learners may or may not respond to the feedback (R. Ellis et al. 2001). However, it has been used extensively in SLA research as a measure of feedback effectiveness. Chaudron (1977), for example, pointed out that 'the main immediate measurement of effectiveness of any type of corrective reaction would be a frequency count of the students' correct responses following each type'. Uptake can be either successful when the learner correctly modifies his or her original utterance or unsuccessful when the learner does not correct his or her erroneous output (R. Ellis et al. 2001). Of course, although the learner may provide uptake in response to feedback, this does not indicate that the learner has acquired the form. It is possible that the learner is simply mimicking the teacher's feedback without much understanding (Gass 2003). However, such learner responses have been considered to contribute to L2 acquisition because they may indicate that the learner has noticed the feedback and has made some use of it (Mackey & Philp 1998).

(1-1) Types of Recasts

Recasts are generally considered as implicit feedback because they imply rather than overtly correct the error. They are also unobtrusive because they rephrase an utterance without breaking the flow of communication. However, such interactional moves are complex, taking many different forms during interaction, differing from one another in terms of their degree of explicitness (Nassaji 2009). For example, recasts may occur in the form of declarative statements to confirm a learner's message (Lyster 1998), in which case they can be considered fairly implicit, as in Example 2. In this example, the teacher provides a recast of the student's utterance but the feedback is implicit; thus, it can be ambiguous in that the student may either interpret the reformulation as corrective feedback or simply as confirming his or her statement. Recasts, however, can also occur in conjunction with additional intonational signals such as added stress, in which case they are more explicit (such as in Example 3). In such cases, the added stress may make the feedback more noticeable, drawing the learners' attention to the correct form more effectively.

Example (2)
TEACHER: OK. Everything was on sale. Why?
STUDENT: Because … baseball winner.
TEACHER: OK. Because they won the Japan series. Do you like baseball?

Example (3)
STUDENT: And she catched her.
TEACHER: She CAUGHT [added stress] her?
STUDENT: Yeah, caught her.

The degree of explicitness of the recast may also vary depending on the number of changes it involves or the length of the feedback. For example, a recast may reformulate part of the utterance or it may correct only one of the errors in a learner's utterance. Alternatively, it may correct multiple errors or even may expand on a learner's utterance by continuing the topic. A shorter recast involving only one correction is relatively more explicit than a longer recast that involves multiple corrections with topic continuation because the former can draw the learner's attention to form more directly than the latter (R. Ellis & Sheen 2006). The following demonstrates an example of a recast correcting a single error and a recast correcting multiple errors with topic continuation.

Example (4)
STUDENT: The boy put the snake in the box and then …
TEACHER: In a box? [Single error corrected]

> **Example (5)**
> NNS: Ohh, she put on the apron?
> NS:　He put an apron on so he wouldn't get messy.
> 　　　[Multiple errors corrected with topic continuation]
> NNS: Cooking?

(2) Clarification Requests

Clarification requests occur when the teacher or an interlocutor does not fully understand a learner's utterance and then asks the learner to rephrase the utterance so that it can be clearer. The request may be motivated by either an error in the learner's utterance or it may be because the utterance is not comprehensible in some other way. The feedback does not provide the learner with the correct form. However, it may indicate to the learner that his or her utterance may contain an error. Since the feedback is interrogative, it provides the learner with an opportunity to self-repair. Clarification requests can be achieved by using phrases such as "pardon me?" or "sorry?" or "excuse me?" etc. The following provides an example of a clarification request.

> **Example (6)**
> STUDENT: I want practice today, today.
> TEACHER: I'm sorry? [Clarification request]

(3) Repetition

Interactional feedback can also occur in the form of **repetition** of all or part of the learner's erroneous utterances with a rising intonation. Like clarification requests, such feedback moves do not provide the learner with the correct form. However, they may indicate that the learner's utterance is erroneous, thus, providing the learner with an opportunity to self-repair. The following provides an example of repetition.

> **Example (7)**
> STUDENT: Oh my God, it is too expensive, I pay only 10 dollars.
> TEACHER: I pay? [Repetition with rising intonation]
> STUDENT 2: Okay let's go.

(4) Metalinguistic Feedback

Metalinguistic feedback refers to feedback that provides the learner with metalinguistic comments (i.e., comments about language) in the form of a statement or a question about the correctness of an utterance. This feedback may either simply involve metalinguistic hints or clues about the location or the nature of the error (e.g., "Can you correct the verb?" or "You need an adverb.") or it may include metalinguistic explanation in conjunction with correction. The following provides examples of a metalinguistic clue and metalinguistic feedback with correction.

Example (8)

STUDENT: I see him in the office yesterday.
TEACHER: You need a past tense. [Metalinguistic clue]

Example (9)

STUDENT: He catch the fish.
TEACHER: Caught is the past tense. [Metalinguistic feedback with correction]

---

(5) Direct Elicitation

Direct elicitation refers to feedback strategies that attempt more overtly to elicit the correct form from the learner. This may take the form of repeating the learner's utterance up to the point where the error has occurred and waiting for the learner to complete the utterance such as "He went … ?" Or it may take the form of a query that asks the learner more directly to repeat his or her utterance such as "Can you repeat what you said?" None of these strategies involves correction, but they may indicate indirectly to the learner that there is something wrong with their utterance. Thus, the feedback may draw the learners' attention to the problematic form and push the learner to self-correct. The following from Nassaji (2007) shows examples of such elicitation strategies.

Example (10)

STUDENT: And when the young girl arrive, ah, beside the old woman.
TEACHER: When the young girl … ?

> **Example (11)**
> STUDENT: She easily catched the girl.
> TEACHER: She catched the girl? I'm sorry, say that again.

(6) Direct Correction

Direct correction refers to feedback that identifies the error and then overtly corrects it. This type of feedback has the advantage of providing the learner with clear information about how to correct the error. However, since the feedback supplies the correction, it does not provide the learner with an opportunity to self-repair. Thus, the feedback may not result in any negotiation or learners' active participation in the feedback process (Lyster 1998). The following provides an example of a direct correction.

> **Example (12)**
> STUDENT: He has catch a cold.
> TEACHER: Not catch, caught. [Direct correction]
> STUDENT: Oh, ok.

(7) Nonverbal Feedback

Feedback can also be provided nonverbally using body movements and signals such as gestures, facial expressions, head, hand, and finger movements. For example, shaking the head or frowning could be used to indicate the presence of an error. Arms, hand, or figure movements could be used to indicate the nature of the error.

> **Example (13)**
> STUDENT: My mom cooks always good food.
> TEACHER: [Crosses over arms in front of the body to indicate word order]

When using nonverbal feedback, it might be useful if the teacher familiarizes students in advance with the kinds of body movements he or she might use. For example, the teacher may inform students that when he or she crosses over his or her arms in front of the body, it indicates a problem with word order.

(D2a) Principles of Error Treatment in the Classroom

Hendrickson (1978) lists the 'five fundamental questions' and reviews the literature that addresses them. Then he predicts that if error correction is done according to the principles described below, it will be effective.

(1) Should errors be corrected?

When error correction 'works', it does so by helping the learner change his or her conscious mental representation of a rule. In other words, it affects learned competence by informing the learner that his or her current version of a conscious rule is wrong. Thus, second language acquisition theory implies that when the goal is learning, errors should indeed be corrected (but not at all times; see below; and not all rules, even if the goal is learning). The theory maintains, however, that error correction is not of use for acquisition. Acquisition occurs, according to the input hypothesis, when acquirers understand input for its meaning, not when they produce output and focus on form.

(2) When should errors be corrected?

Concerning this problem, the most controversial issue is to treat them immediately or to delay. First, we are confronted with a dilemma — fluency versus accuracy. For communicative purpose, delayed correction is usually preferred. Some advanced students believe that when to correct errors is determined by the type of errors committed. For instance, if they are pronunciation or grammatical errors, immediate correction is preferable, for post-correction cannot make learners remember anything. Furthermore, the overall situation in the classroom is also important. When the whole class is familiar with a word, but only one of them is singled out for being corrected, he or she would feel awkward. So, we can see that when to correct is very complicated. Both the teachers' intuition and the feedback from the students are equally important.

(3) Which errors should be corrected?

Learners' errors are usually classified in different categories. Burt (1975) made a distinction between 'global' and 'local' errors. **Global errors** hinder communication and they prevent the learner from comprehending some aspects of the message. **Local errors** only affect a single element of a sentence, but do not prevent a message from being heard. According to Hendrickson (1980), local errors need not be corrected and they are generally held true. But the expressions such as 'a news', or 'an advice' are systematic errors, and they need to be corrected. As for presystematic errors, teachers can simply provide the correct one. For systematic errors, since learners have already had the linguistic competence, they can explain this kind of errors and correct them themselves. So the teacher should consider the purpose of the analysis and analyze them in a systematic way.

(4) How should errors be corrected?

According to James (1998), it is sensible to follow the three principles in error correction. Firstly, the techniques involved in error correction would be able to enhance the students' accuracy in expression. Secondly, the students' affective factors should be taken into consideration and the correction should not be face-threatening to the students. Some scholars believed that teachers' indirect correction is highly appreciated. They either encourage students to do self-correction in heuristic method or present the correct form, so students couldn't feel embarrassed. Compare the two situations:

(1) Student: "What means this word?"
    Teacher: "No, listen, what does this word mean?"
(2) Student: "What means this word?"
    Teacher: "What does it mean? Well, it is difficult to explain, but it means…"

It is obvious that teacher's remodeling in (2) is more natural and sensible than the direct interruption in (1).

(5) Who should correct learner errors?

There are several ways of correction that can be employed in the classroom.

● **Self-correction**:

After the student recognizes what is incorrect in his/her response, s/he should be able to correct him/herself. Self-correction is the best technique, because the student will remember it better.

● **Peer correction**:

If the student cannot correct him/herself the teacher can encourage other students to supply correction. This technique is to be applied tactfully, so that the student who originally made the mistake will not feel humiliated. In the case of errors, it is useful if after peer correction the teacher goes back to the student who made the error and gets him/her to say it correctly. Edge (1990) mentions the following advantages of peer correction: It encourages cooperation, and students get used to the idea that they can learn from each other. Both learners are involved in listening to and thinking about the language. The teacher gets a lot of important information about the learners' ability.

- **Teacher correction**:

If no one can correct, the teacher must realise that the point has not yet been learnt properly. In that case the teacher can re-explain the problematic item of language, especially if he/she sees that the majority of the class has the same problem. We must not forget that the main aim of correction is to facilitate the students to learn the new language item correctly. That is why it is important that after correction the teacher has to ask the student who originally made the error or mistake to give the correct response.

(D3) Responses to Feedback

Uptake is a term that has been used to refer to a discourse move where learners respond to information they have received about some linguistic problem they have experienced. The move typically occurs following corrective feedback, as in Extract 1.

> Extract 1:
> (1) S: I have an ali[bi].
> (2) T: you have what?
> (3) S: an ali[bi].
> (4) T: an alib-? An alib[ay].
> (5) S: ali[bay].
> (6) T: okay, listen, listen, alibi.
> (7) SS: alibi.

The linguistic problem here arises in turn (1), where a student mispronounces the word 'alibi'. The teacher responds in (2) with a request for clarification, signalling that there is a linguistic problem. (3) is an uptake move but the student fails to repair the pronunciation error. This results in explicit correction by the teacher in (4), a further uptake move in (5), which again fails to repair the error, more explicit correction by the teacher in (6), and a final choral uptake move in (7), where the class as a whole now pronounces 'alibi' correctly. From this example, it should be clear that uptake following corrective feedback can be of two basic kinds — 'repair' (as in turn 7) or 'needs repair' (as in turns 3 and 5). Lyster and Ranta (1997) also distinguished different categories of these two basic types, as shown in the following table.

<Types of uptake move (Lyster and Ranta 1997)>

A. Repair
1. Repetition (i.e. the student repeats the teacher's feedback)
2. Incorporation (i.e. the student incorporates repetition of the correct form in a longer utterance)
3. Self-repair (i.e. the student corrects the error in response to teacher feedback that did not supply the correct form)
4. Peer-repair (i.e. a student other than the student who produced the error corrects it in response to teacher feedback)

B. Needs repair
1. Acknowledgement (e.g. the student says 'yes' or 'no')
2. Same error (i.e. the student produces the same error again)
3. Different error (i.e. the student fails to correct the original error and in addition produces a different error)
4. Off-target (i.e. the student responds by circumventing the teacher's linguistic focus)
5. Hesitation (i.e. the student hesitates in response to the teacher's feedback)
6. Partial repair (i.e. the student partly corrects the initial error)

Ellis, Basturkmen and Loewen (2001) defined 'uptake' more broadly. They noted that there are occasions in communicative lessons where teachers or learners themselves pre-empt attention to a linguistic feature (e.g. by asking a question). In student-initiated exchanges, the student still has the opportunity to react, for example, by simply acknowledging the previous move or by attempting to use the feature in focus in his/her own speech. Extract 2 provides an example of this type of uptake (see turn 3). In teacher-initiated exchanges, learner uptake is also possible, for example, when the learner repeats the linguistic form that the teacher has identified as potentially problematic.

Extract 2:
(1) S: You can say just January eighteen<th>?
(2) T: jan- january eighteen?, January eighteen? Mmm It's okay, It's a little casual (.) casual. Friends (.) January eighteen, okay, but usually January THE eighteenth or THE eighteenth of January.
(3) S: January THE eighteenth.
(4) T: the, yeah, good.

To take account of this type of uptake Ellis et al. proposed the following definition:

1. Uptake is a student move.

2. The move is optional (i.e., a focus on form does not obligate the student to provide an uptake move).

3. The uptake move occurs in episodes where learners have demonstrated a gap in their knowledge (e.g. by making an error, by asking a question or by failing to answer a teacher's question).

4. The uptake move occurs as a reaction to some preceding move in which another participant (usually the teacher) either explicitly or implicitly provides information about a linguistic feature.

Uptake is considered successful when it demonstrates that a learner has understood the linguistic form or has corrected the error. On the other hand, uptake is considered unsuccessful when a learner fails to demonstrate the command of the feature (Lyster & Ranta 1997). Successful uptake is also known as repair, referring to 'the correct reformulation of an error as uttered in a single turn and not to the sequence of turns resulting in the correct reformulation; nor does it refer to self-initiated repair'; unsuccessful uptake is also known as needs-repair (Ellis et al. 2001, Lyster & Ranta 1997), referring to uptake that results in an utterance that is still in need of repair.

(E) Communicative Competence

grammatical competence	linguistic knowledge, 'formally possible'
discourse competence	inter-sentential relationship [cohesion, coherence]
sociolinguistic competence	following sociocultural rules, understanding the social context
strategic competence	using verbal/nonverbal tech. to compensate for com. breakdowns

⟨BICS and CALP⟩

In the process of examining components of communicative competence, James Cummins (1979) proposed a distinction between basic interpersonal communicative skills (BICS) and cognitive/academic language proficiency (CALP). BICS is the communicative capacity that all human beings use to function in daily interpersonal exchange. CALP is a specialized dimension of communication used to negotiate typical educational tasks and activities, and often involves a conscious focus on language forms. It is what learners use in classroom exercises, reading assignments, written work, and tests.

Cummins later (1981) modified the notion of BICS and CALP in the form of context-embedded and context-reduced communication, where the former resembles BICS, with the added dimension of considering the context in which language is used, and the latter is similar to CALP. A good share of face-to-face communication with people, because of its social back-and-forth, is context-embedded, while school-oriented language tends to be more context-reduced.

〈Halliday's Seven Functions of Language〉

The functional approach to describing language is one that has its roots in the traditions of British linguist J. R. Firth, who viewed language as interactive and interpersonal, 'a way of behaving and making others behave'. Since then the term 'function' has been variously interpreted. Michael Halliday (1973), who provided one of the best expositions of language functions, used the term to mean the purposive nature of communication, and outlined seven different functions of language:

① **Instrumental**: To manipulate the environment, to cause certain events to happen.

   e.g.) This court finds you guilty. / On your mark, get set, go! / Don't touch the stove.

② **Regulatory**: To control events, to set limits and parameters, and to maintain regulations through approval, disapproval, or setting laws and rules.

   e.g.) Upon good behavior, you will be eligible for parole in 10 months.

   Eat your broccoli or there's no ice cream for dessert.

③ **Representational**: To make statements, convey information and knowledge, or 'represent' reality.

   e.g.) The sun is hot. / The president gave a speech last night.

④ **Interactional**: To ensure social maintenance, phatic communion, to keep channels of communication open.

   e.g.) Oh, I see. / That's interesting. / Hey, how's it going? / Nice weather today.

⑤ **Personal**: To express feelings, emotions, personality, and reaction.

   e.g.) I love you. / I resent that remark. / I feel your pain.

⑥ **Heuristic**: To acquire knowledge, learn, seek (and provide) information, and to form questions designed to elicit information.

   e.g.) Why does water bubble when it gets hot? / How many planets are in our universe?

⑦ **Imaginative**: To create imaginary images, stories, conceptions, or ideas.

   e.g.) fairy tales, jokes, novels, poetry, tongue twisters, puns

Halliday's seven functions of language are neither mutually exclusive nor exhaustive. A single sentence or conversation might incorporate many different functions simultaneously, and a multiplicity of other functions may also be served through language. Yet it is the understanding of how to use linguistic forms to achieve these functions of language that comprises the crux of second language learning.

(F) Discourse Analysis

cohesion	explicit signaler, a property of the text	lexical ~ / grammatical ~
coherence	underlying organizer, the communicators' evaluation of the text	

Discourse is language functioning in its context of use. **Discourse analysis** is the study of these texts, whether spoken or written, and the relationship between the texts and the contexts in which they occur. Discourse analysts are interested in the analysis of real texts — and in this they differ significantly from formal grammarians, whose data for analysis is as often as not derived from their intuitions as from attested examples. In addition, discourse analysts typically study extended stretches of language, with the utterance rather than the sentences as their primary unit of analysis.

The extent to which a stretch of discourse 'means', or 'makes sense', is a measure of its **coherence**, i.e. its capacity to achieve its communicative purpose. A stretch of language achieves coherence to the extent that it 'fits' into both of these levels of context. The use of language in order to achieve this fit is called **cohesion**.

(F1) Cohesion

The child learns to initiate and sustain talk independent of adult support, by incorporating elements from preceding turns in order to create the effect of a cohesive exchange. At the early stages, cohesion from one turn to the next is achieved by exact repetition, but by the age of three this gives way to modifications of the original utterance:

> Adult: You do that one.
> Child: Now I do that one.

Other cohesive devices, such as (in this order) the use of ellipsis, pronominal forms and discourse markers (well, now ⋯), also emerge at an early age, as in these examples:

> Mother: What's George doing?
> Child (aged 2): [*George is*] doing cars
>
> Mother: Let's have some vegetables.
> Child (aged 2 years 8 months): Oh, I'll get *some*.
>
> Silbhan: I want to play with all the Lego.
> Heather (aged 4): *Well*, you can't have that.

In fact, if conversational competence is narrowly defined as the ability to take turns, and to connect successive utterances, then most of the features of adult conversational competence are already in place by the age of four. In this short extract between a mother and her daughter (aged 3.5 years), the cohesive devices the child uses are identified:

> Child: Why d'you never buy me a guitar?
> Mother: Well, I don't know. Would you like one?
> Child: Yes.[1]
> Mother: A little guitar.
> Child: No.[2] A big[3] one[4]. A big one.[5]
> Mother: You wouldn't be able to play a big one.
> Child: I would[6]. I would.[7] I would be able to[8].

Key:

1. adjacency pair (question – answer)
2. adjacency pair (suggestion – refusal)
3. lexical - antonym
4. substitution
5. repetition
6. ellipsis
7. repetition
8. ellipsis

1) Grammatical Cohesion

Categories		Examples
Reference	Personal	I just met your brother. He is a nice guy.
	Demonstrative	You failed the test. This is bad news.
	Comparative	It is the same town we visited last year.
Substitution	Nominal	Can you give me a few nails? I need one.
	Verbal	Did you meet Kate last Sunday? Yes, I did.
	Clause	Will Tom win the match? I hope so.
Ellipsis	Nominal	Jane's paintings are better than Tom's Ø.
	Verbal	Mark will go to the cinema, but I don't think Kate will Ø.
	Clause	Somebody has stolen my car, but who Ø?
Conjunction	Adversative	I didn't study. However, I still passed.
	Additive	He didn't study. And he failed.
	Temporal	She studied hard. Then she sat the test.
	Causal	They studied hard. Therefore, they deserve to pass.

2) Lexical Cohesion

Categories		Examples
Reiteration	Repetition	She had a flower. The beauty of the flower is overwhelming.
	Synonym	I turned to the ascent of the peak. The climb is easy.
	Superordinate	Tom bought a new Mercedes. A color of that car is black.
	General Item	Rebecca is scared of spiders. You should give support to this girl.
Collocation		"Once upon a time, there lived a king named Midas."

(F1a) Creating Cohesion

Coherent texts (that is, sequences of sentences or utterances that seem to 'hang together') contain what were called 'text-forming devices'. These are words and phrases that enable the writer or speaker to establish relationships across sentence or utterance boundaries, and that help to tie the sentences in a text together.

1) Reference

Halliday and Hasan identify three types of cohesive reference: personal, demonstrative, and comparative reference. Personal reference items are realized by pronouns and determiners, and they serve to identify individuals and objects that are named at some other point in the text. Demonstrative reference is realized by determiners and adverbs. This class of reference items can represent a single word or phrase, or much longer chunks of text ranging across several paragraphs or even several pages. Comparative reference is realized through adjectives and adverbs and serves to compare items within a text in terms of identity or similarity. These various devices enable the writer or speaker to make multiple references to people and things within a text. Examples of each type are provided below. (The first part of the referential relationship is underlined, the second is in **bold**.)

- Personal Reference:
  Roni Size peers down from the top floor of a midtown Manhattan hotel at a skyscraper across the street. 'You could fit the whole of Bristol in that,' **he** exclaims.
- Demonstrative Reference:
  Roni Size peers down from the top floor of a midtown Manhattan hotel at a skyscraper across the street.' You could fit the whole of Bristol in **that**,' he exclaims.
- Comparative Reference:
  A: Would you like these seats?
  B: No, as a matter of fact, I'd like **the other seats**.

These devices exist in both spoken and written discourse, as the following conversation illustrates. The cohesive devices in the extract are featured in **bold**.

A: **That**'s a funny looking **bottle**.
B: Yes, **it** is, isn't **it**. **It**'s beautiful. Beer's nice **too**.
A: Oh, gosh, **that**'s **lovely**. Where'd you buy **that**?
B: Oh, there's a little **bottle shop** in the city called the **Wine** … **City Wines**. maybe we'll go **there** tomorrow and have a look.
A: **That**'d be good. I'd love to keep **this bottle**. Wish we could keep **it**.

2) Substitution and Ellipsis

In their 1976 work on cohesion, Halliday and Hasan deal with substitution and ellipsis separately, although they point out that these two types of cohesion are essentially the same. Ellipsis is described as a form of substitution in which the original item is replaced by zero. In a later publication Halliday (1985) combines substitution and ellipsis into a single category. There are three types of substitution: nominal, verbal, and clausal substitution. Examples of each are as follows:

> • Nominal Substitution:
> I'll get you some more bread rolls. These **ones** are stable. (*ones* = bread rolls)
> • Verbal Substitution:
> A: I think you work too hard.
> B: So **do** you! (*do* = work too hard)
> • Clausal Substitution:
> A: Are we going to land soon?
> B: I think **so**. (*so* = we're going to land soon)

In each of these examples, part of the preceding text has been replaced by ***ones, do,*** and ***so,*** respectively (these replacements are indicated in parentheses). Each of these words can only be interpreted with respect to what has gone before.

Ellipsis occurs when some essential structural element is omitted from a sentence or clause and can only be recovered by referring to an element in the preceding text. Consider the following discourse fragment and comprehension question.

> Mary: "I prefer the green."
> Question: Select the correct alternative: Mary prefers the green;
>   (a) hat   (b) dress   (c) shoes

As it stands, the question is impossible to answer. However, if we know what was said before, it becomes a relatively straightforward matter to answer the question.

> Sylvia: I like the blue hat.
> Mary: I prefer the green.

As with substitution, there are three types of ellipsis: nominal, verbal, and clausal ellipsis. Examples of each of these follow (the point at which material has been omitted from the second sentence of each text is marked by (0)). In each example, the second sentence or utterance can only be interpreted with reference to the one that precedes it.

> • Nominal Ellipsis:
> My kids play an awful lot of sport. Both (0) are incredibly energetic.
> • Verbal Ellipsis:
> A: Have you been working?
> B: Yes, I have (0).
> • Clausal Ellipsis:
> A: Why'd you only set three places? Paul's staying for dinner, isn't he?
> B: Is he? He didn't tell me (0).

These elements are all cohesive in that they require other aspects of the discoursal contexts in which they occur to be present in order to be interpretable. Without context, interpretation is impossible.

3) Conjunction

Conjunction differs from reference, substitution, and ellipsis because it is not a device for reminding the reader of previously mentioned items. In other words, it is not what linguists call an **anaphoric relation**. However, it is a cohesive device because it signals relationships that can only be fully understood through reference to other parts of the text. There are four different types of conjunction, and they signal the following semantic relationship: temporality, causality, addition, and adversity. Examples of each type of relationship follow:

> • Adversative:
> "I'm afraid I'll be home late tonight. However, I won't have to go in until late tomorrow."
> "I quite like being chatted up when I'm sitting in a bar having a drink. On the other hand, I hate it if … you know … if the guy starts to make a nuisance of himself."
> • Additive:
> "From a marketing viewpoint, the popular tabloid encourages the reader to read the whole page instead of choosing stories. And isn't that what any publisher wants?"
> • Temporal:
> "Brick tea is a blend that has been compressed into a cake. It is taken mainly by the minority groups in China. First, it is ground to a dust. Then it is usually cooked in milk."
> • Causal:
> Chinese tea is becoming increasingly popular in restaurants, and even in coffee shops. This is because of the growing belief that it has several health giving properties.

4) Lexical Cohesion

Lexical cohesion occurs when two words in a text are semantically related in some way. In other words, they are related in terms of their meaning. In Halliday and Hasan (1976), the two major categories of lexical cohesion are reiteration and collocation. Reiteration includes repetition, a synonym or near synonym, superordinate, and general words.

> • Repetition:
> What we lack in a newspaper is what we should get. In a word, a "popular" newspaper may be the winning ticket.
> • Synonym:
> You could try reversing the car up the slope. The incline isn't all that steep.
> • Superordinate:
> Pneumonia has arrived with the cold and wet conditions. The illness is striking everyone from infants to the elderly.
> • General word:
> A: Did you try the steamed buns?
> B: Yes, I didn't like the things much.

The second underlined word or phrase in each of these texts refers back to the previously mentioned entity. Reiteration thus fulfills a similar semantic function as cohesive reference.

The second type of lexical cohesion is collocation. Collocation can cause major problems for discourse analysis because it includes all those items in a text that are semantically related. In some cases this makes it difficult to decide for certain whether a cohesive relationship exists or not. In the extract below, we could say that the following items are examples of lexical collocation because they all belong to the scientific field of biology.

> plants ⋯ synthesize ⋯ organic ⋯ inorganic ⋯ green plants ⋯ energy ⋯ sunlight ⋯ plants ⋯ energy ⋯ green pigment ⋯ chlorophyll ⋯ photosynthesis ⋯ light synthesis ⋯ self feeding ⋯ autotrophic
>
> Plants characteristically synthesize complex organic substances from simple inorganic raw materials. In green plants, the energy of this process is sunlight. The plants can use this energy because they possess the green pigment chlorophyll. Photosynthesis or "light synthesis," is a "self-feeding," or autotrophic process.

5) Rhetorical patterns in text

Textual coherence is also related to the ways in which information is printed in a text. In his book on patterns of organization in texts, Hoey (1983), argues that the ordering of information in discourse can be accounted for in terms of certain rhetorical relationships such as cause-consequence, problem-solution. He uses the following four sentences to illustrate the ways in which these relationships function in discourse.

> *I opened fire.*
> *I was on sentry duty.*
> *I beat off the attack.*
> *(and) I saw the enemy approaching.*

These four sentences can be sequenced in twenty-four different ways. However, not all of these sequences will be acceptable as coherent discourse, for example "I beat off the attack. I opened fire. I saw the enemy approaching. I was on sentry duty." In fact the twenty-four different versions could probably be graded on a continuum from completely unacceptable to completely acceptable. According to Hoey, only one sequence is completely acceptable: "I was on sentry duty. I saw the enemy approaching. I opened fire. I beat off the attack."

Constraints on the ordering of information within a text, which determine levels of acceptability, are due in part to the relationships that exist between these elements. In the texts we have been considering, there are two particular types of relationship. These are cause-consequence and instrument-achievement relationships.

> *I was on sentry duty.*
> cause → I saw the enemy approaching. → consequence → I opened fire. → instrument → I opened fire. → achievement → I beat off the attack.

There are in fact grammatical devices that can be employed to change the sequencing of the information in the text in acceptable ways. These include subordination ("While I was on sentry duty, I opened fire, because I saw the enemy approaching. I (thereby) beat off the attack.") and conjunction ("I opened fire because I saw the enemy approaching when I was on sentry duty. By this means I beat off the attack.").

(F2) Making Sense: Coherence

Cohesive devices do not always guarantee that a speaker or writer will be understood. Nor does their absence mean that a speaker or writer will not be understood. Consider, for example, the following conversation.

> A: *Where's Rebecca?*
> B: *The rehearsal started tonight.*
> A: *Oh, OK.*

Although the conversational fragment does not contain any of the cohesive devices, most people agree that it makes sense. (The verb ***make*** illustrates the active, constructive nature of the process, in which the reader or listener has to 'work' to interpret the writer or speaker's meaning.) The conversational fragment demonstrates that it is possible to have pieces of coherent discourse that do not contain overt cohesive links. It makes sense, because it is possible to create a context in which it fits together at a functional level.

Utterance	*Function*
A: *Where's Rebecca?*	Request
B: *The rehearsal started tonight.*	Explanation
A: *Oh, OK.*	Acceptance

In creating a meaningful context and identifying the functions of each utterance, coherence is established. As a result, the missing bits of conversation, which would make it cohesive as well as coherent, could be restored. Such a cohesive conversation might run as follows:

> A: *Where's Rebecca? I want to give her her allowance.*
> B: *She's out. You remember that she successfully auditioned for* **The Jungle Book** *— well, the rehearsal started tonight.*
> A: *Oh, OK. I'll leave the money here and she can get it when she comes home.*

The conversation works because, as competent users of the language we expect the function 'request' to be followed by the function 'explanation', in much the same way as we expect a transitive verb to be followed by an object. Initially, this insight led to the belief that discourse could be explained and predicted in the same way as sentences, in terms of rules that specified optional and obligatory conditions determining whether or not they were 'well formed'.

(F2a) Functional Coherence

It is certainly possible to identify regularly recurring patterns and elements within discourse, particularly within contexts where the communicative situation encourages highly predictable, even ritualistic use of language. It is also apparent in other context, particularly transactional encounters involving the exchange of goods and services. In these situations, the negotiation done by the interlocutors pays off. This is not always the case when people converse, however. Cases of pragmatic failure, in which conversations and people fail one another, abound. This is illustrated in the following samples:

1. Context: the upper, nonsmoking deck of a 747 aircraft
   Passenger: I've been smoking for 28 years, and I gave up so I could travel up here.
   Cabin attendant: Sorry?
   Passenger: I said, I've been smoking for 28 years, and I gave up so I could sit up here.
   Cabin attendant: So?
   Passenger: So, I gave up smoking.
   Cabin attendant: What do you want?
   Passenger: I don't want anything.
            (Turns to partner) Well, I won't be traveling with this outfit again.

2. Context: at the end of a shift in a factory
   Native speaker: See you later.
   Non-native speaker: What time.
   Native speaker: What do you mean?

3. Context: during a coffee break at work
   A: I have two tickets for the theatre tonight.
   B: Good for you. What are you going to see?
   A: *Measure for Measure*.
   B: Interesting play. Hope you enjoy it.
   A: Oh, so you're busy tonight. (Widdowson, 1984)

4. Context: A is addressing her husband who is clearing out the garden shed.
   A: Are you wearing gloves?
   B: No.
   A: What about the spiders?
   B: They're not wearing gloves either.

5. Context: in an elementary school classroom
A: Tony, are you talking?
B: Yes, I am.
A: Don't be cheeky.

In none of these interactions is miscommunication caused by the interlocutors getting their linguistic facts wrong. The miscommunication occurs at the level of discourse. Communication breaks down because one person misinterprets the function of the other person's utterance.

In situation 1, the cabin attendant thought that the passenger wanted something (because this is typically why they are addressed by passengers), and assumed the discourse was part of a transactional encounter. In this case, however, the passenger was simply trying to engage in a piece of social interaction.

In situation 2, Speaker B, an immigrant worker, interprets "See you later" as an invitation. In many situations it would be. In this particular cultural context, however, it is a formulaic way of saying "Good-bye".

In situation 3, B, deliberately or otherwise, takes A's utterance as a statement of fact, rather than an invitation.

In 4, the husband, presumably in an attempt at humor, misinterprets the wife's utterance as a simple question rather than a warning.

In situation 5, the schoolchild, perhaps deliberately, misinterprets the teacher's utterance as a question, when in fact it is a command.

What do these situations have in common? All of the participants are either native speakers of English or highly competent users of the language. It is not at the level of grammar or vocabulary that communication breaks down, but at a discoursal/functional level. Granted that grammar is a central, critical, element in functional communication, but it is not the only element. What we need, in teaching grammar, is a functional approach that demonstrates to learners, not only how structures are formed in English but why one form is to be preferred over another in a given context.

It is clear from these examples that interpreting discourse, and thus establishing coherence, is a matter of readers/listeners using their linguistic knowledge to relate the discourse world to entities, events, and states of affairs beyond the text itself. While any piece of language is ultimately interpretable with reference to extralinguistic context, it is going too far to conclude that the language itself is somehow irrelevant or unnecessary.

(F3) Cohesion and coherence: independent but intertwined

Example (1) comes from Enkvist (1978). Cohesive elements, which in this example are all instances of repetition, are in italics:

> (1) The discussions ended last *week*. A *week* has seven *days*. Every *day* I feed my *cat*. *Cats* have four legs. The *cat* is on the *mat*. *Mat* has three letters.

Examples such as (1) demonstrate that a set of sentences, despite abundant cohesive ties, does not form a unified whole if coherence between the propositions is non-existent; in Enkvist's words the text is pseudo-coherent. By contrast, we can consider example (2), presented by Widdowson (1978), which has been used to demonstrate that coherence can be created without cohesion:

> (2) A: That's the telephone.
>   B: I'm in the bath.
>   A: O.K.

There is no surface textual cohesion in this short text, but the three utterances still form a plausible whole, because a situation can easily be imagined in which their propositional content would make sense together, i.e. cohere. Consequently, it was concluded that overt markers of cohesion are only of secondary importance in the creation of unity in text, compared to the covert aboutness created by coherence.

It seems that following the views presented above enables us to make a distinction between cohesion and coherence. Cohesion can be regarded as a property of the text, while coherence depends upon the communicators' evaluation of the text. Cohesive devices, being on the surface of the text, can be observed, counted and analyzed and are therefore more objective. Coherence, on the other hand, is more subjective, and communicators may perceive it in different ways. Although cohesion and coherence will thus be kept separate, it is important to realize that the two phenomena are nonetheless related. There is an interplay between them in that the presence of cohesive devices in a text facilitates the task of recognizing its coherence. In conclusion, it is firmly believed in the present study that successful communication depends on both cohesion and coherence, which are simultaneously independent and intertwined.

(F4) Register

It is well known that different contexts predict different kinds of language use. Systemic Functional Linguistics argues that there is a systematic correlation between context and language, and, specifically, that three different aspects of context correlate with the three different kinds of meaning expressed in language. Halliday (1985) identifies the determining context factors as being:

the *field* of discourse	what is being talked or written about
the *tenor* of discourse	the relationship between the participants
the *mode* of discourse	whether, for example, the language is written or spoken

Together the field, tenor and mode of the situation constitute the ***register variables*** of a situation. Texts whose contexts of situation co-vary in the same way are said to belong to the same ***register***. The concept of register is 'a theoretical explanation of the common-sense observation that we use language differently in different situations'. It is a useful way of explaining and predicting the relationship between features of context and features of text. Thus, the three texts about the hailstorm in the following (the newspaper account, the radio interview and the friendly conversation) all share the same field, in that they are all about the hailstorm. But they differ with regard to their tenor and mode. It is these tenor and mode differences which are reflected in different kinds of grammatical and lexical choices, and which account for such different wordings as the following.

> At Paddington, Ms Jan Mourice said all houses on one side of Prospect Street had windows smashed. [newspaper report]
>
> Steve Simons, a senior forecaster with the Bureau, joins me on the line this morning. [radio interview]
>
> Oh a friend of ours in Paddington, they had to move out of the flat. [conversation]

The way that, within specific cultural contexts, register variables influence how particular texts (whether spoken or written) are structured and have become institutionalized is in the concept of genre. A **genre** is a recognizable language activity, such as a news report, or a conversational story, whose structure has become formalized over time. Speakers of a language know how to perform these language activities in ways that are appropriate to their cultural contexts. For example, they know how to make stories interesting, entertaining or worth listening to. ***Genre theory*** provides semantic and grammatical tools for grouping texts with similar social purposes into text-types.

(F5) Speech Act

locutionary act	performing an act of saying something	language itself
illocutionary act	performing an act in saying something	purpose of the addresser
perlocutionary act	performing an act by saying something	effect on the addressee

When a speech act is uttered, the utterance carries locutionary meaning based on the meaning of the linguistic expression. Thus, an example "I am hungry." is a basic description of the speaker's state. However, it takes on illocutionary force when it acts as a request and the illocutionary force has the intended meaning of "please give me some food." Furthermore, since a speech act is directed toward an addressee who 'suffers the consequences' of the act, it also has perlocutionary force, which is the effect the act has on the addressee. But the individual elements cannot be always separated that easily. Bach and Harnish (1979) say that they are intimately related in a large measure.

(G) Conversation Analysis

The sociological approach to analyzing 'talk-in-interaction' has come to be known as **Conversation Analysis (CA)**, a branch of sociology which posits that it is in and through conversation that most of our routine everyday activities are accomplished. The objective of CA is to describe and explain the orderliness of conversation by reference to the participants' tacit reasoning procedures and sociolinguistic competencies. A researcher within the CA paradigm would be particularly interested in showing how the speakers are oriented to the rules of turntaking and how they accomplish this in an orderly manner. Conversation analysts are also interested in how conversational 'repairs' are achieved, and how these repairs also illustrate the participants' orientation to the basic rules of turntaking, as in this instance when Rob uses the word *tomorrow* to ask about an event that will in fact take place the day after tomorrow:

Rob: So erm they go back to school tomorrow?
Odile: Not tomorrow= =
Rob: = =Monday.
Odile: It's Sunday.
Rob: Monday.

Grace: Monday.
Odile: Monday.
Rob: Mm.
Odile: Yeah.

The repair sequence is interpolated into another sequence, which is the simple, two-part, question-and-answer sequence. The question and the answer would normally constitute what is called an **adjacency pair**, that is a two-part exchange, the second part of which is functionally dependent on the first — as in greetings, invitations, requests, and so on. In this case, a repair sequence is inserted (i.e. it forms an insertion sequence) in the adjacency pair, because the first element of the pair — the question — cannot be answered until the question has been 'repaired'. Conversational analysts are particularly interested in what such sequences demonstrate about the orderliness of conversation, and how the conversational 'work' is co-operatively managed.

Plus

content words vs. function words

Among many features of conversation, repetition, combined with a reliance on a relatively limited number of high frequency words, accounts for the fact that there is typically a lower *lexical density* and less *lexical variety* in conversation than in other registers. Lexical density is a measure of the ratio of the text's *content* words to its *function* words.

Content words	refer to words that carry a high information load, such as nouns, adjectives and lexical verbs.
Function words	refer to words that serve mainly a grammatical purpose, such as articles, auxiliary verbs and prepositions, to which should also be added *inserts*, i.e. words like *hmm, yeah, yuk* and so on, that are inserted freely into talk and which primarily serve an interactional and interpersonal purpose.

The fewer the content words, in proportion to function words and inserts, the lower the lexical density. Of all registers, both spoken and written, conversation has by far the lowest lexical density. This is because talk tends to carry a much lower information load than written text, an effect in large part due to the spontaneity of most speaking compared to the planned nature of most writing.

(G1) Components of conversational competence

conversational competence	Attention getting / Topic nomination / Topic development / Turn-taking / Topic clarification / Repair, Shifting, avoiding and interrupting / Topic termination

(G2) Adjacency Pairs (Preferred / Dispreferred sequences)

One of the most significant contributions of CA is the concept of the adjacency pair. An **adjacency pair** is composed of two turns produced by different speakers which are placed adjacently and where the second utterance is identified as related to the first (Each utterance within this is called a **move**.). Adjacency pairs include such exchanges as question/ answer; complaint/denial; offer/accept; request/grant; compliment/rejection; challenge/ rejection, and instruct/receipt. Adjacency pairs typically have three characteristics:

- They consist of two utterances;
- The utterances are adjacent, that is the first immediately follows the second; and
- Different speakers produce each utterance.

Here are some examples, taken from authentic conversational data:

Question/answer:
A: You don't like the fish?
B: No, it's not that I don't like it, it's the way it is done.

Offer/accept:
A: Now who can I make an iced coffee for?
B: Oh I think you could make one for my fat stomach.

Request/grant:
A: Jerry hi, where's our cake?
B: It's coming, it's coming. [laugh]

Compliment/response:
A: Great haircut.
B: Do you think? The hair colour burnt my scalp!

Instruct/receipt
A: Hand me the knife from the bench, will you.
B: Here you go.

Where there is a choice of responses — as in an invitation or a request, for example — one of these choices typically requires less elaboration than the other. Accepting an invitation, or granting a request, requires less 'face work', that is to say, they are less face-threatening — than refusing either an invitation or a request. The less face-threatening response is referred to as the **preferred sequence**, as in

> A: Would you like to try my Armenian dessert George?
> B: I'll taste it yes, thank you.

whereas a sequence such as:

> A: Why don't we go to see it tonight?
> B: No-way! I just want to collapse in front of tele.

is a '**dispreferred sequence**'. It is often the case that mitigating strategies — such as giving the reason for the refusal or apologizing — are used with dispreferred sequences to ensure conversational co-operativeness.

(G2a) Repair in Conversation Analysis

When an error does cause communication difficulties, there are various ways in which the problem can be sorted out, or 'repaired'. Research on conversation has documented the repair patterns that occur in English.

Think about your own experiences in speaking English with native speakers (or with competent adult non-native speakers). Several questions seem to run quickly through the minds of adult native speakers when a serious communication error is perceived. One question has to do with who will verbally note the existence of the error — the speaker or someone else in the conversation. This issue is referred to as 'self-' or 'other-initiation', since someone must get started on fixing the breakdown, by pointing it out — either verbally or nonverbally. The actual fixing of the error is called 'repair', and it too may be accomplished either by the speaker ('self-repair') or by one of the interlocutors ('other-repair').

Thus there are four possible combinations of initiation and repair involving self or other which occur in ongoing spoken discourse:

1. self-initiated other-repair, in which speakers note breakdowns and request assistance (for example, in a word search — the familiar tip-of-the tongue phenomenon when the speakers cannot produce the word they wish to use);

2. self-initiated self-repair, in which the speakers themselves both notice and correct the errors;

3. other-initiated self-repair, in which the interlocutors note and comment on the errors, but the speakers themselves are able to repair the breakdowns; and

4. other-initiated other-repair, in which people other than the speakers both call attention to the errors and provide the corrections.

By way of illustration, we can consider the following example of native speaker discourse, in which overlapping turns are marked with double slashes:

> **[transcript: Single beds'r awfully thin]**
> Lori: But y'know single beds'r awfully thin tuh sleep on.
> Sam: What?
> Lori: Single beds. // They're
> Ellen: Y'mean narrow?
> Lori: They're awfully narrow // yeah.

Here Sam initiates the repair sequence by asking 'What?' in response to Lori's statement that 'single beds'r awfully thin'. Ellen then supplies the repair, substituting the lexical item **narrow** for **thin**. This is an example of other-initiated other-repair.

Research into English conversations has shown a strong propensity for self-initiated self-repair: speakers normally notice and fix breakdowns as they occur. At other times, other-initiated self-repair is used, where the listener seeks clarification or repetition, which is then supplied by the original speaker. However, other-initiated other-repair (such as the example given in the above transcript) is relatively rare in normal conversation among linguistic equals.

How do these patterns of normal conversational repair relate to second language learning and teaching? Gaskill (1980) investigated initiation and repair strategies in conversations among native and non-native speakers of English. He found that other-initiated corrections were relatively infrequent. In Kasper's work (1985), the concept of 'trouble source' (that is, the problem that provokes the initiation and subsequent repair) is much broader than the concept of error which we are using here. Kasper divided the lessons in her data base into segments with a language-centered phase and those with a content-centered phase. She found that repair in the content-centered phase was similar to that in non-educational discourse among speakers of equal status: 'self-initiated and self-completed repair is preferred by both learners and teacher'. In the language-centered phases, trouble sources were identified by the teacher and repaired by the teacher or another learner, rather than the original speaker.

Given the findings from these studies and our experience, we can suggest that one characteristic of language classes that marks them as somehow different from 'real life' is the preponderance of other-initiated other-repair: teachers often tell learners that they have made errors and then tell them what to say instead.

(G3) IRF

In classroom organizations, such as pair and group work, where the teacher-led IRF-type discourse structures no longer operate, researchers have found a marked improvement both in the quality and quantity of language produced. Ellis (1994), summarizing the findings, comments that 'it seems reasonable to conclude that interaction between learners can provide the interactional conditions which have been hypothesized to facilitate acquisition more readily than can interaction involving teachers'. These interactional conditions include repair negotiation, which Porter (1986) found to be present in learner-learner interactions during task-centered discussions in ESL classrooms.

Nevertheless, there is considerable evidence to suggest that expert teachers are capable of exploiting learning opportunities in conversational discourse, without subverting the learners' own communicative agenda. One way they do this is by reformulating their learners' contributions in such a way as to align these contributions more closely to what has been said, and also to provide a springboard into the next stage of the talk. Cullen (2002) shows how one teacher achieves this through her skilful use of the F (follow-up) move in the traditional IRF routine. In this sequence, taken from a recording of an English lesson in a government secondary school in Tanzania, the teacher is preparing the class (of some 40 girls) to read a text about a plane hijacking:

> T: Now suppose you were inside the plane and this was happening. What would you do? You have to imagine yourself now, you are in the plane. Now I'll give you two minutes to discuss it with your friend. Two minutes. OK. Yes, please?
> S8: I shall pray my God because I know it is my final time. [laughter]
> T: She says she's going to kneel down and say, 'please God, forgive my sins'. [laughter]
> T: Yes?
> S9: I won't do anything. I'm going to die.
> T: She won't do anything. She'll just close her eyes [laughter] and say, 'take me if you want. If you don't want, leave me'.
> T: Yes?
> S10: I will shout.
> T: You will shout. Aagh! [laughter] I don't know if Heaven will hear you. [laughter]

Cullen comments that the teacher's follow-up moves play a crucial part in clarifying and building on the ideas that the students express in their responses, and in developing a meaningful dialogue between teacher and class. In doing so, the teacher supports learning by creating an environment which is rich in language and humour. Cullen identifies at least four specific strategies that the teacher uses in her follow-ups: **reformulation, elaboration, comment** and **repetition**. A reformulation is a more accurate or more appropriate rewording, by the teacher, of the learner's utterance (also called a **recast**). An elaboration extends or embellishes the reformulation (as in the teacher's second turn in the above extract). A comment, on the other hand, is the teacher's own personal response to the learner's utterance, as when the teacher in the above extract comments: *I don't know if Heaven will hear you*. The purpose of repeating a learner's utterance (sometimes called, disparagingly, **echoing**) is 'to confirm, question, or express surprise'.

(G4) Talk at school

Referential questions	not knowing the answer in advance (= Genuine Q / Information Q)
Display questions	knowing the answer in advance
Open questions	→ longer and more complex answers w/ explanation & reasoning
Closed questions	→ simple one-word responses, quick and easy to respond

The teacher and class are talking about seasons; Betty is five and a half:

> Teacher: Now when winter is over a new season will start. Do you know the name of that season?
> Betty: January
> Teacher: No, that's the name of the month. What season will it be? After winter will be s---?
> Betty: Spring
> Teacher: Good girl springtime

Even in this short extract a number of typical features of teacher talk are represented. The teacher's questions are all **display questions**, that is questions designed to elicit knowledge from the learners (as opposed to **referential questions**, where the asker does not know the answer). They are also *closed* in that they elicit short — characteristically one-word — answers. Because of this, the teacher contributes a greater quantity of talk to the interaction than the learner. The questions are all initiated by the teacher (there are no learner-initiated exchanges), a reflection of the unequal distribution of speaking rights. Each question forms the opening move in an IRF sequence (I=*initiate*, R=*response*, F=*follow up*, or *feedback*). The feedback is evaluative, commenting on the correctness or not of the response (No ⋯ good girl), rather than on its meaning. IRF sequences are often chained together to form large chunks of lesson time. Although there is no information about the pause lengths in the extract, it is likely that the teacher didn't allow a great deal of *wait time* between the initiating move and the response. In classrooms, there is typically little or no time for learners to formulate longer, more complex, more reflective responses, or to initiate their own topics.

None of these features of teacher talk are alien to caretaker talk: parents, too, ask display questions, give evaluative feedback, and tend to initiate exchanges. But children also participate in conversations with their caregivers where they play a far less passive role, and where there is a greater symmetry in the distribution and initiation of turns. On the other hand, the demands of the classroom situation, including the large number of learners that the teacher has to deal with, and the pedagogic motivation of classroom discourse, often mean that learners are exposed to very little other than the kind of interaction exemplified above. In itself, this might not seem to be a problem, especially if children are getting plentiful opportunities to participate more reciprocally and more actively in conversations outside the classroom. However, there are strong arguments to suggest that conversation 'when engaged in collaboratively, ⋯ can be an effective medium for learning and teaching'. By extension, a learning environment in which there are few or no conversational opportunities will be an impoverished one.

⟨Types of teacher questions⟩

on frame of lesson	Procedural questions	classroom procedure, routines, & management
on content of lesson	Convergent questions	similar and short student responses
	Divergent questions	diverse and not short student response

There are many different ways to classify questions, and as researchers have observed it is sometimes difficult to arrive at discrete and directly observable categories. For the purposes of examining the role of questions in the classroom, three kinds of questions are distinguished here — procedural, convergent, and divergent.

1) Procedural questions

Procedural questions have to do with classroom procedures and routines, and classroom management, as opposed to the content of learning. For example, the following questions occurred in classrooms while teachers were checking that assignments had been completed, that instructions for a task were clear, and that students were ready for a new task.

> Did everyone bring their homework?
> Do you all understand what I want you to do?
> How much more time do you need?
> Can you all read what I've written on the blackboard?
> Did anyone bring a dictionary to class?
> Why aren't you doing the assignment?

Procedural questions have a different function from questions designed to help students master the content of a lesson. Many of the questions teachers ask are designed to engage students in the content of the lesson, to facilitate their comprehension, and to promote classroom interaction. These questions can be classified into two types — convergent questions and divergent questions, depending on the kind of answer they are intended to elicit.

2) Convergent questions

Convergent questions encourage similar student responses, or responses which focus on a central theme. These responses are often short answers, such as 'yes' or 'no' or short statements. They do not usually require students to engage in higher-level thinking in order to come up with a response but often focus on the recall of previously presented information. Language teachers often ask a rapid sequence of convergent questions to help develop aural skills and vocabulary and to encourage whole-class participation before moving on to some other teaching technique. For example, the following questions were used by a teacher in introducing a reading lesson focusing on the effects of computers on everyday life. Before the teacher began the lesson she led students into the topic of the reading by asking the following convergent questions:

> How many of you have a personal computer in your home?
> Do you use it every day?
> What do you mainly use it for?
> What are some other machines that you have in your home?
> What are the names of some computer companies?
> What is the difference between software and hardware?

3) Divergent questions

Divergent questions are the opposite of convergent questions. They encourage diverse student responses which are not short answers and which require students to engage in higher-level thinking. They encourage students to provide their own information rather than to recall previously presented information. For example, after asking the convergent questions above, the teacher went on to ask divergent questions such as the following:

> How have computers had an economic impact on society?
> How would businesses today function without computers?
> Do you think computers have had any negative effects on society?
> What are the best ways of promoting the use of computers in education?

(G5) Foreigner Talk vs. Teacher Talk

Teacher Talk is usually highly grammatical as opposed to often ungrammatical Foreigner Talk.

Teacher talk	the language used by teachers while addressing their students
Foreigner talk	the language used by native speakers while addressing non-native speakers
Caregiver talk	the language used in addressing young children

A major portion of class time in teaching is taken up by teachers talking in front of the class. No matter what teaching strategies or methods a teacher uses, it is necessary to give directions, explain activities, clarify the procedures students should use on an activity, and check students' understanding.

A large proportion of the teacher's total communicative efforts can be taken up with coaxing along the communicative process itself, especially when the learners are relative beginners. The teacher has to get the pupils' attention, monitor their understanding by constant checking, clarify, explain, define and when appropriate summarise. (Ellis 1984)

This is seen in the following examples of a teacher explaining a textbook exercise to students and monitoring the students' progress.

> T: Have you finished yet? Have you completed the questions at the bottom of the page?
> S1: Not yet.
> T: [*to another student*] Where are you up to, Juan? Are you finished yet?
> S2: No, not yet.
> T: Try to finish up to here [*points at book*].
> T: Write your answers on a separate piece of paper, Akito, don't do it in your book.
> T: You work together with Akito now and check your answers. Do you understand?
> S3: OK. Check answers.
> T: Yes. Check your answers. You and Akito check your answers together.

The repetitive nature of the teacher's requests and instructions in this example is characteristic of what happens in teaching. Repetition is one of the many strategies teachers use to make their directions and instructions understandable to the learners. Other strategies (Chaudron 1988) include:

Speaking more slowly. When teachers speak to language learners in the classroom, they often use a slower rate of speech than they would use in other situations.

Using pauses. Teachers tend to pause more and to use longer pauses when teaching language learners, particularly lower-level students. These pauses give learners more time to process what the teacher has said and hence facilitate their comprehension.

Changing pronunciation. Teachers may sometimes use a clearer articulation or a more standard style of speech, one which contains fewer reductions and contractions than they would use outside of a teaching situation. For example, instead of saying, "Couldja read that line, Juan?" the teacher might more carefully enunciate "Could you ...?"

Modifying vocabulary. Teachers often replace a difficult word with what they think is a more commonly used word. For example, the teacher might ask, "What do you think this picture ***shows***?" instead of "What do you think this picture ***depicts***?" However, teachers sometimes unwittingly 'complicate' vocabulary instead of simplifying it. For example, teachers might say, "What do you think this picture ***is about***?" supplying an idiomatic (but not necessarily simpler) replacement for ***depicts***.

Modifying grammar. Language teachers often simplify the grammatical structure of sentences in the classroom. For example, teachers may use fewer subordinate clauses in a classroom situation than in other contexts, or avoid using complex tenses.

Modifying discourse. Teachers may repeat themselves or answer their own questions in order to make themselves understood, as we saw in the dialogue earlier.

These kinds of modifications in teachers' speech can lead to a special type of discourse which has been referred to as **teacher talk**. When teachers use teacher talk they are trying to make themselves as easy to understand as possible, and effective teacher talk may provide essential support to facilitate both language comprehension and learner production. Krashen (1985) argues that this is how teachers provide learners with 'comprehensible input' (input which is finely tuned to the learner's level of comprehension), which he sees as 'the essential ingredient for second language acquisition'. However, sometimes teachers may develop a variety of teacher talk which would not sound natural outside of the classroom. The following are examples of teachers using this variety of teacher talk when teaching low-level ESL learners.

In your house, you ... a tub ... you (gestures) *wash.* (The teacher is explaining the meaning of 'wash'.)

I want to speak another person. He not here. What good thing for say now? (The teacher is explaining how to take telephone messages.)

Not other students listen. I no want. Necessary you speak. Maybe I say what is your name. The writing not important. (The teacher is explaining an interview procedure.)

The book ... we have ... (holds up book) *... book is necessary for class. Right ... necessary for school. You have book.* (The teacher is reminding the students to bring their books to class.)

Although these examples may be extreme, they illustrate that in their efforts to provide students with comprehensible input, teachers may sometimes develop a style of speaking that does not reflect natural speech.

(H) Types of Nonverbal Communication

Kinesics	body movements and posture including gestures, head movements and posture, eye contact, and facial expressions
Kinesthetics	(= haptics) touch behaviors
Vocalics	the vocalized but not verbal aspects
Proxemics	the use of space and distance
Chronemics	the study of how time affects communication
Personal presentation and environment	the use of objects

(I) Genre Analysis

Genre Analysis attempts to identify the textual patterns and regularities and show how such text types (or genres) are determined by their contexts of use. The analysis of a spoken genre involves a number of steps:

- identifying a 'chunk' of talk that is amenable to a generic description;
- defining the social purpose of the genre;
- differentiating the different stages (the macro-structure), including specifying obligatory and optional stages; and
- analyzing the linguistic features of each stage.

The first stage in genre analysis is the identification of chunks of text that have internal consistency, and seem to move through predictable stages. This is where one participant holds the floor for a period, for example to tell a story, to gossip etc. When reporting conversations, people will often say things like *Chris told us this amazing* story *about when he was hitchhiking in Italy*, or *We had a good* gossip *about work while Jack was in the men's room*. These conversational chunks are often monologic, as is the case of stories, and once initiated, constrain the other interactants to yield the floor until all the stages of the sequence have been realized.

Having identified a chunk, the second stage in genre analysis is to define its social purpose in terms of its typical contexts of use, and, at the same time, to supply it with a functional label that reflects this purpose. Is the text's function to inform, to amuse, to criticize, to warn, for example? Simply 'telling a story' is too broad a description of the genre's purpose, and does not necessarily capture the way that social reality is constructed by means of telling and being told stories. Speaker-hearer conceptions of the kind of social activity taking place and its social purpose determine the way that the discourse is structured. Stories are told for different purposes, and the functional label needs to reflect each purpose accurately.

The third stage in genre analysis is the identification and differentiation of the genre's constituent stages. These are best labelled in terms of their function, too. A widely accepted model of the narrative structure of personal anecdotes is that described by Labov and Waletzky (1967):

> (Abstract) ^ Orientation ^ Complication ^ Evaluation ^ Resolution ^ Coda
> where ^ = is followed by.

The stages are written in a linear sequence and the symbol ^ is placed between them to indicate how they are ordered with respect to one another.

The final stage in the analysis of a genre is a description of the micro-features of the genre, specifically the lexico-grammatical features that characterize the genre, and which serve both to differentiate the genre from other genres, and to differentiate the stages within the genre from each other. The micro-analysis stage needs to take account of typical features as well as variants within generic models. As in the case of the macro-structure, a micro-analysis should try to identify obligatory and optional elements at each stage. But identification alone is not enough: according to genre theory, the analysis should also explain the effect of these lexico-grammatical choices and relate these effects to the overall function of the text.

최서원 전공영어 영어교육학 PRACTICAL

Chapter 04 Mind Map

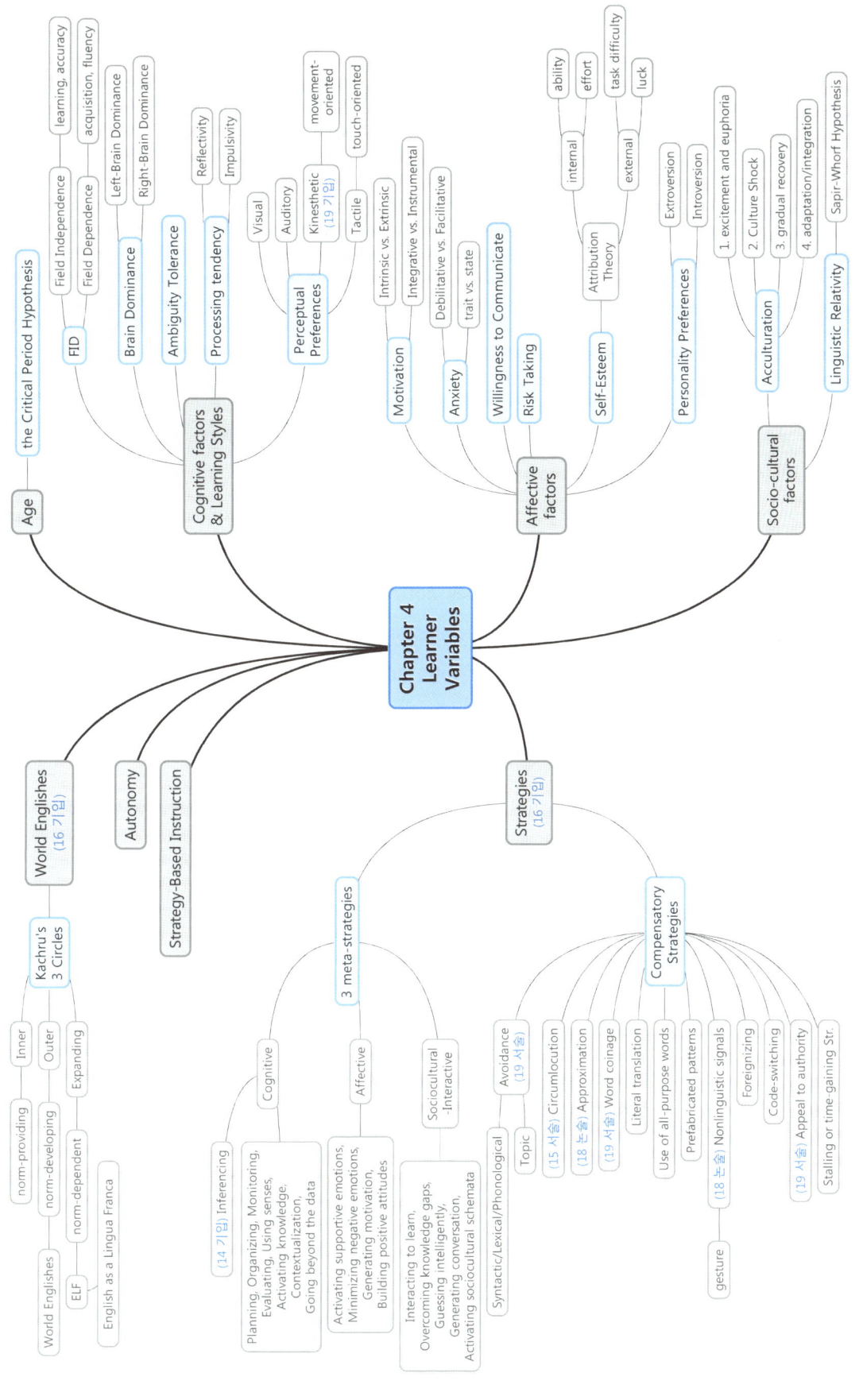

Chapter 04   Learner Variables

(A) Age & Critical Period Hypothesis

The effect of age on acquisition has been extensively documented, the issue being whether younger learners acquire a second language more efficiently and effectively than older learners. Research to date has not conclusively settled the issue of age one way or another, largely because, from a research perspective, the issue is more complex than it might seem at first. As Ellis (1985), points out, it is necessary to distinguish between the effect of age on the route of acquisition (whether the same target language items are acquired in the same order for different learners), the rate (how rapidly the learners acquire the language), and ultimate attainment (how proficient they end up being). Ellis concludes (from his review of the available literature) that, while age does not alter the route of acquisition, it does have a marked effect on the rate and ultimate success. However, the results are by no means straightforward. For example, in terms of rate, adults appear to do better than children (6 to 10 years), while teenagers (12 to 15 years) appear to outperform both adults and children. Ellis concludes that:

- Starting age does not affect the route of SLA. Although there may be differences in the acquisitional order, these are not the result of age.

- Starting age affects the rate of learning. When grammar and vocabulary are concerned, adolescent learners do better than either children or adults, when the length of exposure is held constant. When pronunciation is concerned, there is no appreciable difference.

- Both number of years of exposure and starting age affect the level of success. The number of years' exposure contributes greatly to the overall communicative fluency of the learners, but starting age determines the levels of accuracy achieved, particularly in pronunciation.

These age-related differences have been explained in terms of a biological mechanism known as the '**critical period**'. This construct refers to a limited period of time in the development of an organism during which a particular behavior can be acquired. It has been argued that the optimum age for acquiring another language is in the first ten years of life because it is then that the brain retains its maximum 'plasticity' or flexibility (the plasticity metaphor, suggesting as it does that the brain is like a lump of plasticine that gradually hardens with age. It is suggested that, at around puberty, the brain loses its plasticity, the two hemispheres of the brain become much more independent of one another, and the language function is largely established in the left hemisphere. The CPH argues that, after these neurological changes have taken place, acquiring another language becomes increasingly difficult.

The hypothesis, however, is not without its critics. As Ellis (1985) points out, it is only partially correct to suggest that acquisition is easier for younger children. In fact, pronunciation is the only area where the younger the start the better, and the hypothesis is at a loss to explain why the loss of plasticity only affects pronunciation.

(B) Cognitive factors & Learning Styles

We can outline three categories of learner styles thought to represent natural orientations of learners:

1. *Perceptual preferences*

This involves whether or when learners tend to learn by listening (auditory style), seeing (visual style), or doing (kinesthetic style). For example, a learner with a visual style might prefer to learn vocabulary by reading new words rather than by hearing them.

2. *Personality preferences*

This involves learners' degree of openness to new experiences and their extroversion versus introversion. For example, learners might prefer to learn by looking outward in social contexts (extroverted style) or looking inward (introverted style). If asked to perform a role play in front of the class, learners with an introverted style might feel embarrassed, causing their performance to suffer.

3. *Processing preferences*

This concerns whether or when learners prefer to process information by seeing the big picture (global-oriented style) versus the specifics (detail-oriented style), by figuring out rules from examples (inductive style) versus learning the rules and applying them to examples (deductive style), or by bringing the parts together to determine the whole (synthetic style) versus disassembling the whole into parts (analytic style). For example, a learner with a global-oriented style might prefer to begin a new lesson by looking over the entire unit to get the big picture before attending to specifics.

<Table> Common Learner Styles

\<Perceptual preferences\>		
Style	Description	Example learner self-report
Auditory	Prefers learning by hearing.	I learn better by hearing someone explain it.
Visual	Prefers learning by seeing.	I learn better by reading it.
Kinesthetic	Prefers learning by doing.	I learn better when I experience doing it myself.

\<Personality preferences\>		
Style	Description	Example learner self-report
Extroverted	Prefers to learn by looking outward.	I learn better by working with others.
Introverted	Prefers learning by looking inward.	I learn better by working alone.

\<Processing preferences\>		
Style	Description	Example learner self-report
Global-oriented	Prefers focusing on the big picture (top-down); gravitates first toward the main ideas, then the details.	I learn better by summarizing the information.
Detail-oriented	Prefers focusing on the specifics (bottom-up); gravitates first toward the details, then the main ideas.	I learn better by understanding the specifics.
Inductive	Prefers to start with examples so generalizations can be made from the patterns.	I learn better by figuring out the rules from examples in the language.
Deductive	Prefers to start with the rules or theories so they can be applied to examples.	I learn better when I have the language rules before applying them.
Synthetic	Prefers to bring the parts together to construct new ideas.	I learn better by summarizing what has been said.
Analytic	Prefers to break information down into components so the relationships can be identified and understood.	I learn better by looking at the parts so I can analyze and understand them.
Field-sensitive	Prefers to get information in context.	I learn better if I see new words, structures, or ideas in context.
Field-insensitive	Prefers to get information in the abstract rather than in concrete situations.	I learn better if new words, structures, or ideas are explained without reference to context.

(B1) Field Independence vs. Field Dependence

Field Independence	step by step & with sequential instruction, more accurate learners
Field Dependence	information presented in context, more fluent learners

Field independence has its origins in visual perception. It distinguishes individuals dichotomously as to whether or not they are dependent on a prevailing visual field. If an individual is dependent on the prevailing visual, she or he cannot see something right in front of them. On the other hand, those who are field-independent are better able to notice details outside of the prevailing visual object and are not dependent on that object. Some individuals are better at finding objects in the middle of clutter (*field-independent*), whereas others (*field-dependent*) cannot see things that may be obvious to those with a field-independent orientation. In other words, the 'field' (surroundings) gets in the way of field-dependent individuals. In a review of the literature, Johnson, Prior, and Artuso (2000) report that field independents are, in general, better at performing cognitive tasks, but Chapelle (1995) pointed out that those who are field-dependent have an orientation that might be deemed more interpersonal and more sensitive to the social context. This would certainly have importance for their differential role in interaction studies. It would be predicted that field-dependent individuals would be more sensitive to implicit feedback than field-independent individuals and would, as a result, benefit more from interactions.

A common thread that runs through most of the senses of field independence is that the field-independent person tends to be highly analytic, ignoring potentially confusing information in the context (this is the inspiration for the term itself), and self-reliant. The field-dependent person, on the other hand, tends to pay great attention to context. These patterns are apparently robust over many different tasks and hence may be considered a personality trait.

Given this background, predictions can be made about the effects of this personality trait on second language learning. Logically, one might expect that field-independent individuals would be better at analytical tasks in second language learning. This would appear to be an advantage. On the other hand, field dependence would seem to help in social interactions. Linguists have often argued that the context provides much of the meaning that is missing in just the actual linguistic text itself. If field-dependent individuals pay more attention to the context, then this would seem to aid in context-dependent tasks.

Some studies reported correlations in the expected directions. Others found little support for a relationship at all. To summarize the debate, there is no evidence for any personality trait that predicts overall success in second language learning. Certain personality traits appear helpful in completing certain tasks that may play a role in second language learning. Thus, the value of the trait to the learner depends on how important the facilitated tasks may be. This depends on the teaching methods the student is subjected to (assuming formal instruction) and the particular way the student goes about learning another language. Personality is perhaps better investigated within the context of the contributions learners, teachers, methods, and materials make to the learning situation.

(B2) Left-Brain Dominance vs. Right-Brain Dominance

Left-Brain	associated with logical, analytical thought, with mathematical and linear processing of information
Reflectivity	perceiving and remembering visual, tactile, and auditory images efficient in processing holistic, integrative, and emotional information

(B3) Ambiguity Tolerance

Ambiguity Tolerance	cognitive willingness to tolerate ideas against his/her belief system

(B4) Reflectivity & Impulsivity

Impulsivity	making a quick or gambling guess at an answer to a problem
Reflectivity	making a slow, more calculated decision to a problem

(B5) Perceptual preferences

Visual	preferring reading charts, drawings, and other graphic information
Auditory	preferring listening to lectures and audiotapes
Kinesthetic	movement-oriented, preferring demonstrations and physical activities
Tactile	touch-oriented

(C) Affective factors

(C1) Motivation

Intrinsic motivation	motivated by the activity itself
Extrinsic motivation	motivated by a reward from outside and beyond the self
Instrumental motivation	for practical goals
Integrative motivation	for social interchange

(C2) Anxiety

helpful	Facilitative anxiety	Debilitative anxiety	harmful

(C3) Willingness to Communicate

Willingness to Communicate	the intention to initiate communication, given a choice

(C4) Risk Taking

Risk Taking	trying out hunches about the language and taking the risk of being wrong

(C5) Self-Esteem / Attribution Theory & Self-Efficacy

Internal factors	Ability	Task difficulty	External factors
	Effort *	Luck	

(C6) Personality preferences

from other people	Extroversion	Introversion	from their own self

(D) Socio-cultural factors

(D1) Acculturation

Stage 1	(excitement and euphoria)	over newness of the surroundings
Stage 2	(culture shock)	feeling the intrusion of cultural differences
Stage 3	(gradual recovery)	gradual, tentative and vacillating recovery
Stage 4	(adaptation / integration)	either assimilation or adaptation

(D2) Linguistic Relativity (Sapir-Whorf Hypothesis)

Linguistic Relativity	language not 'determines' but 'influences'

(E) Techniques in teaching culture

AMU	TPR adaptation	
Culture Assimilator	self-instructional	using 'critical incident' techniques
Cultural Drama	student participation	
Culture Capsule	w/ visual aids and realia, and explanation	
Culture Island	a classroom atmosphere	

⟨Audio-motor Unit⟩

    The **audio-motor unit** is designed primarily to teach listening comprehension. It consists of a series of oral commands to which students are instructed to react physically. It is an application of TPR to teaching culture. When the commands contain culturally related material, this highly motivating technique immediately demonstrates the cultural phenomena through the physical responses. The example shown below illustrates four characteristics of Spanish table manner of eating meat, the position of the hands when not in use, the role of wine at mealtime, and the manner of eating bread.

You are at a restaurant.	Chew it.
Pick up your napkin.	Swallow it.
Unfold it.	Put down your knife and fork.
Leave your hands on the table.	You want some bread. Break off a piece.
Pour a glass of wine.	Eat it.
Take a sip.	Pick up the bill.
Put it on your lap.	Look at it.
Pick up your fork in your left hand.	Take out your wallet.
Pick up your knife in your right hand.	Pay the bill.
Cut a piece of meat.	Leave a tip.
Put it in your mouth.	Leave the restaurant.

‹Culture Assimilator›

Based on critical incident techniques, **culture assimilators** provide an excellent self-instructional source for learning cultural concepts. Each episode consists of an incident presented in narrative or dialogue format in which a foreigner comes face to face with a conflict in the target culture. After reading the episode, students select one of four possible explanations. Each choice is accompanied by appropriate feedback. The reader should note that even the feedback for the wrong choices provides interesting cultural information. The sample here is 'burp episode'.

> Minsu has recently arrived to study in the US. When he was enrolling for classes, he met Ken, an American student. Ken invited him to dinner. Ken also invited several of his American friends so that Minsu could meet some more Americans. During dinner, Minsu was telling the Americans about Korea and about the differences he noticed between two cultures. When he finished his dinner, Minsu burped loudly. The Americans looked shocked and Minsu became uncomfortable, wondering if he had said anything to offend anyone.
> How would you explain this to Minsu?
>
> a) Americans are offended by this kind of talk at the dinner table.
> b) He should have expressed his appreciation of the meal while he was eating, not afterwards.
> c) He didn't burp loudly enough, so the Americans thought he didn't like the food.
> d) Americans find burping offensive when in the company of others.
>
> Feedback:
> a) This kind of talk is very normal and often welcomed at American dinner tables. There is a more appropriate answer. Please choose again.

> b) Normally, a guest would express his/her appreciation after the meal, although it would not be unusual to express their appreciation during the meal. This would not account for the shock that the Americans expressed. Please try again.
>
> c) The loudness of a burp has no particular mean for the reaction of the American hosts, but the burp itself does. Please see answer 4 for a complete explanation.
>
> d) This is the best answer. Burping is a habit that is considered rude in any situation in American culture, but it is especially rude at the dinner table. Americans are taught from an early age that burping in front of others is unacceptable. If it is necessary to burp, a hand covering one's mouth while burping is acceptable.

<Cultural Minidrama>

Using critical incident techniques similar to the culture assimilator the minidrama presents an example of a miscommunication in the form of a dramatization. This is followed by teacher-led discussion to help students discover the cause of the miscommunication. Minidramas provide an excellent opportunity for student participation not only through the attempt to solve the problem but also through staging the dramatization.

<Culture Capsule>

The culture capsule was designed to explain a specific cultural difference between a learner and a foreign custom. Using a variety of visual aids and realia, the teacher provides a brief oral explanation of the foreign custom and contrasts it with a related custom of the learner. This is followed by a series of content-related questions and appropriate student activities. Some publishers have produced sets of culture capsules based on this original model and designed for supplementary use. Unfortunately, most of them have been written in L1, reinforcing the notion that culture should not necessarily be taught in the target language. The culture capsule need not be limited to oral presentation by the teacher nor restricted to presentation in L1.

(F) World Englishes

In the past, the field of English language teaching was divided into teaching **English as a second language** (**ESL**) and teaching **English as a foreign language** (**EFL**). ESL was for immigrants to English-speaking countries or for citizens of countries where English was a widely used second language (L2). EFL was taught as a foreign language in countries where

English had no official internal use (i.e., it was an academic subject at school). It is now necessary to go well beyond the English as a second versus foreign language distinction. English has, over the past century, gradually become the most widely taught language in the world. It has also become the most widely used language for most purposes of communication in international diplomacy, business, science, education, and entertainment. English is also more widely dispersed geographically than any other language. These facts prompted Ferguson (1971) to claim that English has become a language of wider communication, or (in more recent terminology) what S. L. McKay (2012) calls **English as an international language** (**EIL**).

World Englishes are regionally distinct varieties of English that have arisen in areas of Asia, Africa, and Oceania, where there is a long (often colonial) history of English being widely used in education, commerce, and government. Over time this widespread use of English (spoken side by side with local languages) has given rise to local varieties of English with their own standards. Examples of World Englishes are Indian English, West African English, Filipino English, and Singapore English. Examples of features of these varieties of English include more frequent use of the progressive aspect (*be ... -ing*) in Indian English (e.g., ***Whatever you are wanting, I am not having***), the use of ***isn't it?*** as the invariant tag in Nigerian English (e.g., ***Our team won the football game, isn't it?***), and the use of ***lah*** as marker of solidarity in Singapore English (e.g., ***No problem lah. I go there anyway.***).

Although English can be used as the lingua franca between a native English speaker and a non-native speaker, the prototypical use of **English as a lingua franca** (**ELF**) occurs in communication between two non-native speakers of English who do not share a common L1. Furthermore, in a majority of environments, it is now more common to have an English teacher who is a non-native speaker than a teacher who is a native speaker. It is thus often more realistic in such contexts to teach English so that learners can communicate with other non-native speakers rather than with native speakers. This represents a fundamental shift in orientation in that most previous EFL instruction assumed that communication with native speakers was the primary learning objective.

The one major problem that has been raised with respect to these established varieties is that they are often not fully intelligible to users of other varieties of English. Kirkpatrick (2007) proposes a scale that characterizes this problem. At one extreme, we have the goal of national or regional identity; people use a regional variety of English with its specific grammar, lexicon, and phonology to affirm their own national or ethnic identity. At the other end of the scale, we have the goal of intelligibility; users of a regional variety should ideally still be readily intelligible to other users of English everywhere else in the world to fully participate in the use of English as an international language. The challenge is to find a good balance between the identity-intelligibility extremes on Kirkpatrick's scale. Effective users may engage in a certain amount of code-switching (i.e., using English and another language in the same discourse unit). Based on the situational context, they may use a strongly local version of the regional variety to communicate with fellow users of the local variety and a weaker, more formal version when communicating with users of other varieties, when international intelligibility is necessary.

(F1) Kachru's Three Circles of English

Inner Circle	UK, USA, Australia, New Zealand, Ireland, etc.	'norm-providing'
Outer Circle	(World Englishes) India, Nigeria, Pakistan, etc.	'norm-developing'
Expanding Circle	(ELF) Korea, China, Japan, Russia, Egypt, etc.	'norm-dependent'

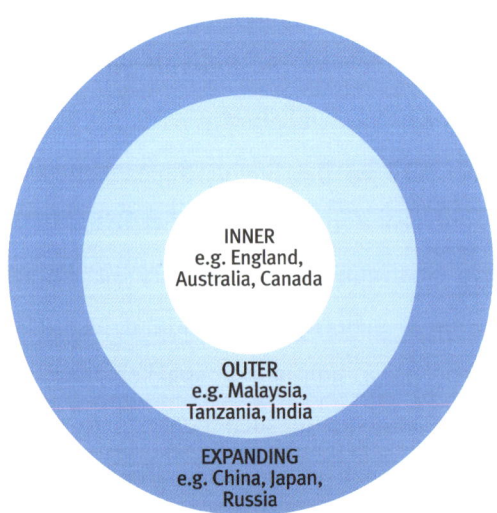

(F2) Bilingual Education

The widely accepted view within the English as a Second Language (ESL) research and pedagogical community is that the ideal for all English language learners is to maintain or enrich their native languages while acquiring ESL (Gass & Neu 1995).

(F2a) Classifications of bilingualism

Reflecting the multidimensionality of bilingualism, we can see that different classifications have been proposed focusing on different dimensions of bilingualism. Such dimensions include: the relationship between language proficiencies in two languages (as seen in balanced and dominant bilinguals); the functional ability (receptive and productive bilinguals); the age of acquisition (simultaneous, sequential, and late bilinguals); the organization of linguistic codes and meaning units (compound, coordinate, and subordinate bilinguals); the effect of L2 learning on the retention of L1 (additive and subtractive bilinguals), and so forth.

before critical period	Early	Late	after critical period
both proficient	Balanced	Dominant	unbalanced
2 codes w/ 1 meaning	Compound	Coordinate	2 codes w/ 2 meanings
w/o losing L1	Additive	Subtractive	w/ losing L1

(1) Early and Late Bilinguals

Bilinguals can be categorized into early and late bilinguals, according to the age of exposure to two (or more) languages. ***Early bilingualism*** is defined as the acquisition of more than one language in the pre-adolescent phase of life (Baetens Beardsmore 1986). ***Late bilingualism*** has been defined as the acquisition of one language before and the other language after the age of 8 years.

Early bilingualism can also be classified into two types. ***Simultaneous early bilingualism*** occurs in situations when a child learns two languages at the same time, from birth. This often produces a strong bilingualism. ***Successive early bilingualism*** occurs in situations when a child who has already partially acquired a L1 (first language) and then learns a L2 (second language) early in childhood; an example can be when a child moves to another place where the dominant language is not his native language. This usually results in the production of a strong bilingualism, but the child needs time to learn the L2.

Late bilingualism refers to the bilinguals who have learned their L2 after the critical period, especially when L2 is learned in adulthood or adolescence. Late bilingualism in fact is a successive bilingualism which occurs after the acquisition of L1.

(2) Balanced and Dominant Bilinguals

The distinction between balanced and dominant (or unbalanced) bilinguals (Peal and

Lambert 1962) is based on the relationship between the fluency and proficiencies of the respective languages which bilinguals master. Those who acquire similar degrees of proficiency and mastery in both languages are defined as ***balanced bilinguals***, while on the contrary, ***dominant*** (or ***unbalanced***) ***bilinguals*** are those individuals whose proficiency in one language is higher than that in the other language(s).

(3) Compound, Coordinate, and Subordinate Bilinguals

According to Weinreich (1953), compound, coordinate, and subordinate distinctions deal with the properties of how two or more linguistic codes are organized and stored by individuals. In ***compound bilinguals***, two sets of linguistic codes are stored in one meaning unit; in other words, have one system of meaning for words which is used for both L1 and L2, while on the contrary, in ***coordinate bilinguals***, each linguistic code is stored and organized separately in two meaning units and the bilinguals have two systems of meanings for words. Furthermore, in subordinate bilinguals, linguistic codes of bilinguals' second language (L2) are assumed to be understood and interpreted through their first language (L1). Specifically, they are considered to possess two sets of linguistic codes, however, only one meaning unit, which is accessible merely through their L1. Nowadays only first two kinds i.e. coordinate and compound bilinguals are endorsed by the researchers and experts in the field, while the third one is dropped.

(4) Additive Bilinguals and Subtractive Bilinguals

Lambert (1974) depicts that depending on how one's L2 influences the retention of one's L1, bilinguals can be classified into additive bilinguals and subtractive bilinguals. Bilinguals who improve their L2 without losing their L1 proficiency are called ***additive bilinguals***. On the contrary, those whose L2 is acquired or learned at the cost of losing their L1 are called as ***subtractive bilinguals***. For being additive bilinguals, both of the languages learned by individuals should be valued in the society in which they live.

(F2b) Bilingual teaching and learning & Functional bilingualism

One of the current trends in teaching foreign languages is 'bilingual teaching', meaning that the language is no longer the subject matter of education, but serves as the medium of instruction in science and art classrooms around the world. Creating and preserving a bilingual education system, where the mother tongue is used together with the L2 as a means of instruction, multicultural education is advocated as the main trend of the modern education system. Leaving aside the problem of bilingual education employing minority languages, the present research focuses on English as a lingua franca. It is not a secret that English currently seems to be the 'unofficial' language not only of the European Union but of Russia as well, at least in academia. European bilingual education models are currently exemplified by CLIL – Content and Language Integrated Learning, a new generic and/or umbrella term for bilingual education, which has been rapidly spreading throughout Europe since the mid-nineties. Generally, the basis of this educational approach is that disciplines such as history, math, geography, etc. are taught in a foreign language instead of in the mother tongue, thus exposing the students to the foreign language in a much more authentic and holistic way. Such an approach, as described in Eurydice's (2006) report Content and Language Integrated Learning (CLIL) at School in Europe, involves learning and teaching one or more 'non-language' disciplines not simply in, but also with and through a foreign language.

As a result of bilingual teaching, functional bilingualism is becoming extremely wide spread. **Functional bilingualism** is one's ability to use and produce both languages across 'an encyclopedia of everyday events' (Baker 1993). Functional bilingualism implies that languages of an individual are only his/her tools, which are used to fulfill a certain linguistic need or a need for interaction with an environment. The term 'functional' is bound to competent use of one language to another if necessary. The essence of this type of bilingualism is that the L2 is used for special purposes, mostly study. In accordance with the traditional diverse classification of bilinguals the students involved in bilingual teaching and defined as having functional bilingualism could be also referred to as dominant (or unbalanced), late sequential, coordinate, and productive and additive bilinguals. For example, some students of an ESL program are immersed in a foreign language environment, having 6-8 classes a day in English (both language and non-language), but their L1 proficiency is still higher than that of their L2 (dominant). Most students were exposed to a foreign language and have been productive in it since 10-12 years old (sequential, late, productive bilingualism), L2 being as enrichment without loss of L1 (additive).

(G) Autonomy

Autonomy	learner-centered

Closely linked to the concept of autonomy is the demand on learners to become aware of their own processes of learning. Now, with the backdrop of a good deal of research on awareness and 'consciousness raising', language programs are offering more occasions for learners to develop a metacognitive awareness of their ongoing learning (Byram 2012). The supporting research stockpile is growing on ***awareness-raising*** among L2 learners in classrooms around the world (Lightbown & Spada 2000, Rosa & Leow 2004). These studies found that an optimal level of awareness serves learners. Too much awareness, overattention to monitoring for correctness, or explicit focus on grammar will smother a learner's yearning to simply *use* language. Even too much thinking about strategic options — with too little intuitive, subconscious communication — can block open communication. On the other hand, some levels of awareness are clearly warranted, and teachers need to take the conscious application of appropriate strategies.

(H) Strategies

Cognitive strategies	constructing, transforming, and applying L2 knowledge
Affective strategies	employing beneficial emotional energy, forming positive attitudes, and generating and maintaining motivation
Sociocultural-Interactive strategies	generating and maintaining interactive communication within a cultural context
Compensatory strategies	making up for gaps in one's ability

Cognitive Strategies and tactics	
Planning	Previewing, reviewing, setting schedules, deciding to attend to a specific aspect of language input, planning for and rehearsing linguistic components necessary to carry out an upcoming language task, deciding to postpone speaking
Organizing	Deciding to attend to specific aspects of language input or situational details that will cue the retention of language input, reordering, classifying, labeling items in the language
Monitoring	Correcting one's speech for accuracy in pronunciation, grammar, vocabulary, imitating a language model, including silent rehearsal, and self-checking
Evaluating	Checking the outcomes of one's own language learning against an internal measure of completeness and accuracy

Using senses	Creating visualizations and pictures to remember, noticing phonological sounds, acting out a word or sentence
Activating knowledge	Using the first language for comparison/contrast to remember words and forms, applying rules by deduction, using translation to remember a new word
Contextualization	Placing a word or phrase in a meaningful language sequence, relating new information to other concepts in memory
Going beyond the data	Guessing meanings of new items, predicting words or forms from the context
Affective Strategies and tactics	
Activating supportive emotion	Encouraging oneself, making positive statements, making lists of one's abilities, rewarding oneself for accomplishments, noticing what one has accomplished to build self-confidence, writing a language learning diary
minimizing negative emotions	Using relaxation to lower fear or anxiety, using positive self-talk to lower self-doubt, generating interesting charts, images, or dialogues to lower boredom, making a list of "to do" items to avoid feeling overwhelmed
Generating motivation	Learning about the culture of a language, setting personal goals and monitoring their accomplishment, listing specific accomplishments, turning attention away from tests and toward what one can do with the language
Building positive attitudes	Using relaxation to lower fear or anxiety, generating interesting activities to lower boredom, empathizing with others to develop cultural understanding
Sociocultural-interactive strategies and tactics	
Interacting to learn	Cooperating with one or more peers to obtain feedback, pool information, or model a language activity
Overcoming knowledge gaps	Asking a teacher or other native speaker for repetition, paraphrasing, explanation, and/or examples, questioning for clarification, using memorized chunks of language to initiate or maintain communication
Guessing intelligently	Using linguistic clues in lexicon, grammar, or phonology to predict, using discourse markers to comprehend
Generating conversation	Initiating conversation with known discourse gambits, maintaining conversation with affirmations, verbal and nonverbal attention signals, asking questions
Activating socio-cultural schemata	Asking questions about culture, customs, etc., reading about culture (customs, history, music, art)

Compensatory strategies	
Avoidance	Avoiding a topic, concept, grammatical construction, or phonological element that poses difficulty
Circumlocution	Describing or exemplifying the target object or action (e.g. *the thing you open bottles with* for *corkscrew*)
Approximation	Using an alternative term which expresses the meaning of the target lexical items as closely as possible (e.g. *ship* for *sailboat*)
Word coinage	Creating a nonexisting L2 word based on a supposed rule (e.g. *vegetarianist* for *vegetarian*)
Nonverbal signals	Mime, gesture, facial expression, or sound imitation
Prefabricated patterns	Using memorized stock phrases, usually for 'survival' purposes (e.g. *Where is the _____?, How much does this cost?*)
Code-switching	Using a L1 word with L1 pronunciation or a L3 word with L3 pronunciation while speaking in L2
Appeal to authority	Asking for aid from the interlocutor either directly (e.g. *What do you call ...?*) or indirectly (e.g. rising intonation, pause, eye contact, puzzled expression)
Keeping the floor	Using fillers or hesitation devices to fill pauses and to gain time to think (e.g. *well, now let's see, uh, as a matter of fact*)

According to Nunan (2004), language learning activities, or tasks, can be divided into five different groups according to what kind of strategies are the base for the tasks. The five strategies are the cognitive, interpersonal, linguistic, affective and creative strategies.

- The cognitive strategy is the base for a task, and it means that the task has the students manipulate the input they receive in some way, for example by classifying things into categories, or by just taking notes.
- The interpersonal strategy includes tasks which require communication with another person, such as in role playing.
- With the linguistic strategy, the main focus is on the language. Summarizing and doing controlled language exercises are examples of this.
- The affective strategy includes tasks with which the students have to understand their own feelings and opinions and use them in order to finish the task. Reflecting is an example of this.
- With the creative strategy, as the name suggests, the students create something new, be it a play or just for example brainstorming.

COGNITIVE

CLASSIFYING: Putting things that are similar together in groups
   Example: Study a list of names and classify them into male and female.

PREDICTING: Predicting what is to come in the learning process
   Example: Look at the unit title and objectives and predict what will be learned.

INDUCING: Looking for patterns and regularities
   Example: Study a conversation and discover the rule for forming the simple past tense.

TAKING NOTES: Writing down the important information in a text in your own words

CONCEPT MAPPING: Showing the main ideas in a text in the form of a map

INFERENCING: Using what you know to learn something new

DISCRIMINATING: Distinguishing between the main idea and supporting information

DIAGRAMMING: Using information from a text to label a diagram

INTERPERSONAL

CO-OPERATING: Sharing ideas and learning with other students
   Example: Work in small groups to read a text and complete a table.

ROLE PLAYING: Pretending to be somebody else and using the language for the situation you are in
   Example: You are a reporter. Use the information from the reading to interview the writer.

LINGUISTIC

CONVERSATIONAL PATTERNS: Using expressions to start conversations and keep them going
   Example: Match formulaic expressions to situations.

PRACTISING: Doing controlled exercises to improve knowledge and skills
   Example: Listen to a conversation, and practice it with a partner.

USING CONTEXT: Using the surrounding context to guess the meaning of an unknown word, phrase, or concept

SUMMARIZING: Picking out and presenting the major points in a text in summary form

SELECTIVE LISTENING: Listening for key information without trying to understand every word
   Example: Listen to a conversation and identify the number of speakers.

SKIMMING: Reading quickly to get a general idea of a text
   Example: Decide if a text is a newspaper article, a letter or an advertisement.

AFFECTIVE

PERSONALIZING: Learners share their own opinions, feelings and ideas about a subject.
   Example: Read a letter from a friend in need and give advice.

SELF-EVALUATING: Thinking about how well you did on a learning task, and rating yourself on a scale

REFLECTING: Thinking about ways you learn best

> **CREATIVE**
>
> BRAINSTORMING: Thinking of as many new words and ideas as one can
>   Example: Work in a group and think of as many occupations as you can.

1) Classifying

Tasks such as the following that require learners to put vocabulary items into their semantic groups are classification tasks. Classifying helps learners because it is easier to memorize items that are grouped together in meaningful ways than trying to remember isolated items.

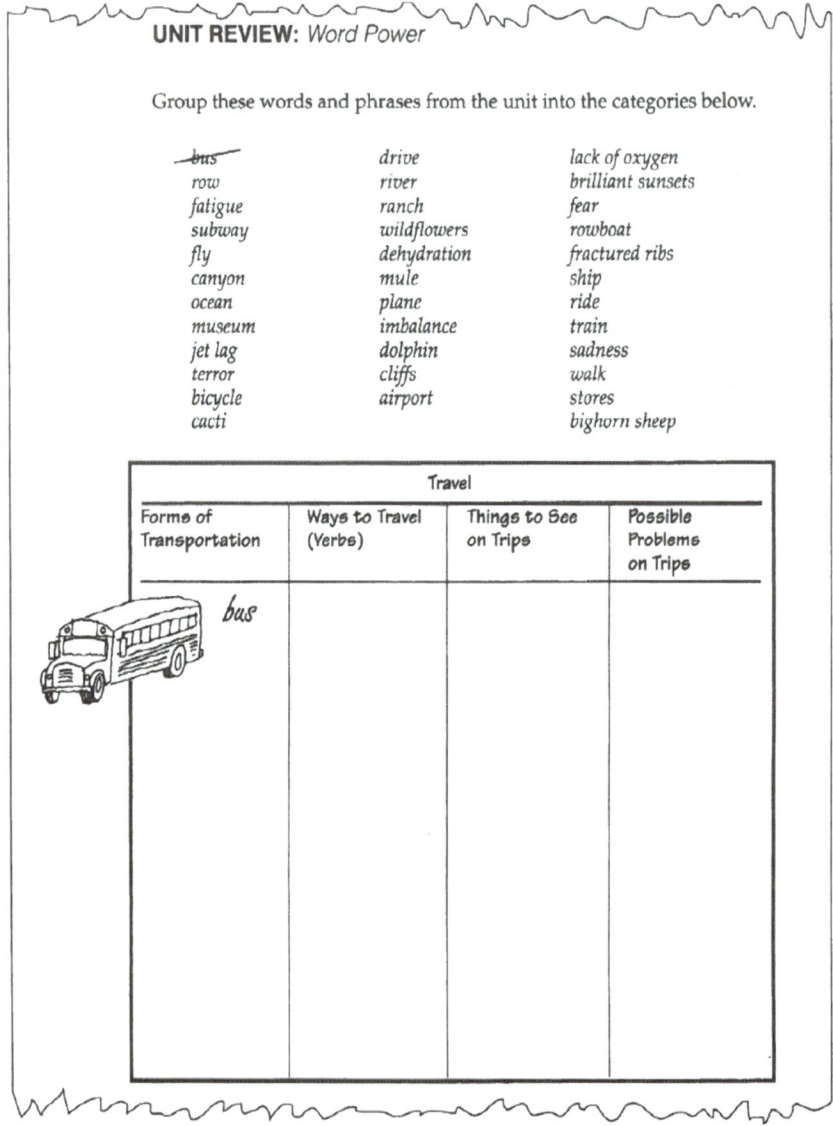

2) Predicting

Predicting, or looking ahead, helps learners to anticipate what is to come. This results in more effective learning, because the learners are adequately prepared for the new material.

3) Inductive Reasoning

In an inductive approach to learning, students are given access to data, and are provided with structured opportunities to work out rules, principles, and so on for themselves. The idea here is that information will be more deeply processed and stored if learners are given an opportunity to work things out for themselves, rather than simply being told.

> **3** **Pair Work** Draw a line to show where each adverb should go in each sentence.
>
> a Is it warm in the evening?　　usually
> b It is cold in Rio de Janeiro.　　rarely
> c Does it snow in New York?　　often
> d It is wet in London.　　always
> e It snows in Sydney.　　never

4) Inferencing

Inferencing involves using what you know to learn something new. Because learning is basically making links between what is new and what is already known, inferencing is an extremely important strategy.

> **8. Class Work.** Writers often suggest what they mean rather than stating it directly. Readers must then make inferences, or draw logical conclusions, based on the available information. What inferences can you make about the slave traders and the Ibo people based on the information in the sentences below?
>
> | READING STRATEGY: Making Inferences See page 225. |
>
> a. While the slave traders were in Africa, they went by the Ibo tribe, and they found eighteen grown people. They fooled them. They told them, "We want you to go to America to work."
>
> What inferences can you make about the slave traders from the information in these sentences?
>
> *The slave traders weren't honest.*
>
> _____
>
> b. When these people got to St. Simon's Island, they found out that they had been tricked and they were going to be sold as slaves. Then all eighteen of these people agreed together. They all said, "No! Rather than be a slave here in America, we would rather be dead."
>
> What inferences can you make about the people from the Ibo tribe based on the information in these sentences?
>
> _____
> _____

5) Discriminating

Discriminating means distinguishing between the main idea and supporting information in both aural and written texts. Learners who are skilled at identifying the most important information in a text are more effective listeners and readers. They can process language more quickly, and are able to identify and remember the speaker or reader's central message more effectively.

• A. Reading Overview: Main Idea, Details, and Summary

Read the passage again. As you read, underline what you think are the most important ideas in the reading. Then, in one or two sentences, write the main idea of the reading. *Use your own words.*

Main idea:
_____
_____
_____

Details:

Use the chart below to organize the information in the article. Refer back to the information you underlined in the passage as a guide. When you have finished, write a brief summary of the reading. *Use your own words.*

A Nuclear Graveyard

The Nuclear Repository Controversy: To Use or Not to Use the Yucca Mountain Site	
Arguments Against Using This Site	Arguments in Favor of Using This Site

6) Cooperating

When we cooperate, we share ideas and learn with other students. This principle exploits the old saying that 'two heads are better than one'. It is particularly effective in language learning, because students are required to communicate with each other in order to cooperate.

PLAN A TRIP

With a group of three students, consult the information from the tables above, and choose a city that you would like to visit. Describe to your class your choice of destination and the reasons your group chose it. Next, as a group, write a letter to its tourist board (addresses below), or visit a local travel agency to get more information. When you receive the information, read it, and create a poster advertising your destination. Include information from the tables in this chapter, as well as photos or information included in the promotional literature you received in the mail.

Argentinean Tourist Information
330 West 58th Street
New York, NY 10019

Brazilian Consulate General
3810 Wilshire Blvd.
Los Angeles, CA 90010

British Tourist Authority
40 West 57th Street
New York, NY 10019

Egyptian Tourist Authority
323 Geary Street
San Francisco, CA 94102

French Government Tourist Office
610 Fifth Avenue
New York, NY 10020

Hong Kong Tourist Association
548 5th Avenue
New York, NY 10036

Italian Government Travel Office
630 Fifth Avenue
New York, NY 10111

Japan National Tourist Office
360 Post Street
San Francisco, CA 94108

Mexican Tourist Office
10100 Santa Monica Boulevard
Los Angeles, CA 90067

Russian Intourist
630 Fifth Avenue
New York, NY 10111

Singapore Tourist Board
342 Madison Avenue
New York, NY 10173

Spanish Tourist Office
665 Fifth Avenue
New York, NY 10022

Thailand Tourism Authority
3440 Wilshire Blvd.
Los Angeles, CA 90010

7) **Practicing**

An essential strategy for developing skills is practicing. Practicing means doing controlled exercises to improve knowledge and skills.

The Sound of It: Understanding Intonation in Negative Questions

People often use statement word order to ask a negative question if they think the answer will be "no." Their intonation goes up. Here's an example from Conversation 1.

EXAMPLE: Question: You don't have one?

In many languages, people answer "yes" because they're thinking, "Yes, that's right. I don't have one." But in English the answer is "no."

EXAMPLE: Question: You don't have one?
Answer: No (I don't).

A. With a partner, take turns asking and answering these questions. In each case, answer "no" and give the correct answer. Then listen and check your answers.

EXAMPLE: a: The main language of Quebec isn't English?
b: _No, it's French_   (French)

1. a: It's not strange to experience culture shock?
   b: _____ (normal)
2. a: Osaka isn't the capital of Japan?
   b: _____ (Tokyo)
3. a: Men don't usually talk much at home?
   b: _____ (in public)
4. a: Women don't usually talk much in public?
   b: _____ (at home)
5. a: English isn't easy?
   b: _____ (hard)
6. a: You're not from Canada?
   b: _____

8) Selective Listening

A key strategy for learners is listening for key information without trying to understand every word. This strategy is essential if learners are to cope effectively in genuine communicative situations outside the classroom. It is important for learners to realize that native speakers use this strategy quite naturally when communicating with one another, that it is, in fact, impossible as well as unnecessary to process every single word in most listening situations.

E. Listen for Numbers

Read these questions about the story asking *How far* and *How long*. Then listen to the story again and answer with the questions.

1. How long are they going to be on vacation? _____
2. How far is it from Ohio to the Shenandoah National Park? _____
3. How long are they going to stay at the park? _____
4. How far is it from the park to Wilmington? _____
5. How long are they going to stay in North Carolina? _____
6. How far is it from Wilmington to Orlando? _____
7. How far are they staying from Disney World? _____
8. How far is it from Orlando back to Columbus? _____

⟨Compensatory Strategies⟩

Tarone (1980) summarizes types of communication strategies under five main categories, along with their subcategories. The list goes as follows:

A. Paraphrase

Paraphrase includes three subcategories which are described below.

(a) Approximation: The use of a target language vocabulary item or structure, which the learner knows is not correct, but which shares semantic features with the desired item to satisfy the speaker (e.g. 'pipe' for 'water pipe')

(b) Word coinage: The learner's making up a new word in order to communicate a desired concept (e.g. 'airball' for 'balloon')

(c) Circumlocution: The learner's describing the characteristics or elements of an object or action instead of using the appropriate TL structure (e.g. "She is, uh, smoking something. I don't know what's its name. That's, uh, Persian, and we use in Turkey, a lot of")

B. Transfer

Transfer has two elements in it.

(a) Literal translation: The learner's translating word for word from the native language (e.g. "He invites him to drink" for "They toast one another")

(b) Language switch: The learner's using the NL (native language) term without bothering to translate (e.g. 'balon' for 'balloon' or 'tirtil' for 'turtle')

C. Appeal for Assistance

This refers to the learner's asking for the correct term or structure (e.g. "What is this?").

D. Mime

Mime refers to the learner's using non-verbal strategies in place of a meaning structure (e.g. clapping one's hands to illustrate applause).

E. Avoidance

Avoidance consists of two subcategories described below.

(a) Topic avoidance: The learner's bypassing concepts for which the vocabulary or other meaning structures are not known to them.

(b) Message abandonment: The learner's beginning to talk about a concept but being unable to continue due to lack of meaning structure, and stopping in mid-utterance.

(I) Strategies-based Instruction

Strategies-based instruction is a learner-centered approach to teaching that has two major components: (1) students are explicitly taught how, when, and why strategies can be used to facilitate language learning and language use tasks, and (2) strategies are integrated into everyday class materials, and may be explicitly or implicitly embedded into the language tasks. The first of these components has often stood alone as the approach when strategies are included in the language classroom. The field has referred to this approach as 'strategy training', 'strategies instruction', or 'learner training'. In a typical classroom strategy training situation, the teachers describe, model, and give examples of potentially useful strategies; they elicit additional examples from students based on the students' own learning experiences; they lead small-group / whole class discussions about strategies (e.g., the rationale behind strategy use, planning an approach to a specific activity, evaluating the effectiveness of chosen strategies); and they encourage their students to experiment with a broad range of strategies.

The second component focuses on integrating and embedding strategies into classroom language tasks. In order to do so, teachers may start with a set of strategies that they wish to focus on and design activities to introduce and/or reinforce them, start with the established course materials and then determine which strategies might be inserted, or insert strategies spontaneously into the lessons whenever it seems appropriate (e.g., to help students overcome problems with difficult material or to speed up the lesson). In all likelihood, teachers will be engaged in strategies-based instruction with an explicit focus on strategies only part of the time, while the rest of the time the strategies will be implicitly embedded into the language tasks.

The goal of this kind of instruction is to help foreign language students become more aware of the ways in which they learn most effectively, ways in which they can enhance their own comprehension and production of the target language, and ways in which they can continue to learn on their own and communicate in the target language after they leave the language classroom. In other words, strategies-based instruction aims to assist learners in becoming more responsible for their efforts in learning and using the target language. It also aims to assist them in becoming more effective learners by allowing them to individualize the language learning experience.

(I1) SBI Model

Chamot, Barnhardt, El-Dinary, and Robbins (1999) developed a model as an overall guide to SBI implementation. Each session starts with the preparation stage to warm up and activate background knowledge. The teacher next explains the strategy of the week and models its use, normally by thinking aloud. Students are then given worksheets and tasks to practice the strategy in question. Each session ends with a summary and evaluation phase. Students take away homework with similar tasks for strategy expansion. Teachers are also encouraged to give students opportunities to use the strategy of the week in all other English language classes. From the preparation stage to the expansion stage, responsibility of strategy use is gradually shifted from teachers to learners.

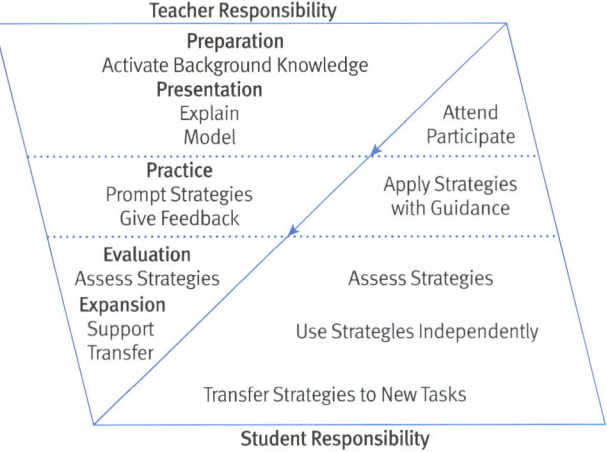

<A Strategy instruction Framework>

The Chamot et al. (1999) model was crystallised into the following procedures for each SBI session like the following.

<Structure of an SBI Lesson>

Preparation		5 minutes
Presentation	• Step 1: Explaining • Step 2: Modelling	15 minutes
Practice		25 minutes
Evaluation		10 minutes
Expansion	• Similar tasks in assignment • Other EL lessons	

최지원 **전공영어 영어교육학 PRACTICAL**

Chapter 05 Mind Map

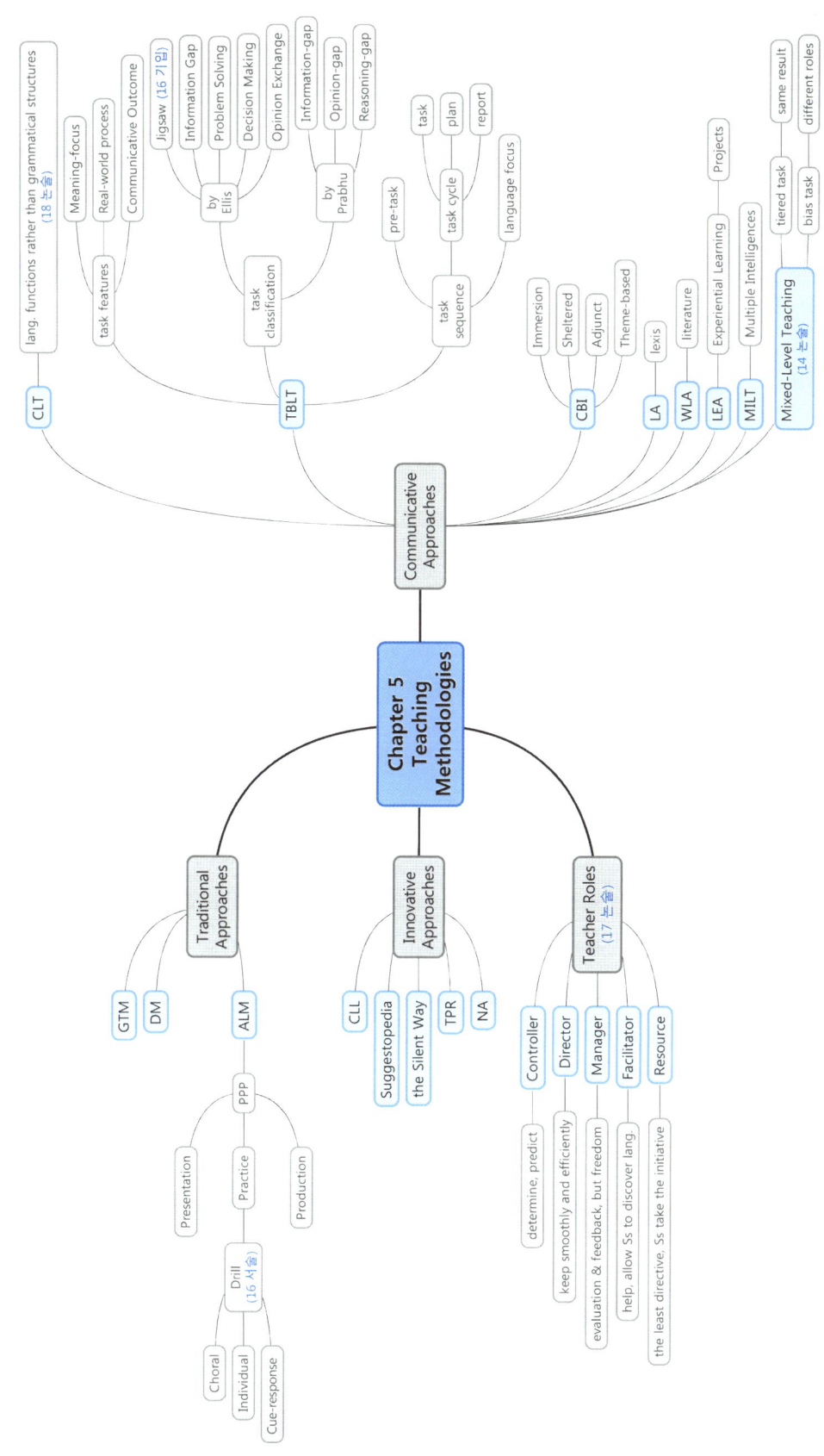

Chapter 05 Teaching Methodologies

(A) Traditional Approaches

(A1) GTM, DM, & ALM

(A1a) GTM

The grammar translation method is a foreign language teaching method derived from the classical (also called traditional) method of teaching Greek and Latin. The method requires students to translate whole texts word for word and memorize numerous grammatical rules and exceptions as well as enormous vocabulary lists. The goal of this method is to be able to read and translate literary masterpieces and classics. In America, the basic foundations of this method were used in most high school and college classrooms and were eventually replaced by the audio-lingual method among others.

(A1b) ALM

The audio-lingual method, Army Method, or New Key, is based on behaviorist theory, which professes that certain traits of living things, and in this case humans, could be trained through a system of reinforcement — correct use of a trait would receive positive feedback while incorrect use of that trait would receive negative feedback.

This approach was similar to another, earlier method called the direct method. Like the direct method, ALM advised that students be taught a language directly, without using the students' native language to explain new words or grammar in the target language. However, unlike the direct method, ALM didn't focus on teaching vocabulary. Rather, the teacher drilled students in the use of grammar.

In ALM, there is no explicit grammar instruction — everything is simply memorized in form. The idea is for the students to practice the particular construct until they can use it spontaneously. In this manner, the lessons are built on static drills in which the students have little or no control on their own output. This type of activity, for the foundation of language learning, is in direct opposition with CLT.

(A1c) Drills

Drill	Choral repetition → Individual repetition → Cue-response drill

	control of response	comprehension of stimulus	number of answers
Mechanical drill	○	×	only one
Meaningful drill	○	○	(more than) one
Communicative drill	×	○	free

Paulston said that there are at least 'two levels of language' or 'two methods of learning': one that is characterized by mechanical skill and one that involves thought or understanding (1976). She pushed for an eclectic approach that included grammatical rules and drills that moved from mechanical practice to communicative practice:

> ... a grammar lesson should consist of grammatical ... rules which explain the particularities of the structural pattern to be learned plus a series of drills from a mechanical level to a communicative in order to give students optimum practice in language production. (Paulston 1976)

Paulston proposed a theoretical classification of three types of drills necessary for language learning: mechanical, meaningful, and communicative drills. She defined a mechanical drill as one in which there is complete control of the response and only one correct way of responding. Furthermore, because of the ***complete*** control of the response, students do not even need to comprehend the stimulus to successfully complete the drill. Then, she provides the following activity on the concord of person and noun in Spanish as examples of a mechanical memorizing drill:

```
Model: andar      (tu) Response: andas
       cantar     (tu) Response: cantas
Continue the drill:
Cue: trabajar    (tu) [Response]
     hablar      (tu) [Response]
```

The purpose of this kind of drills is to help students memorize the pattern with virtually no possibility for mistakes, and even the reader who does not know Spanish can complete the drill above correctly.

Meaningful drills are also very controlled and have one right or wrong answer. However, the learner must also comprehend the stimulus. The following examples will make it easy to understand.

> A. Situation: (A female student is outside the classroom.)
>   Teacher: She's outside.
>   Student 1: Where is she?
>   Student 2: She's outside.
>
> B. Situation: (A female student is sitting on a chair. She is writing in a book.)
>   Teacher: What's she doing?
>   Student 1: She's sitting on the chair.
>   Student 2: She's writing in the book.

In example (A), Student 2's response is not meaningful; it is merely a repetition. While in example (B), Student 2's response is more meaningful. He or she cannot complete this drill without fully understanding structurally and semantically what is being said or questioned. The results in example (A) come very close to being vocabulary drills; while in example (B) it may have the check for feedback which shows that the student really understands the patterns built into the lexical components. In other words, it is more situational and meaningful.

In a meaningful drill, there is still control of the response although it might be correctly expressed in more than one way and as such is less suitable for choral drilling. There is a right answer and the student is supplied with the information necessary for responding, either by the teacher, the classroom situation, or the assigned reading; but in all cases the teacher always knows what the student ought to answer.

At this point, there is still no real communication taking place. Students have a tendency to learn what they are taught rather than what the teacher thinks he or she is teaching. The expected terminal behavior in communicative drills is normal speech for communication or, if one prefers, the free transfer of learned language patterns to appropriate situations. The degree of control in a communicative drill is a moot point. Paulston originally stated that there is no control of the response, that the students have a free choice to say whatever they want. However, this turns out not to be true. All classroom teachers, using this system of sequencing drills, have reported that there is indeed control, not of lexical items as we had at first thought but of structural patterns. Compare the following examples.

> A. Situation: (A female student wears a white shirt.)
>   Teacher: What color is your shirt?
>   Student: ... [response]
>
> B. Situation: (Teacher asks about what will be on the next Saturday night.)
>   Teacher: Do you have a date for Saturday night?
>   Student: ... [response]

In example (A), it is merely meaningful; the situation supplies the information, and the teacher knows the answer as well as the student. The example (B) is more communicative; here the class gets a piece of information it did not have before.

Communicative drills require learners to also supply information that is not known prior to the drill. Thus, in a communicative drill, there is no right or wrong answer except in terms of grammatical well-formedness. For example, "Where do you think John puts his books when he gets home?" Here students may respond with "He puts them on the kitchen counter," "He leaves them on a chair," "He puts them on his desk," and so on. Communicative drills are the most time-consuming and the most difficult to arrange, but if we want fluency in expressing personal opinions, we must teach that. It should be emphasized that these drills do not involve free communication, and that if that is the ultimate goal of the class, then these drills should be followed by interaction activities, situations so structured that the students learn through free communication with their peers.

(B) Innovative Approaches

CLL	counseling, tape recording	
Suggestopedia	music, physical environment	
Silent Way	T's non-involvement, Cuisenaire rods	
TPR	physical movement, T commands, Ss listen and perform	comprehension-based approach
NA	comprehension – early speech – speech emergence	

(1) Community Language Learning (Curran, 1976)

Sitting in a circle, and with the session being recorded, students decide what they want to say. The teacher as counselor-facilitator then translates and gets learners to practice in the target language the material that was elicited. Later at the board, the teacher goes over the words and structures the class is learning and provides explanations in the L1 as needed.

(2) Suggestology, Suggestopedia, or Accelerated Learning (Lozanov, 1978)

In a setting more like a living room than a classroom, learners sit in easy chairs and assume a new identity; the teacher, using only the target language, presents a script two times over two days, accompanied by music. This is followed by group or choral reading of the script on the first day, along with songs and games. On the second day, the students elaborate on the script to tell an anecdote or story. The learners have copies of the script along with an L1 translation juxtaposed on the same page. The process continues with new scripts.

(3) Silent Way (Gattegno, 1976)

Using an array of visuals (e.g., rods of different shapes and colors, and charts with words or color-coded sounds), the teacher gets students to practice and learn a new language while saying very little in the process. The method is inductive, and only the target language is used.

(4) Total Physical Response (Asher, 1996)

The teacher gives commands, "Stand up!" "Sit down!" and so on and shows learners how to demonstrate comprehension by doing the appropriate physical action as a response. New structures and vocabulary are introduced this way for an extended time. When learners are ready to speak, they begin to give each other commands. Only the target language is used.

(C) Communicative Approaches

(C1) CLT

CLT	task, communication, meaningfulness

(C2) TBLT

Target tasks	refer to uses of language in the world beyond the classroom.
Pedagogical tasks	are those that occur in the classroom.

(C2a) Criterial features of a task

The following criterial features of a task can be identified:

① **A task is a workplan.**

A task constitutes a plan for learner activity. This workplan takes the form of teaching materials or of ad hoc plans for activities that arise in the course of teaching. The actual activity that results may or may not match that intended by the plan. A task, therefore, may not result in communicative behaviour.

② **A task involves a primary focus on meaning.**

A task seeks to engage learners in using language pragmatically rather than displaying language. It seeks to develop L2 proficiency through communicating. Thus, it requires a primary focus on meaning. To this end, a task will incorporate some kind of 'gap', i.e. an information, opinion, or reasoning gap. The gap motivates learners to use language in order to close it. The participants choose the linguistic and non-linguistic resources needed to complete the task. The workplan does not ***specify*** what language the task participants should use but rather allows them to choose the language needed to achieve the outcome of the task. However, a task creates a certain semantic space and also the need for certain cognitive processes, which are linked to linguistic options. Thus, a task ***constrains*** what linguistic forms learners need to use, while allowing them the final choice. As Kumaravadivelu (1991) puts it, tasks 'indicate' the content but 'the actual language to be negotiated in the classroom is left to the teacher and the learner'. However, as we shall shortly see, one type of task can be designed in such a way as to predispose learners to use a specific linguistic form, for example, a particular grammatical structure. This task type is discussed below. Even in this kind of task, however, the final choice of what resources to use is left up to the learner.

③ **(A task allows the participants to choose the linguistic resources to use.)**

④ **A task involves real-world processes of language use.**

The workplan may require learners to engage in a language activity such as that found in the real world, for example, completing a form, or it may involve them in language activity that is artificial, for example, determining whether two pictures are the same or different. However, the processes of language use that result from performing a task, for example, asking and answering questions or dealing with misunderstandings, will reflect those that occur in real-world communication.

⑤ **A task can involve any of the four language skills.**

The workplan may require learners to: (1) listen to or read a text and display their understanding, (2) produce an oral or written text, or (3) employ a combination of receptive and productive skills. A task may require dialogic or monologic language use. In this respect, of course, tasks are no different from exercises.

⑥ **A task engages cognitive processes.**

The workplan requires learners to employ cognitive processes such as selecting, classifying, ordering, reasoning, and evaluating information in order to carry out the task. These processes influence but do not determine the choice of language; they circumscribe the range of linguistic forms a user will need to complete the task but allow the actual choice of forms to remain with the learner.

⑦ **A task has a clearly defined communicative outcome.**

The workplan stipulates the non-linguistic outcome of the task, which serves as the goal of the activity for the learners. The stated outcome of a task serves as the means for determining when participants have completed a task.

The following provides examples of language teaching activities. The extent to which these activities can be called 'tasks' can be determined by evaluating whether they satisfy the criterial features of a task given above.

<Activity 1> A dangerous moment

Student A	Student B
Have you ever been in a situation where you felt your life was in danger? Describe the situation to your partner. Tell him/her what happened. Give an account of how you felt when you were in danger and afterwards.	Listen to your partner tell you about a dangerous moment in his/her life. Draw a picture or show what happened to your partner. Show him/her your picture when you have finished it.

Activity 1, 'A dangerous moment', is the kind of task favoured by sociolinguists who wish to elicit samples of vernacular language use. They argue that people are more likely to talk spontaneously when they are recounting a traumatic experience. This activity has all the characteristics of a task.

<Activity 2> The same or different?

Work with a partner. Take it in turn to describe your pictures. Does your partner have the same picture as you or a different one? Ask your partner questions about the picture if you are not sure.

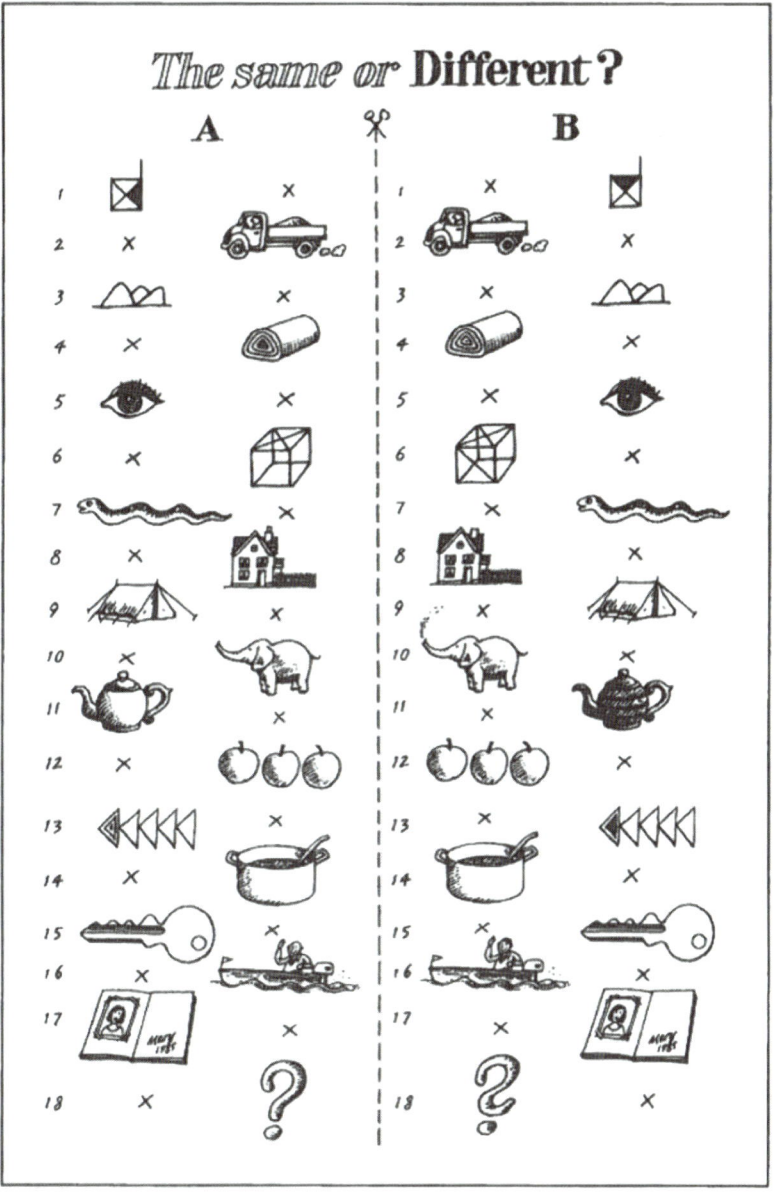

Activity 2, 'The same or different', is a popular language teaching activity and has also been used quite widely in research. The activity requires learners to describe their pictures with sufficient precision to enable their partners to decide whether they are holding the same or different pictures. It displays all the features of a 'task'.

<Activity 3> New students

Here are some information cards for four new students in Level 2 at the English Language Academy. Some information is missing from them. Listen to the conversation and write in the missing information about the new students.

Name: *Gabriela*
Country: *Portugal*
Birth date: *8/25/50*
Married ■ / Single □
Occupation: *doctor*
Interest and hobbies: *reading&photography*

Name: *Samuel*
Country: ____
Birth date: *2/4/65*
Married □ / Single □
Occupation: *student*
Interest and hobbies: *classical music*

Name: *Kuniko*
Country: *Japan*
Birth date: ____
Married □ / Single □
Occupation: ____
Interest and hobbies: *volleyball&swimming*

Name: ____
Country: *Morocco*
Birth date: ____
Married □ / Single □
Occupation: *doctor*
Interest and hobbies: ____

Complete the following summary about Kuniko:

Kuniko is ____ Japan. She was born on ____. She ____ married. She ____ Japanese. She is a student and she ____ to play volleyball and swim.

Now find out the same information about some of your classmates by interviewing each other. Complete an information card for each classmate you interview.

Activity 3, 'New students', entails three separate activities. The first requires students to listen to some information about four people and fill in missing information on forms. The second requires students to fill in the missing words in a short written passage. The third asks students to ask their classmates questions in order to fill in forms. The first activity satisfies the defining characteristics of a task. (1) It constitutes a workplan. (2) the focus is on meaning. (3) The learners have to make their own selection of what words to use, as opposed to being provided with, say, multiple choice answers. (4) The kind of language behaviour required is artificial but related to natural language use. (5) It is a listening activity. (6) It involves the cognitive process of identifying specific information. (7) There is a definite outcome, i.e. the completed forms. The third activity similarly functions as a task, in this case, though, an interactive one involving speaking.

The second activity in 'New students', however, seems more like an exercise. In this case, the workplan focuses learners' attention primarily on grammatical form as most of the blanks in the text require function words like 'from' or 'is' rather than content words. Except for the words needed to fill in the blanks, the learners have no choice over the linguistic resources to be used. It is difficult to see how filling in blanks in a passage manifests 'some sort of relationship to the real world'. Finally, the only outcome is the completed passage, i.e. the outcome cannot be established separately from the language that is produced. Of course, the fact that this activity is an exercise does not denigrate its worth as a language-learning activity. Indeed, theoretical grounds can be found for including exercises alongside tasks, a teaching strategy quite widely favoured.

<Activity 4> Asking for help

Work in pairs. One student looks at the card A. The other looks at the card B. Practise the conversation.

Card A	Card B
You are a student. You want your friend to help you with some homework.	You are a student. Your friend wants you to help him/her with homework. You are not keen.
A: Check if B is busy. B: _____. A: Ask him/her to help you. B: _____. A: Try to persuade him/her. B: _____. A: Thank him/her.	A: _____. B: Tell him/her you are not doing anything. A: _____. B: Refuse. Give a reason. A: _____. B: Agree reluctantly. A: _____.

Activity 4, 'Asking for help', is an example of a cue-card activity. This has some of the features of a task. For example, it provides a workplan for an oral interaction and, to some extent at least, the participants are free to choose the linguistic resources, i.e. they decide how to request help, refuse, persuade, etc. Also, the resulting interaction may bear some resemblance to an authentic conversation. However, the intended primary focus is on form rather than meaning — the meanings of the utterances are given so that all the learners have to do is find the linguistic forms to encode the stated functions. Also, the only outcome is the performance of the activity itself; the oral interaction does not result in an outcome to show that the activity has been completed. This kind of cue-card activity, while of potential value for practicing language, does not constitute a task.

<Activity 5> Going shopping

Look at Mary's shopping list. Then look at the list of items in Abdullah's store.

- Mary's shopping list

| 1 oranges | 2 eggs | 3 flour | 4 powdered milk | 5 biscuits | 6 jam |

- Abdullah's store

| 1 bread | 2 salt | 3 apples | 4 tins of fish | 5 Coca Cola | 6 flour | 7 mealie meal flour |
| 8 sugar | 9 curry powder | 10 biscuits | 11 powdered milk | 12 dried beans |

Work with a partner. One person be Mary and the other be Abdullah. Make conversations like this:

Mary: Good morning. Do you have any flour?
Abdullah: Yes, I do.
or
Mary: Good morning. Do you have any jam?
Abdullah: No, I'm sorry. I don't have any.

Activity 5, 'Going shopping', is even more obviously an exercise. The workplan requires learners to attend to form — the use of 'any' and 'some' in questions and replies; it asks them only to substitute items in sentences they are given; it is not likely to lead to the kind of language use found in the real world; it is cognitively undemanding; and the outcome of the activity does not involve a definite product. However, as Johnson (1982) has shown, exercises like this can easily be made more task-like by splitting the information. Thus, if Student A had Mary's shopping list and Student B the list of items in Abdullah's store, the resulting 'gap' would require a focus on meaning. The participants could be left to choose their own linguistic resources by removing the model sentences. Finally, a definite outcome could be introduced by requesting the students to write down what items Mary was able to buy.

The discussion of these five language-learning activities, which are representative of the kinds of workplans found in teaching materials, demonstrates the essential differences between a task and an exercise. Moreover, the discussion shows that some language-teaching activities cannot easily be classified as a 'task' or an 'exercise' as they manifest features of both. We have also seen that it may be possible to make an activity more task-like by making adjustments to the way it is designed.

The discussion also indicated that some of the criteria are more important for judging whether an activity is a task than others. The key criterion is (2), the need for a primary focus on meaning. As Stern (1992) has pointed out, 'a task stops being communicative only if the choice of activity has been prompted by purely linguistic considerations'. Also important are (3), (4), and (7). In contrast, (1), (5), and (6) would seem to apply to all kinds of teaching materials, including exercises. The following, then, is the definition of a task:

A task is a workplan that requires learners to process language pragmatically in order to achieve an outcome that can be evaluated in terms of whether the correct or appropriate propositional content has been conveyed. To this end, it requires them to give primary attention to meaning and to make use of their own linguistic resources, although the design of the task may predispose them to choose particular forms. A task is intended to result in language use that bears a resemblance, direct or indirect, to the way language is used in the real world. Like other language activities, a task can engage productive or receptive, and oral or written skills, and also various cognitive processes.

(C2b) Classification of tasks 1 — by Ellis

	Interactant relationship	Interaction requirement	Goal orientation	Outcome options
Jigsaw	two-way	required	convergent	closed
Information gap	one-way or two-way	required	convergent	closed
Problem solving	one-way or two-way	optional	convergent	closed
Decision making	one-way or two-way	optional	convergent	open
Opinion exchange	one-way or two-way	optional	divergent	open

(C2c) Classification of tasks 2 - by Prabhu

An information-gap activity	Exchange of information among participants
An opinion-gap activity	Exchange of personal preferences, feelings, or attitudes
A reasoning-gap activity	Deriving some new info. by inferring it from the old info.

(C2c1) Classification of tasks 3 - by Willis

Willis (1996) offers a pedagogic classification of tasks. The types reflect the kind of operations learners are required to carry out in performing tasks.

1) Listing:

Listing tasks may seem unimaginative, but in practice, tend to get a lot to talk as learners explain their ideas. The types involve brainstorming, in which learners draw on their own knowledge and experience either as a class or in pairs/groups; fact-finding, in which learners find things out by asking each other or other people, etc.

> In pairs, agree on a list of four or five people who were famous in the 20th century and give at least one reason for including each person.

2) Ordering and sorting:

Ordering and sorting tasks involve four main types: sequencing items, actions or events in a logical or chronological order; ranking items, according to personal values or specified criteria; categorizing items in given groups or grouping them under given headings; classifying items in different ways, where the categories are not given.

> In pairs, look at your list of famous people. Which people are most likely to remain popular and become 20th century icons? Rank them from most popular to least popular, and be prepared to justify your order to another pair.

3) Comparing:

Broadly, comparing tasks involve comparing information of a similar nature but from different sources or versions in order to identify common points and/or differences. The processes involved matching to identify specific points and relate them to each other; finding similarities and things in common; finding differences.

> Compare your list of possible 20th century icons with your partner's list. Did you have any people in common? Tell each other why you chose them. How many reasons did you both think of? Finally, combine your two lists, but keep it to five people.

4) Problem solving:

Problem-solving tasks make demands upon people's intellectual and reasoning powers, and though challenging, they are engaging and often satisfying to solve. The processes and time scale will vary enormously depending in the type and complexity of the problem. Real-life problems may involve expressing hypotheses, describing experiences, comparing alternatives and evaluating and agreeing a solution. Completion tasks are often based on short extracts from texts, where the learners predict the ending or piece together clues to guess it. The classification ends with case studies, which are more complex, entail an in-depth consideration of many criteria, and often involve additional fact-finding and investigating.

> Think of a town centre where there is too much traffic. In twos, think of three alternative solutions to this problem. List the advantages and disadvantages of each alternative. Then decide which alternative would be the cheapest one, the most innovative one, and the most environmentally friendly one. Report your decisions to another pair / group / the class, and discuss with them which solution would be the best one to put forward to the local government.

5) Sharing personal experiences:

Tasks of sharing personal experiences encourage learners to talk more freely about themselves and share their experiences with others. For example, after reading a selected material about one's childhood, learners can be encouraged to tell their own childhood. The resulting interaction is closer to casual social conversation in that it is not as directly goal-oriented as in other tasks. For that very reason, however, these open tasks may be more difficult to get going in the classroom.

6) Creative tasks:

These are often called projects and involve pairs or groups of learners in some kind of freer creative work. They also tend to have more stages than other tasks and can involve combinations of task types above. Out-of-class research is sometimes needed. Organizational skills and teamwork are important in getting the task done. The outcome can often be appreciated by a wider audience than the students who produced it.

(C2d) TBLT framework (by Willis)

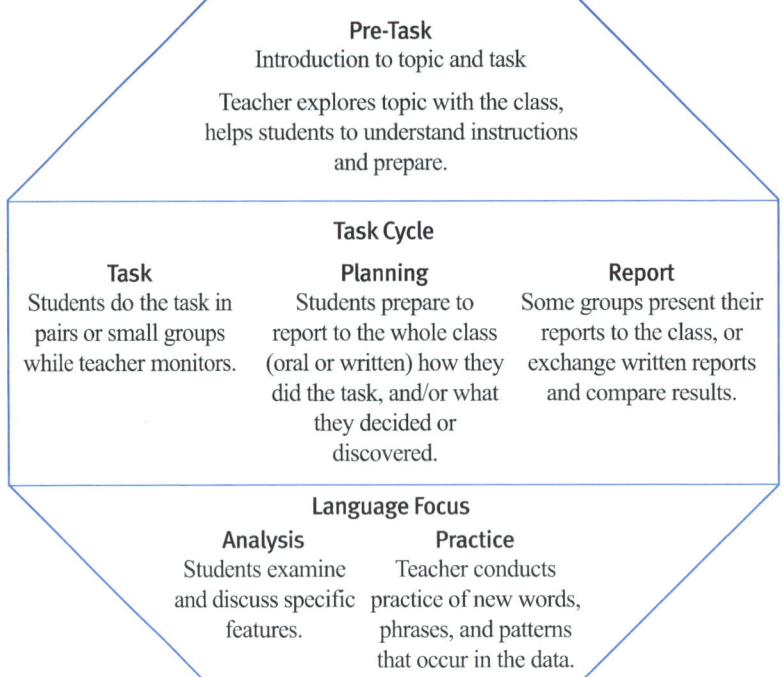

(C2e) A task framework (by David Nunan)

The point of departure for task-based language teaching is real-world or target tasks. These are the hundred and one things we do with language in everyday life, from writing a poem to confirming an airline reservation to exchanging personal information with a new acquaintance. These three examples, by the way, illustrate Michael Halliday's three macrofunctions of language. Halliday argues that at a very general level, we do three things with language: we use it to exchange goods and services (this is the transactional or service macrofunction), we use it to socialize with others (this is the interpersonal or social macrofunction), and we use it for enjoyment (this is the aesthetic macrofunction).

Typically, in everyday interactions, the macrofunctions are interwoven, as in the following (invented) example:

A: Nice day.
B: That it is. What can I do for you?
A: I'd like a round-trip ticket to the airport, please.

In order to create learning opportunities in the classroom, we must transform these real-world tasks into pedagogical tasks. Such tasks can be placed on a continuum from rehearsal tasks to activation tasks.

1) Pedagogical task: rehearsal rationale

A rehearsal task bears a clear and obvious relationship to its corresponding real-world counterpart. For example, the other day I was teaching on a course designed to help my students develop job-seeking skills. The task that my students had to complete was as follows.

> <Pedagogical task: rehearsal rationale>
> Write your resumé and exchange it with a partner. Study the positions available in the newspaper advertisements and find three that would be suitable for your partner. Then compare your choices with the actual choice made by your partner.

This task has a *rehearsal* rationale. If someone were to visit my classroom and ask why the students were doing this task, my reply would be something along the lines of, 'Well, I'm getting them, in the security of the classroom, to rehearse something they're going to need to do outside the classroom.'

Notice that the task has been transformed. It is not identical to the process of actually applying for a job in the world outside the classroom. In addition to the work with a partner, the students will be able to get feedback and advice from me, the teacher, as well as drawing on other resources.

2) Pedagogical task: activation rationale

Not all pedagogical tasks have such a clear and obvious relationship to the real world. Many role plays, simulations, problem-solving tasks and information exchange tasks have what I call an *activation* rationale. The task is designed not to provide learners with an opportunity to rehearse some out-of-class performance but to activate their emerging language skills. In performing such tasks, learners begin to move from reproductive language use — in which they are reproducing and manipulating language models provided by the teacher, the textbook or the tape — to creative language use in which they are recombining familiar words, structures and expressions in novel ways. I believe that it is when users begin to use language creatively that they are maximally engaged in language acquisition because they are required to draw on their emerging language skills and resources in an integrated way.

Here is an example of an activation task. It is one I observed a group of students carrying out in a secondary school classroom. It formed the basis of an extremely engaging lesson to which all students actively and animatedly contributed.

> <Pedagogical task: activation rationale>
> Work with three other students. You are on a ship that is sinking. You have to swim to a nearby island. You have a waterproof container, but can only carry 20 kilos of items in it. Decide which of the following items you will take. (Remember, you can't take more than 20 kilos with you.)
>
> | | |
> |---|---|
> | • Axe (8 kilos) | • Box of novels and magazines (3 kilos) |
> | • Cans of food (500 grams each) | • Packets of sugar, flour, rice, powdered milk, coffee, tea (each packet weighs 500 grams) |
> | • Bottles of water (1.5 kilos each) | • Medical kit (2 kilos) |
> | • Short-wave radio (12 kilos) | • Portable CD player and CDs (4 kilos) |
> | • Firelighting kits (500 grams each) | • Rope (6 kilos) |
> | • Notebook computer (3.5 kilos) | • Waterproof sheets of fabric (3 kilos each) |

This task, which worked very well, does not have a rehearsal rationale in that the teacher was not expecting the students to be shipwrecked in the foreseeable future. The aim of the task was to encourage students to activate a range of language functions and structures including making suggestions, agreeing, disagreeing, talking about quantity, how much / how many, wh-questions, etc. (It is worth noting, however, that learners are not constrained to using a particular set of lexical and grammatical resources. They are free to use any linguistic means at their disposal to complete the task.)

One interpretation of TBLT is that communicative involvement in pedagogical tasks of the kind described and illustrated above is the necessary and sufficient condition of successful second language acquisition. This 'strong' interpretation has it that language acquisition is a subconscious process in which the conscious teaching of grammar is unnecessary: 'Language is best taught when it is being used to transmit messages, not when it is explicitly taught for conscious learning.'

The argument by proponents of a 'strong' interpretation of TBLT is that the classroom should attempt to simulate natural processes of acquisition, and that form-focused exercises are unnecessary. Elsewhere, Krashen argues that there is a role for grammar, but that this role is to provide affective support to the learner — in other words it makes them feel better because, for most learners, a focus on form is what language learning is all about, but it does not fuel the acquisition process. In fact, Krashen and Terrell argue that even speaking is unnecessary for acquisition: 'We acquire from what we hear (or read), not from what we say.' The role of a focus on form remains controversial.

My own view is that language classrooms are unnatural by design, and that they exist precisely to provide for learners the kinds of practice opportunities that do not exist outside the classroom. Learners, particularly those in the early stages of the learning process, can benefit from a focus on form, and learners should not be expected to generate language that has not been made accessible to them in some way. In fact, what is needed is a pedagogy that reveals to learners systematic interrelationships between form, meaning and use (Larsen-Freeman 2001).

In the TBLT framework presented here, form-focused work is presented in the form of enabling skills, so called because they are designed to develop skills and knowledge that will ultimately facilitate the process of authentic communication. In the framework, enabling skills are of two kinds: *language exercises* and *communicative activities*.

3) Language exercises

Language exercises come in many shapes and forms and can focus on lexical, phonological or grammatical systems. Here are examples of lexically and grammatically focused language exercises:

<Language exercise>

[Language exercise: lexical focus]

(A) Complete the word map with jobs from the list.

> Architect, receptionist, company director, flight attendant, supervisor, engineer, salesperson, secretary, professor, sales manager, security guard, word processor

Professionals
architect
....
....
....
....

Service occupations
flight attendant
....
....
....
....

JOBS

Management positions
company director
....
....
....

Office work
receptionist
....
....
....

(B) Add two jobs to each category. Then compare with a partner.

[Language exercise: grammatical focus]

(A) Complete the conversation. Then practise with a partner.

> A: What _____ you _____?
> B: I'm a student. I study business.
> A: And _____ do you _____ to school?
> B: I _____ to Jefferson College.
> A: _____ do you like your classes?
> B: I _____ them a lot.

The essential difference between these practice opportunities and those afforded by pedagogical tasks has to do with outcomes. In each case above, success will be determined in linguistic terms: 'Did the learners get the language right?' In pedagogical tasks, however, there is an outcome that transcends language: 'Did the learners select the correct article of clothing according to the weather forecast?' 'Did they manage to get from the hotel to the bank?' 'Did they select food and drink items for a class party that were appropriate and within their budget?'

4) Communicative activities

Communicative activities represent a kind of 'half-way house' between language exercises and pedagogical tasks. They are similar to language exercises in that they provide manipulative practice of a restricted set of language items. They resemble pedagogical tasks in that they have an element of meaningful communication. In the example that follows, students are manipulating the forms 'Have you ever ...?', 'Yes, I have' and 'No, I haven't.' However, there is also an element of authentic communication because, presumably, they can not be absolutely sure of how their interlocutors are going to respond.

<Communicative activity>

Look at the survey chart and add three more items to the list. Now, go around the class and collect as many names as you can.

Find someone who has ...	Name
... driven a racing car	
... been to a Grand Prix race	
... played squash	
... run a marathon	
... had music lessons	
... ridden a motorcycle	
... flown an airplane	
... been to a bullfight	
... been scuba diving	

These then are the basic building blocks of TBLT. These elements can be combined to form units of work. The framework described in this section is represented diagrammatically on the following.

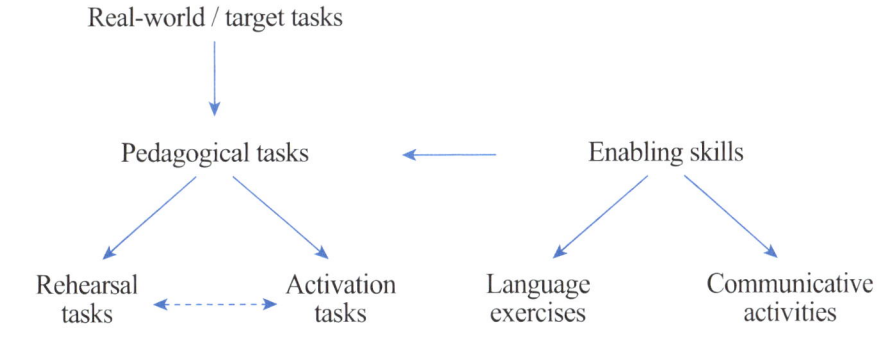

A framework for TBLT

(C3) CBI

CONTENT DRIVEN			LANGUAGE DRIVEN
Immersion	Sheltered	Adjunct	Theme-based

In language immersion, academic subjects are learned through the medium of a foreign language. In Canada, successful second language immersion programs, in which Anglophone children learn their academic subjects in French, have existed for many years. Snow has referred to content-based instruction as a method with many faces.

Another content-based instruction 'face', where content and language instruction have been integrated, is the adjunct model. In the adjunct model, students enroll in a regular academic course. In addition, they take a language course that is linked to the academic course. Then, during the language class, the language teacher's focus is on helping students process the language in order to understand the academic content presented by the subject teacher. The language teacher also helps students to complete academic tasks such as writing term papers, improving their note-taking abilities, and reading academic textbooks assigned by the content teacher.

In sheltered-language instruction in a second language environment, a third model of content-based instruction has been used. Both native speakers and non-native speakers of a particular language follow a regular academic curriculum. For classes with non-native speakers, however, 'sheltered' instruction is geared to students' developing second language proficiency. Sheltered-language instructors support their students through the use of particular instructional techniques and materials. It offers the significant advantage that second language students do not have to postpone their academic study until their language control reaches a high level. It follows that students are often highly motivated because they are learning content that is relevant to the academic requirements of the programs in which they are enrolled.

Finally, it should be noted that the focus need not be academic for these same motivational benefits to be derived. For example, competency-based instruction, an effective form of content-based instruction for adult immigrants, offers students an opportunity to develop their second language skills at the same time that they are learning vital 'life-coping' or 'survival' skills such as filling out job applications or using the telephone.

In sum, what all models of content-based instruction have in common is learning both specific content and related language skills. "In content-based language teaching, the claim in a sense is that students get 'two-for-one' — both content knowledge and increased language proficiency" (Wesche 1993).

(C4) LA

In arguing for a more lexical approach to teaching language, Lewis (1997) advocated the use of 'lexical chants', that is, rhythmic chants that are composed entirely of lexical phrases. If these are dialogic in form, such as the following, they can be chanted by alternating groups:

Group A:	Group B:
I was going to say …	Do go on.
I meant to tell you …	Don't mind me.
A funny thing happened …	Take your time.
You'll never believe it …	I entirely agree.
And the funny thing was …	What do you mean?
How can I put it?	I haven't a clue.
Believe it or not …	Sorry, I'm lost.
Do you see what I mean?	Not at all. Do you?

The use of such chants may suggest a return to the somewhat mindless and hence discredited techniques associated with audiolingualism. However, there is growing evidence supporting the value of repetition of 'chunks'. N. Ellis (2005), for example, describes 'ways that chunking and sequence repetition lead to the consolidation of memorized whole utterances'.

(C5) WLA

WLA	under the umbrella of CLT, using 'literature', integration

(C6) Experiential Learning & Project-Based Learning

LEA	'learning by doing' by J. Dewey, inductive learning by discovery

(C6a) Project

Projects are one useful way of providing an ongoing 'threat' to classroom work. They supply a longer term goal to focus on, and students can invest their energy in something that has a tangible outcome. They also offer a valuable chance for learners of mixed levels to work on something at their own current ability level. Projects are usually task-oriented rather than language-oriented; in other words, the learners focus on doing something practical rather than directly on studying language. They typically involve learners in decisions about precisely what is done and how to do it, as well as in collecting information, solving problems and presenting the final outcome as a written or performed presentation. The planning, decision-making, ideas-collecting, structuring, discussion, negotiation, problem-solving, etc are all an integral part of the work. The language learning arises from learners having a reason to communicate authentically in English to achieve a specific goal. Projects often also have a strong group-building outcome.

Teachers often fear that a project will be troublesome to organise, especially as they may involve different groups of learners working on quite different things. This sounds like it may require a lot more teacher preparation. In fact, it rarely does, because projects quickly become very learner-centered, and learners generally require guidance and advice rather than to have work specially devised for them. The most demanding part of a project for a teacher is in the initial planning and then in the starting-off phase.

Most projects will work best if undertaken by small groups of three or four learners. Individuals could do one, but it can be isolating, and learners on their own tend to lose motivation and focus as time goes on. Working together provides mutual support and a wider range of ideas.

(C6b) Project-based instruction

Project-based instruction has a great deal in common with the two preceding approaches: topic-based/theme-based instruction and content-based instruction. Projects can be thought of as 'maxi-tasks', that is a collection of sequenced and integrated tasks that all add up to a final project. For example, a simulation project such as 'buying a new car,' might include the following subsidiary tasks:

1. Evaluating available options and selecting a suitable model based on price, features and so on.
2. Selecting an appropriate car firm from a series of classified advertisements.
3. Arranging for a bank loan through negotiation with a bank or finance house.
4. Role-playing between purchaser and salesperson for purchase of the car.

Ribe and Vidal (1993) argue that project-based instruction has evolved through three 'generations' of tasks. (Slightly confusingly, they tend to use the terms 'project' and 'task' interchangeably.) First-generation tasks focus primarily on the development of communicative ability. These are similar to tasks as they have been conventionally defined in this book.

> *Example of a first-generation task*
>
> Problem-solving
> The students have a map with bus and underground routes. They discuss and select the best route for going from one point to another according to a set of given variables (price, time, distance, comfort, etc.)
> (Ribe and Vidal 1993)

Second-generation tasks are designed to develop not only communicative competence but also cognitive aspects of the learner as well. They thus incorporate a learning strategies dimension, developing thinking skills, cognitive strategies for handling and organizing information and so on.

> *Example of a second-generation task*
>
> Through foreigners' eyes
>
> The objective of this task is to collect and analyse information on what tourists of different nationalities think of the students' country/city/town.
>
> 1. Students decide (a) what they need to know; (b) how to get the information (interviews, questionnaires, tourist brochures, etc.); (c) where to get the information (airport, beach, library, tourist information office, etc.); (d) when to obtain the information; (e) what grids / database format they want to use to collate the information; (f) the kind of questionnaires / interviews they want to devise; (g) the language they need to carry out the interviews.
> 2. Students carry out the research, transcribe the interviews and put the information together.
> 3. Students select relevant data, decide on a format (posters, dossier, etc.) for their presentation.
> 4. Students make a report and present it.
> (Ribe and Vidal 1993)

Just as second-generation tasks incorporate the characteristics of first generation tasks, so third-generation tasks incorporate the characteristics of first- and second-generation tasks. In addition to fostering communicative competence and cognitive development, they also aim at personality development through foreign language education. Third generation tasks fulfill wider educational objectives (attitudinal change and motivation, learner awareness, etc.) and so are especially appropriate for the school setting, where motivation for the learning of the foreign language needs to be enhanced.

> ***Example of a third-generation task***
>
> Designing an alternative world
>
> 1. Students and teachers brainstorm aspects of their environment they like and those they would most like to see improved. These may include changes to the geographical setting, nature, animal life, housing, society, family, leisure activities, politics, etc.
> 2. Students are put into groups according to common interests. The groups identify the language and information they need. The students carry out individual and group research on selected topics. The students discuss aspects of this 'alternative reality' and then report back. They decide on the different ways (stories, recordings, games, etc.) to link all the research and present the final product.
> 3. Students present the topic and evaluate the activity. (Ribe and Vidal 1993)

Projects, then, are integrated 'maxi-tasks' that could last over the course of a semester, or even over a year. A project can either constitute the main element of instruction to a foreign language class, or run in parallel with more traditional instructions. Regardless of how it fits into the curriculum, Ribe and Vidal (1993) recommend the following ten-step sequence for implementing project-based instruction.

> 1. create a good class atmosphere
> 2. get the class interested
> 3. select the topic
> 4. create a general outline of the project
> 5. do basic research around the topic
> 6. report to the class
> 7. process feedback
> 8. put it all together
> 9. present the project
> 10. assess and evaluate the project

(C7) MILT

1. Logical/mathematical	5. Interpersonal
2. Visual/spatial	6. Intrapersonal
3. Body/kinesthetic	7. Verbal/linguistic
4. Musical/rhythmic	8. Naturalist

(C8) Episode Hypothesis

Episode Hypothesis	beyond context, a logical structure and conclusion

According to John Oller and his episode hypothesis, "texts (oral or written forms of discourse) which are more episodically organized can be stored and recalled more easily than less episodically organized material" (Oller 1983). In other words, it is easier for students to learn a language if they are given connected sentences that have a logical structure and a story line, instead of disconnected, randomly organized phrases. Of course it has been stated many times before that vocabulary and language can be learnt in context; however, Oller goes one step further and states that context in itself is not sufficient (i.e. a simple dialogue). What is essential is that the dialogue or text should have a logical structure and a logical conclusion. This way the students can follow the story line step by step and can recall its structure more easily because logic helps them, and they do not have to rely only on memory. Brown (1994) points out, since stories are universal, students from different cultures can understand their structure and can identify with the characters, which helps them to acquire vocabulary, grammatical and communicative competence, and provides them with special cultural knowledge as well.

Now, it must be noted that the reality of the language classroom is such that not every aspect of language can be embedded in gripping dramatic episodes that have students yearning for the next day's events, as they might with a favorite soap opera! But to the extent that a curriculum allows it, episodic teaching and testing may offer a rewarding alternative to sprinkle into your daily diet of teaching technique.

(C9) Mixed-Level Teaching: Tiered Tasks and Bias Tasks

Tiered Task	Different level, but the same result
Bias Task	Mixed-level, different roles for members

(C9a) Tiered Tasks

The following three task sheets all accompany a reading about *The Spirit of London* exhibit at Madame Tussaud's museum in London.

<Example 1>

- Top Tier

Task A: for Weaker Students
  1. How much of London's history does *The Spirit of London* show?
  2. How do you go around it?
  3. What special effects does it have?
  4. What can you see in the modern-day section?
Answers
  1. Lights, sound, music, and smells
  2. Police, punks, and tourists
  3. More than 400 years
  4. In a taxi

- Middle Tier

Task B: for Midlevel Students
  1. How much of London's history does *The Spirit of London* show?
     a. 400 years
     b. more than 400 years
     c. 399 years
  2. How do you go around it?
     a. in a taxi
     b. in a train
     c. on foot
  3. What special effects does it have?
     a. light
     b. sound and music
     c. smells
  4. What can you see in the modern-day section?
     a. police
     b. punks
     c. tourists

- Bottom Tier

> Task C: for Stronger Students
> 1. How much of London's history does *The Spirit of London* show?
> 2. How do you go around it?
> 3. What special effects does it have?
> 4. What can you see in the modern-day section?

- Task A gives all the answers on the page for support. They are jumbled for challenge. Weaker students manipulate the given material, and can use logic to help match the task items, together with the information in the reading text.

- Task B gives multiple-choice answers to help the average students. This is slightly different from the conventional 'one answer only is correct' multiple choice, since in questions 3 and 4 there is more than one correct answer.

- Task C gives open questions — with no extra support — to challenge the strongest students in the group.

A useful feature of a tiered task activity is that, whichever level of task students get, the result is the same or similar for all. Oral feedback can therefore take place with the whole class.

We ourselves can assign task sheets to individual students, based on our knowledge of students' abilities. (Sometimes the teacher knows best, especially after conducting a diagnostic test, or after working with a class for a long period of time!)

Alternatively, we can let students choose the lettered tasks, unseen, according to whether they want a lot of help, some help, or no help with the reading activity. Initially, students may overestimate their abilities and choose the most difficult task, or they may play safe and take the easy task. However, when we have offered students a choice of tasks in the classroom a number of times — perhaps with some advice — they will begin to select a realistic task for their level: one that is achievable, yet challenging and not boring.

<Example 2>

Another very simple form of tiered task which works on two levels is a dual-choice gapfill. It is good to vary things by dividing the class into two groups from time to time instead of three. As with all level grouping, where exactly we draw the line is a subjective decision. What follows is the first part of a dual-choice gapfill that accompanies a rap.

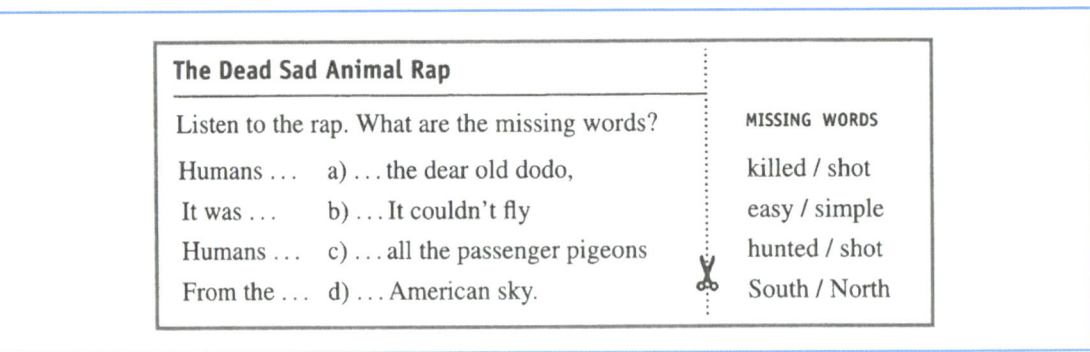

As they listen, weaker students circle one of the words in the box to fill each gap. Stronger students get the same task sheet, but with the missing words box cut off. The task is therefore more challenging for them.

(C9b) Bias Tasks

Now let us look at bias tasks. The following two task sheets accompany a Penpal Ad Page reading text.

<Example 1>

Task A: for Weaker Students	Task B: for Stronger Students
1. How many of the young people are 13 years old? (Three ⋯)	Write questions for these answers, based on the Penpal Page.
2. How many boys are there?	1. How many of them are 13? *Three of them are.*
3. Who doesn't eat meat?	2. ………………………………? *There are four.*
4. Who likes football?	3. ………………………………? *Eloise doesn't.*
5. Who lives in the country?	4. ………………………………? *James does.*
	5. ………………………………? *Chris does.*

With Task A, weaker students answer questions about the text. With Task B, stronger students write questions for given answers related to the text.

Because the answers to these two tasks are complementary, it would not be an efficient use of class time for the teacher to conduct postactivity feedback with the whole class. Instead, student-student feedback would be a good idea, with the students in AB pairs. The teacher should naturally be available as an arbiter if there are any questions. These may come from stronger students — who might come up with alternative questions of their own. If these are grammatically correct, and fit the given answers, the teacher should confirm them as also correct.

This type of feedback, in weak/strong pairs, is very motivating for the weaker students. They have got the difficult questions that the strong students have struggled to reconstruct. For weak students, already knowing key information is a pleasant change from traditional whole-class oral feedback, which often turns into a dialogue between the teacher and the brightest and most forthcoming students, while the weaker students feel left out.

<Example 2>

Another very simple form of bias task activity is a jigsawed gapfill. To prepare a jigsawed gapfill of a song, photocopy the lyrics twice. Label one photocopy 'A' and the other 'B'. On photocopy A, blank out with correction fluid nine words. On photocopy B, blank out eleven words, making sure that the gaps on photocopy A are in different places from the gaps on photocopy B. In this example, photocopy B is the high-level task (with more gaps to fill), and photocopy A is the low-level task (with fewer gaps). The simplicity or complexity of the words you gap can also make the task easier or more difficult.

A positive feature of this kind of bias activity is that, because the jigsawed gaps are in different places, students are not necessarily aware of who has more gaps and who has fewer. We could easily add a third task sheet (C) for the weakest students, with six gaps in different places from the gaps on photocopies A and B. This would mean conducting feedback in groups of three.

(C10) Cooperative Language Learning

Cooperative Language Learning (**CLL**) is part of a more general instructional approach also known as **Collaborative Learning** (**CL**). Cooperative Learning is an approach to teaching that makes maximum use of cooperative activities involving pairs and small groups of learners in the classroom. The success of CL is crucially dependent on the nature and organization of group work. This requires a structured program of learning carefully designed so that learners interact with each other and are motivated to increase each other's learning. Olsen and Kagan (1992) propose the following key elements of successful group-based learning in CL:

> ① Positive interdependence
> ② Group formation
> ③ Individual accountability
> ④ Social skills
> ⑤ Structuring and structures

① ***Positive interdependence***: It occurs when group members feel that what helps one member helps all and what hurts one member hurts all. It is created by the structure of CL tasks and by building a spirit of mutual support within the group.

② ***Group formation:*** It is an important factor in creating positive interdependence. Factors involved in setting up groups include:

- deciding on the size of the group: This will depend on the tasks they have to carry out, the age of the learners, and time limits for the lesson. Typical group size is from two to four.

- assigning students to groups: Groups can be teacher-selected, random, or student-selected, although teacher-selected is recommended as the usual mode so as to create groups that are heterogeneous on such variables as past achievement, ethnicity, or sex.

- student roles in groups: Each group member has a specific role to play in a group, such as noise monitor, turn-taker monitor, recorder, or summarizer.

③ ***Individual accountability***: It involves both group and individual performance, for example, by assigning each student a grade on his or her portion of a team project or by calling on a student at random to share with the whole class, with group members, or with another group.

④ ***Social skills:*** They determine the way students interact with each other as teammates. Usually some explicit instruction in social skills is needed to ensure successful interaction.

⑤ ***Structuring and Structures:*** These refer to ways of organizing student interaction and different ways students are to interact such as Three-step interview or Round Robin.

Coelho (1992) describes three major kinds of cooperative learning tasks and their learning focus, each of which has many variations.

(1) Team practice

(from common input; skills development and mastery of facts)

- All students work on the same material.
- The task is to make sure that everyone in the group knows the answer to a question and can explain how the answer was obtained or understands the material. Because students want their team to do well, they coach and tutor each other to make sure that any member of the group could answer for all of them and explain their team's answer.
- When the teacher takes up the question or assignment, anyone in a group may be called on to answer for the team.
- This technique is good for review and for practice tests; the group takes the practice test together, but each student will eventually do an assignment or take a test individually.
- This technique is effective in situations where the composition of the groups is unstable (in adult programs, for example). Students can form new groups every day.

(2) Jigsaw

(differentiated but predetermined input; evaluation and synthesis of facts and opinions)

- Each group member receives a different piece of the information.
- Students regroup in topic groups (expert groups) composed of people with the same piece to master the material and prepare to teach it.
- Students return to home groups to share their information with each other.
- Students synthesize the information through discussion.
- Each student produces an assignment of part of a group project, or takes a test, to demonstrate synthesis of all the information presented by all group members.
- This method may require team-building activities for both home groups and topic groups, long-term group involvement, and rehearsal of presentation methods.
- This method is very useful in the multilevel class, allowing for both homogeneous and heterogeneous grouping in terms of English proficiency.

- Information-gap activities in language teaching are jigsaw activities in the form of pair work. Partners have data (in the form of text, tables, charts, etc.) with missing information to be supplied during interaction with another partner.

(3) Cooperative projects

(topics/resources selected by students; discovery learning)

- Topics may be different for each group.
- Students identify subtopics for each group member.
- Steering committee may coordinate the work of the class as a whole.
- Students research the information using resources such as library reference or interviews.
- Students synthesize their information for a group presentation: oral and/or written. Each group member plays a part in the presentation.
- Each group presents to the whole class.
- This method places greater emphasis on individualization and students' interests. Each student's assignment is unique.
- Students need plenty of previous experience with more structured group work for this to be effective.

(D) Roles of the Interactive Teacher

directive				non-directive
Controller	Director	Manager	Facilitator	Resource

Chapter 06 Mind Map

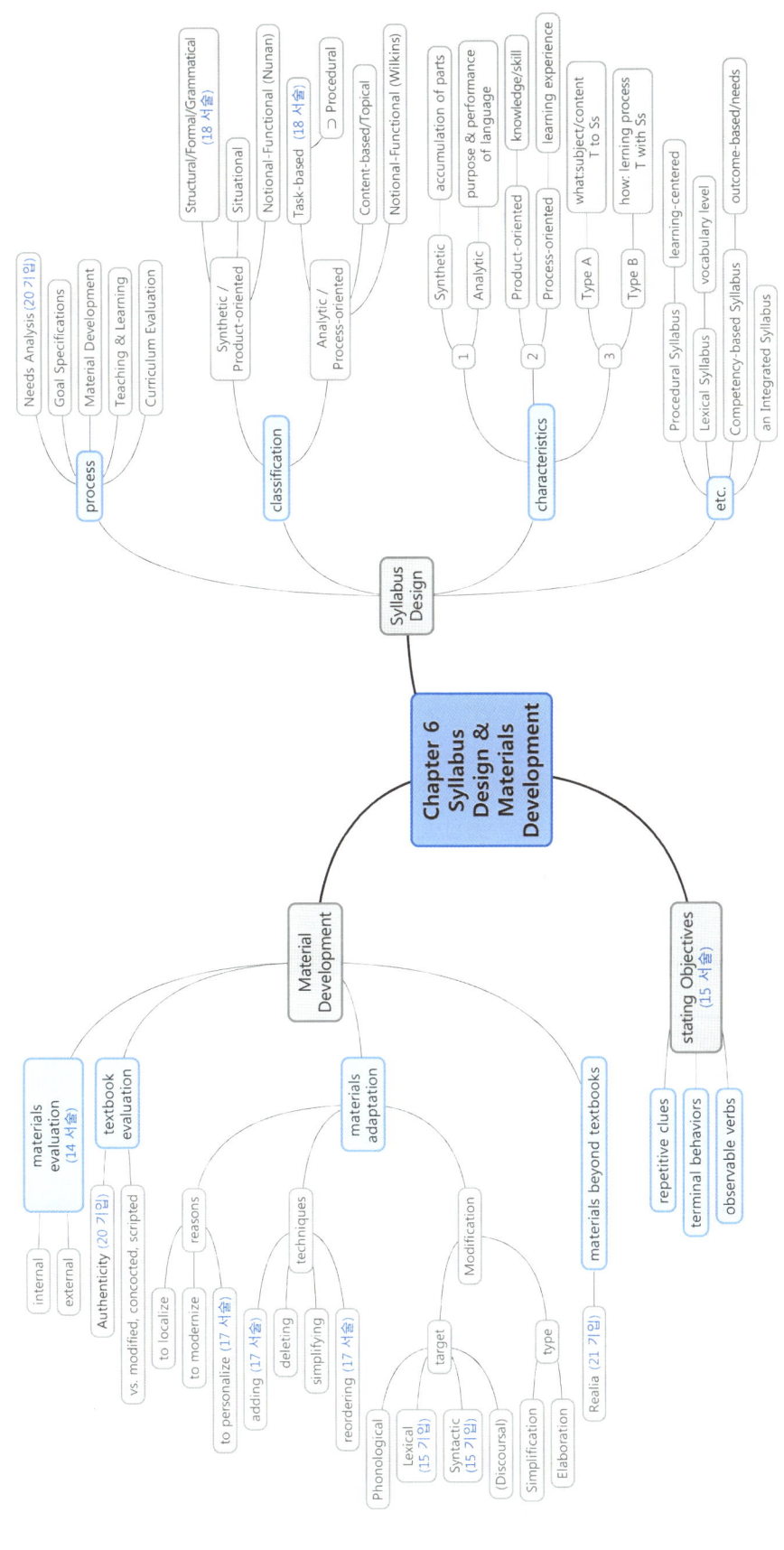

Chapter 06
Syllabus Design and Material Development

(A) Curriculum components

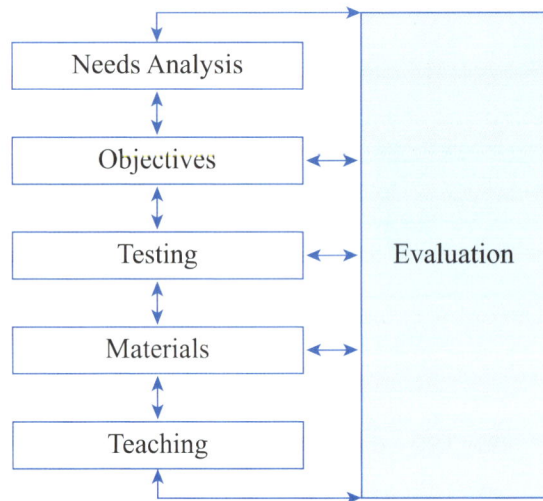

(B) Classification of Syllabus

A syllabus describes the major elements that will be used in planning a language course and provides the basis for its instructional focus and content.

accumulation of parts	Synthetic syllabuses	Analytic syllabuses	purpose & performance of language
knowledge / skill	Product-oriented syllabuses	Process-oriented syllabuses	learning experience
what: subject / content, T to Ss	Type A syllabuses	Type B syllabuses	how: learning process, T with Ss

Synthetic/Product-oriented syllabuses	Analytic/Process-oriented syllabuses
• Structural/formal syllabus • Situational syllabus • Notional-functional syllabus (Widdowson)	• Task-based syllabus • Procedural syllabus • Content-based syllabus • Notional-functional syllabus (Wilkins)

(C) Types of Syllabus

(C1) Grammatical (Structural/Formal) syllabus

It is organized around grammatical items. Traditionally, **grammatical syllabuses** have been used as the basis for planning general courses, particularly for beginning-level learners. In developing a grammatical syllabus, the syllabus planner seeks to solve the following problems:

- to select sufficient patterns to support the amount of teaching time available,
- to arrange items into a sequence that facilitates learning,
- to identify a productive range of grammatical items that will allow for the development of basic communicative skills.

Choice and sequencing of grammatical items in a grammar syllabus reflect not only the intrinsic ease or difficulty of items but their relationship to other aspects of a syllabus that may be being developed simultaneously. The syllabus planner is typically mapping out grammar together with potential lesson content in the form of topics, skills, and activities, and for this reason grammatical syllabuses often differ from one course to the next even when targeting the same proficiency level. The following presents the grammatical syllabus underlying a typical first-year EFL course.

> 1. Present verb *be*
> 2. Subject pronouns
> 3. Possessive adjectives
> 4. Indefinite article: *a/an*
> 5. Plural nouns: *-s, -ies, -es* …

Grammatical syllabuses have been criticized on the following grounds:

- They represent only a partial dimension of language proficiency.
- They do not reflect the acquisition sequences seen in naturalistic SLA.
- They focus on the sentence rather than on longer units of discourse.
- They focus on form rather than meaning.
- They do not address communicative skills.

These objections are true for traditional grammar-based courses and few language courses today are planned solely around grammatical criteria. Indeed, it is doubtful if they ever were. However, grammar remains a core component of many language courses. Typically, however, they are seen as one stream of a multiskilled or integrated syllabus rather than as the sole basis for a syllabus.

(C2) Situational syllabus

It is organized around the language needed for different situations such as **at the airport** or **at hotel**. A situation is a setting in which particular communicative acts typically occur. A situational syllabus identifies the situations in which the learner will use the language and the typical communicative acts and language used in that setting. Situational syllabuses have been a familiar feature of language teaching textbooks for centuries and are often used in travel books and books that focus on mastering expressions frequently encountered in particular situations. An example of a recent situationally organized textbook on English for travel is **Passport**, which contains the following situational syllabus:

> 1. On an airplane
> 2. At an immigration counter
> 3. At a bank
> 4. On the telephone
> 5. On the street …

Situational syllabuses have the advantage of presenting language in context and teaching language of immediate practical use. However, they are also subject to the following criticisms:

- Little is known about the language used in different situations, so selection of teaching items is typically based on intuition.
- Language used in specific situations may not transfer to other situations.
- Situational syllabuses often lead to a phrase-book approach.
- Grammar is dealt with incidentally, so a situational syllabus may result in gaps in a student's grammatical knowledge.

The role of situations in syllabus design has recently reentered language teaching, albeit in a different form from traditional situational syllabuses, with the emergence of communicative approaches to syllabus design and ESP. ESP approaches to curriculum development attribute a central role to the situation or setting in which communication takes place and to the following elements of the situation: the participants, their role relations, the transactions they engage in, the skills or behaviors involved in each transaction, the kinds of oral and written texts that are produced, and the linguistic features of the text.

Competency-based language teaching is an approach to teaching that focuses on transactions that occur in particular situations and their related skills and behaviors. The notion of situation has thus been incorporated as an element of more comprehensive approaches to syllabus design.

(C3) (Notional-) Functional syllabus

It is organized around communicative **functions** such as ***requesting, complaining, suggesting, agreeing***. A **functional syllabus** seeks to analyze the concept of communicative competence into its different components on the assumption that mastery of individual functions will result in overall communicative ability. Functional syllabuses were first proposed in the 1970s as part of the communicative language teaching movement and have formed the basis for many language courses and textbooks from that time. They were one of the first proposals for a communicative syllabus, that is, one that addresses communicative competence rather than linguistic competence. In ***Threshold Level English***, basic functions were identified through analysis of the purposes for which learners use English, particularly younger learners up to the intermediate level using a language for social survival and travel purposes. This resulted in a widely used functional syllabus that consists of 126 functions grouped into the following categories: imparting and seeking factual information, expressing and finding out attitudes, deciding on courses of action, socializing, structuring discourse, and communication repair.

Functional syllabuses such as ***Threshold Level*** provided the first serious alternative to a grammatical syllabus as a basis for general-purpose course design, and major courses published from the 1980s increasingly employed functional syllabuses, sometimes linked to a parallel grammatical syllabus. Because they often focus on communication skills, functional syllabuses are particularly suited to the organization of courses in spoken English. Functional syllabuses have proved very popular as a basis for organizing courses and materials for the following reasons:

- They reflect a more comprehensive view of language than grammar syllabuses and focus on the use of the language rather than linguistic form.

- They can readily be linked to other types of syllabus content (e.g., topics, grammar, vocabulary)
- They provide a convenient framework for the design of teaching materials, particularly in the domains of listening and speaking.

Functional syllabuses have also been criticized for the following reasons:

- There are no clear criteria for selecting or grading functions.
- They represent a simplistic view of communicative competence and fail to address the processes of communication.
- They represent an atomistic approach to language, which assumes that language ability can be broken down into discrete components that can be taught separately.
- They often lead to a phrase-book approach to teaching that concentrates on teaching expressions and idioms used for different functions.
- Students learning from a functional course may have considerable gaps in their grammatical competence because some important grammatical structures may not be elicited by the functions that are taught in the syllabus.

These objections can be regarded as issues that need to be resolved in implementing a functional syllabus. Since their inception and enthusiastic reception in the 1980s, functional syllabuses are now generally regarded as only a partial component of a communicative syllabus. Alternative proposals for communicative syllabus design include task-based and text-based syllabuses.

(C4) Task-based syllabus

It is organized around tasks that students will complete in the target language. A **task** is an activity or goal that is carried out using language such as finding a solution to a puzzle, reading a map and giving directions, or reading a set of instructions and assembling a toy. "Tasks are activities which have meaning as their primary focus. Success in tasks is evaluated in terms of achievement of an outcome, and tasks generally bear some resemblance to real-life language use" (Skehan 1996). While carrying out the tasks, learners are said to receive comprehensible input and modified output, processes believed central to SLA.

The basic claims made for a **task-based syllabus** are:

- Tasks are activities that drive the SLA process.
- Grammar teaching is not central with this approach because learners will acquire grammar as a by-product of carrying out tasks.

- Tasks are motivating for learners and engage them in meaningful communication.

At present, however, task-based syllabuses have not been widely implemented in language teaching. Among the concerns they raise are:

- ***definition of task***: Definitions of tasks are sometimes so broad as to include almost anything that involves learners doing something.
- ***design and selection of tasks***: Procedures for the design and selection of tasks remain unclear.
- ***development of accuracy***: Excessive use of communicative tasks may encourage fluency at the expense of accuracy.

Although the notion of task appears useful as a component of methodology, it has yet to be widely adopted as a unit of syllabus design.

(C5) Procedural syllabus

Procedural syllabus	learning centered approach, a kind of task-based syllabus
Process syllabus	negotiated syllabus

(C6) Content-based (Topical) syllabus

It is organized around themes, topics, or other units of content. With a **topical syllabus**, content rather than grammar, functions, or situations is the starting point in syllabus design. Content may provide the sole criterion for organizing the syllabus or a framework for linking a variety of different syllabus strands together. "It is the teaching of content or information in the language being learned with little or no direct effort to teach the language separately from the content being taught" (Krahnke 1987). All language courses, no matter what kind of syllabus they are based on, must include some form of content. But with other approaches to syllabus design, content is incidental and serves merely as the vehicle for practicing language structures, functions, or skills. In a topic-based syllabus, in contrast, content provides the vehicle for the presentation of language rather than the other way around.

Topic-based syllabuses have often been a feature of ESL programs in elementary or secondary schools where the teaching of English is integrated with science, mathematics, and social sciences, as well as of ESL programs for students at the university level.

Although choosing appropriate content is an issue in the design of any language course, using topics as the overarching criterion in planning a course leaves other questions unresolved because decisions must still be made concerning the selection of grammar, functions, or skills. It may also be difficult to develop a logical or learnable sequence for other syllabus components if topics are the sole framework. Different topics may require language of differing levels of complexity and, as a consequence, it may not always be possible to reconcile the different strands of the syllabus.

The following describes how a topical syllabus was used in developing speaking skills.

> 1. Music   2. Work   3. Shopping   4. Making friends   5. Clothes ⋯

(C7) Lexical syllabus

It identifies a target vocabulary to be taught normally arranged according to levels such as the first 500, 1,000, 1,500, 2,000 words. Today there is a large degree of consensus in English-language teaching concerning targets for vocabulary teaching at different levels and textbook and materials writers tend to keep materials within target vocabulary bands. Typical vocabulary targets for a general English course are:

> • Elementary level: 1,000 words
> • Intermediate level: an additional 2,000 words
> • Upper Intermediate level: an additional 2,000 words
> • Advanced level: an additional 2,000+ words

Because vocabulary is involved in the presentation of any type of language content, a **lexical syllabus** can only be considered as one strand of a more comprehensive syllabus.

(C8) Competency-based syllabus

An alternative to the use of objectives in program planning is to describe learning outcomes in terms of competencies, an approach associated with **Competency-Based Language Teaching** (**CBLT**). CBLT seeks to make a focus on the outcomes of learning a central planning stage in the development of language programs. Traditionally, in language teaching planners have focused to a large extent on the content of teaching (as reflected in a concern for different types of syllabuses) or on the process of teaching (as reflected in a concern for different types of teaching methods). Critics of this approach argue that this concern with content or process focuses on the means of learning rather than its ends. CBLT shifts the focus to the ends of learning rather than the means. As a general educational and training approach, CBLT seeks to improve accountability in teaching through linking instruction to measurable outcomes and performance standards.

Competency-based syllabus is one based on a specification of the competencies learners are expected to master in relation to specific situations and activities. **Competencies** are a description of the essential skills, knowledge, and attitudes required for effective performance of particular tasks and activities. Competency-based syllabuses are widely used in social survival and work-oriented language programs. Examples of competencies related to the topic of 'telephoning' are:

1. Read and dial telephone numbers
2. Identify oneself on the telephone when answering and calling
3. Request to speak to someone
4. Respond to request to hold
5. Respond to offer to take message

(C9) An Integrated syllabus

Decisions about a suitable syllabus framework for a course reflect different priorities in teaching rather than absolute choices. The issue is, which foci will be central in planning the syllabus and which will be secondary? In most courses there will generally be a number of different syllabus strands, such as *grammar* linked to *skills* and *texts*, *tasks* linked to *topics* and *functions*, or *skills* linked to *topics* and *texts*. In arriving at a decision about which approach to syllabus planning to take, the course planners need to decide between macrolevel and microlevel planning units in the course. For example, a reading course might first be planned in terms of reading skills (the macrolevel category) and then further planned in terms of text types, vocabulary, and grammar (the microlevel category). A syllabus might be organized grammatically at the first level and then the grammar presented functionally. Or the first level of organization might be functional with grammar items selected according to the grammatical demands of different functions. In practical terms, therefore, all syllabuses reflect some degree of integration.

(D) Material Development

Objectives of adaptation	Personalization, Localization, Modernization
Techniques for adaptation	Adding, Deleting, Simplifying, Reordering, Replacing

target of adaptation (what is modified?)	phonological modification
	lexical modification
	syntactic modification
	discourse modification (= interactional modification)
type of adaptation (how is it modified?)	simplification
	elaboration (= elaborative/elaborated modification)

⟨Adoption vs. Adaptation⟩

Whereas adoption is concerned with whole coursebook, adaptation concerns the parts that make up that whole. Teachers do not always have direct involvement: they may well influence decisions about whole textbooks only if they are part of a ministry of education team concerned with training or writing materials. A far more widespread and necessary activity among teachers is therefore that of adaptation, because the smaller-scale process of changing or adjusting the various parts of a course book is more closely related to the reality of dealing with learners in the dynamic environment of the classroom. Evaluation as an exercise can help us develop insights into different views of language and learning and into the principles of materials design and is something we do against the background of a knowledge of our learners and of the demands and potential of our teaching situation. To adapt materials is to try to bring together these individual elements under each heading or combinations of them so that they match each other as closely as possible.

⟨Evaluating Materials⟩

1) External Evaluation

The aim of an external evaluation is to examine the organization of materials as stated by the author. A look at the 'blurb' on the cover as well as the introduction and table of contents shows 'what the books say about themselves' (Cunningsworth 1984). The external evaluation looks at claims and promises made by the author/publisher to better understand the objectives of the coursebook. McDonough and Shaw (2003) assert that the table of contents often serves as a link between the external claims and the materials presented within the book.

The factors in external evaluation are:

- The cover of the book
- Introduction and table of contents: - the intended audience, the proficiency level, the context in which the materials are to be used
- How the language has been presented and organized into teachable units
- The author's view on language and methodology
- Date of publication
- The main core course or to be supplementary?
- Is the teacher's book in print locally available?
- Is a vocabulary list included?
- What visual materials does the book contain?
- Layout
- Too culturally biased or specific?
- Do the materials represent minority groups and/or women in a negative way?
- The inclusion of audio/video material
- The inclusion of tests in the teaching material

2) Internal Evaluation

An internal evaluation occurs after a coursebook has experienced an external evaluation and is deemed potentially appropriate and worthy for a particular group of learners thus far (McDonough and Shaw 2003). This type of evaluation is valuable in establishing the extent to which external factors and the internal organization of the material match. An investigation into two units or more is recommended to determine the validity of the authors' claims.

The factors in internal evaluation are:

- The presentation of skills
- The grading and sequencing of the materials
- Authentic or artificial?
- Suitable for different learning styles
- Sufficiently transparent to motivate both students and teachers

3) Overall evaluation factors

- The usability factor (integration of the material into a particular syllabus)
- The generalizability factor (useful for a group or not in general)
- The adaptability factor (feasibility of adaptation)
- The flexibility factor (how the materials can be used in different ways)

최서원 **전공영어 영어교육학** PRACTICAL

Chapter 07 Mind Map

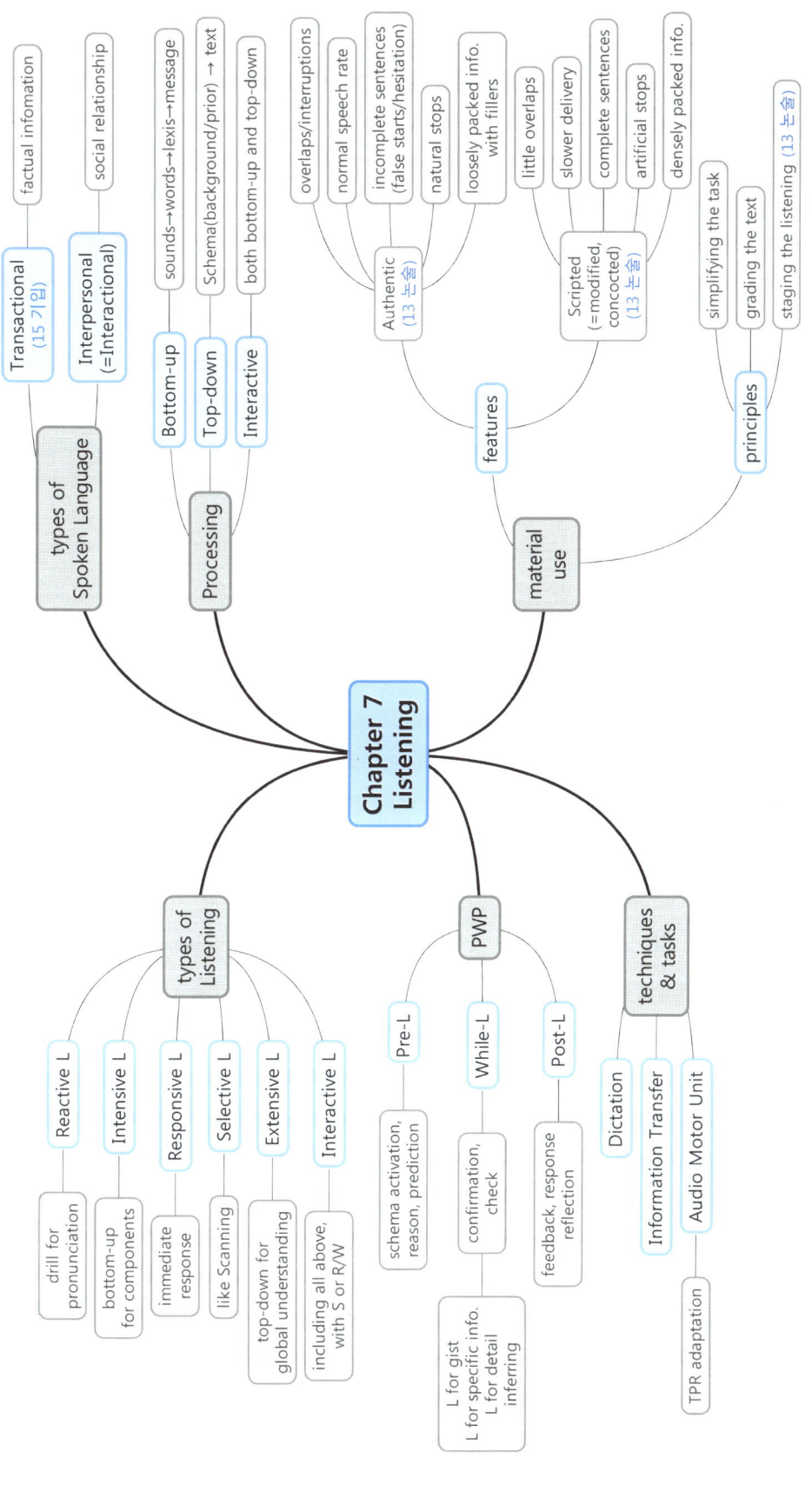

Chapter 07   Teaching Listening

(A) Types of Spoken Language (L/S)

Transactional	conveying propositional/factual information, message-oriented
Interactional (Interpersonal)	promoting social relationship, listener-oriented

The function of service encounters (such as those that take place in shops) is primarily **transactional**: the speakers have a practical goal to achieve, and the success of the exchange depends on the achievement of that goal. Typical transactional exchanges include such events as buying a train ticket, negotiating a loan or returning a damaged item to a store. To a certain extent it could be argued that the radio interview (between a radio talk show host and a spokesman from the Weather Bureau on the hailstorm in the previous day) is transactional, too, but, rather than the transaction of goods or services, it is the transaction of information that is the objective. The same argument might apply also to the interaction that characterizes classrooms (including language classrooms), another context in which rights are not equally distributed and where information is being transacted — typically in the form of facts.

What is at stake in casual conversation, however, is the social well-being of the participants, the aim being essentially *phatic*, i.e. to signal friendship and to strengthen the bonds within social groups. Rather than being directed at the achievement of some practical goal, the talk is primarily directed at the establishing and servicing of social relationships. For this reason conversation has been labelled **interactional** as opposed to **transactional**. Brown and Yule refine the distinction between these two purposes:

> We could say that primarily interactional language is primarily *listener-oriented*, whereas primarily transactional language is primarily *message-oriented*.

Because it emphasizes the personal element, we will use the term **interpersonal** in preference to **interactional**. This is also consistent with Halliday's use of the term to identify one of language's metafunctions: 'Interpersonal meaning is meaning as a form of action: the speaker or writer doing something to the listener or reader by means of language'. The 'something' that a speaker is doing in conversation is social 'work'—the establishing and maintaining of social ties.

It is important to emphasize that talk is seldom purely transactional or purely interpersonal, but that both functions are typically interwoven in spoken language: even the most straightforward transactions are tempered with interpersonal language (such as greetings) and chat amongst friends would be ultimately unrewarding without some kind of information exchange taking place. Nevertheless, the ***primary*** purpose of a shopping exchange is not social, and nor is the primary purpose of a chat conversation to exchange factual information.

(B) Bottom-up vs. Top-down Processing (L/R)

Bottom-up processing	sounds → words → lexis → a final message
Top-down processing	schema (background/prior knowledge) → text
Interactive processing	both bottom-up and top-down

It used to be believed that listeners built up their understanding of a text by working out what each individual sound was, then adding these up into a word, understanding the word, checking the meaning of that word with the words around them, etc (a bit like building up a wall from the individual bricks). Although this theory, known as 'bottom-up' (ie building up the messages from the individual small pieces), may initially sound appealing, it is virtually impossible to do.

Spoken English probably comes at you too fast to be able to adopt such an item-by-item approach on its own. It seems likely that we make use of 'bottom-up' skills more to fill in missing gaps rather than as a general approach to comprehension word by word.

The alternative theory is that when we listen to a new dialogue, we start processing the text using skills associated with a second theory ('top-down'), ie making use of what we already know to help us predict the structure and content of the text, and getting a general overall impression of the message.

Do the following represent use of top-down or bottom-up strategies?

1. Before we start listening, we can already predict some possible words and phrases that might be used because of our knowledge of lexical sets associated with the topic.
2. We listen carefully to a recording several times so that we can find a word we can't catch clearly.
3. When we don't clearly catch some of what people say, we hypothesise what we have missed and reinstate what we think was there, based on our knowledge of similar conversations.
4. We know the typical pattern some interactions follow (eg the typical sequence of exchanges when ordering a taxi on the phone), and this helps us understand these when they are spoken.

Strategy 2 is bottom-up. Strategies 1, 3 and 4 are examples of top-down strategies, and we do a lot more of this kind of processing that you might expect. Using background knowledge, prediction and 'filling-in' gaps are all important listening skills.

We don't come to a new piece of listening completely from a 'zero' starting point. We bring our previous knowledge to it, even before it's started. Making a good prediction of the content or the shape of a listening text will definitely help us to make better sense of it when it happens.

Things that could help include:

- having some idea what the topic being discussed will be;
- knowing something about that topic;
- knowing the typical sequence of exchanges that is used in a dialogue like this;
- predicting issues likely to be raised;
- being quickly able to get an overview of the general direction of the conversation;
- knowing any general rules or guidelines for what can/can't be said in conversations of this type;
- understanding the attitudes of the participants;
- knowing some words or phrases that are commonly used in conversation of this type.

Making a good prediction of the content or the shape of a listening text will definitely help us to make better sense of it when it happens. Rather than having to start from scratch, the listening may fall neatly into an imagined framework we have already set out for it. Of course, we can't be ready for everything, but anything that we have correctly expected frees up our energy to pay attention to things that require more intensive listening. This is summed up in the following figure.

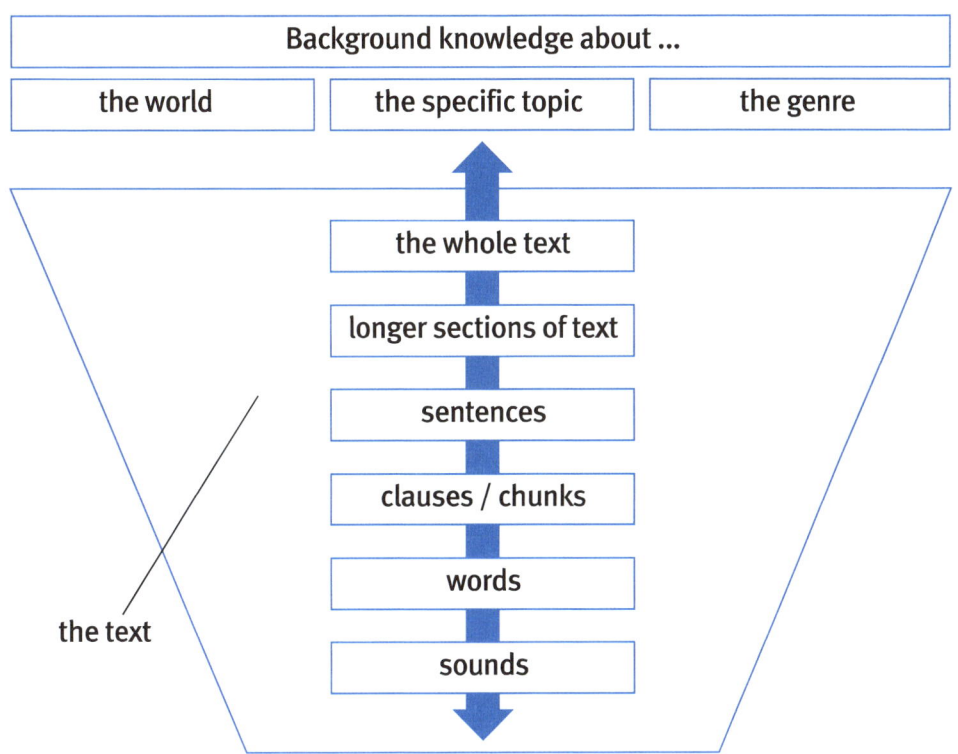

(C) Features of Authentic Materials in Listening

Authentic	Scripted
Overlaps and interruptions between speakers	Little overlap between speakers
Normal rate of speech delivery	Slower (maybe monotonous) delivery
Relatively unstructured language	Structured language, more like written English
Incomplete sentences, with false starts, hesitation, etc.	Complete sentences
Background noise and voices	No background noise
Natural stops and starts that reflect the speaker's train of thought and the listener's ongoing response	Artificial stops and starts that reflect an idealised version of communication (in which misunderstandings, false starts, etc. never occur)
Loosely packed information, padded out with fillers	Densely packed information

(C1) Using authentic materials in listening

simplifying the task	"If one notches up the text, one notches down the task."
grading the text	in accordance with the proficiency level of Ss
staging the listening	progressing to the tasks that are more demanding

One of the developments from the traditional listening lesson sequence has been the increased use of authentic material. Recordings of spontaneous speech expose learners to the rhythms of natural everyday English in a way that scripted materials cannot, however good the actors. Furthermore, authentic passages where the language has not been graded to reflect the learners' level of English afford a listening experience much closer to a real-life one. It is vital that students of a language be given practice in dealing with texts where they understand only part of what is said.

For these two reasons (naturalness of language and real-life listening experience), it is advisable to introduce authentic materials early on in a language course. In general, students are not daunted or discouraged by authentic materials — provided they are told in advance not to expect to understand everything. Indeed, they find it motivating to discover that they can extract information from an ungraded passage. The essence of the approach is as follows: ***Instead of simplifying the language of the text, simplify the task that is demanded of the student.*** With a text above the language level of the class, one demands only shallow comprehension. One might play a recording of a real-life stall holder in a market and simply ask the class, to write down all the vegetables that are mentioned.

Students may have difficulty in adjusting to authentic conversational materials after hearing scripted ones. It is worthwhile introducing your learners systematically to those features of conversational speech which they may find unfamiliar — hesitations, stuttering, false starts, and long, loosely structured sentences. Choose a few examples of a single feature from a piece of authentic speech, play then to the class, and ask them to try to transcribe them.

(D) Types of Listening Performance

Reactive L	drill for pronunciation
Intensive L	bottom-up for language components
Responsive L	immediate response
Selective L	specific information in longer texts (like scanning in R)
Extensive L	top-down for global understanding
Interactive L	including all above, with S or R/W

(D1) Listening skills

As a guide for teachers to plan listening tasks, Vandergrift and Goh (2012) identify six core skills that are integral to the listening process:

(1) *Listen for details*

Identify specific information that is relevant to the listening goal, such as key words, numbers, names, dates, and places.

(2) *Listen selectively*

Pay attention to particular parts of the text and ignore others that are not relevant to listening goals or that contain too much information to attend to at the same time.

(3) *Listen for global understanding*

Understand the overall general idea, such as the theme, topic, and purpose.

(4) *Listen for main ideas*

Understand the key points or propositions in a text, such as points in support of an argument, directions for doing something, and important events in a story.

(5) *Listen and infer*

Make up for information that is missing, unclear, or ambiguous in the text by using different resources, such as background knowledge, visual clues, and speaker's tone.

(6) *Listening and predict*

Anticipate what is going to be said before or during listening by using clues from the context, from background knowledge, or knowledge about the speaker.

(E) PWP (Process Listening)

Pre-listening	1. Activate schemata: What do I know? 2. Reason: Why listen? 3. Prediction: What can I expect to hear?
While-listening	1. Monitor (1): Are my expectations met? 2. Monitor (2): Am I succeeding in the task?
Post-listening	1. Feedback: Did I fulfill the task? 2. Response: How can I respond?

(E1) Current format for a listening lesson

The lesson format used by many teachers in early days was a relatively rigid one which reflected the structuralist orthodoxy of the time.

[Early format for a listening lesson]

Pre-listening
  Pre-teach vocabulary 'to ensure maximum understanding'

Listening
  Extensive listening followed by general questions on context
  Intensive listening followed by detailed comprehension questions

Post-listening
  Teach any new vocabulary
  Analyse language (*Why did the speaker use the Present Perfect here?*)
  Paused play; Students listen and repeat

Over the years, the original model has been modified. The listening lesson that one encounters in good ELT practice today has a rather different structure, which includes some or most of the elements shown in the following table. Let us consider the rationale behind the changes.

> **[Current format for a listening lesson]**
>
> **Pre-listening**
>   Establish context
>   Create motivation for listening
>   Pre-teach only critical vocabulary
>
> **Extensive listening**
>   General questions on context and attitude of speakers
>
> **Intensive listening**
>   Pre-set questions
>   Intensive listening
>   Checking answers to questions
>
> **Post listening (optional)**
>   Functional language in listening passage
>   Learners infer the meaning of unknown words from the sentences in which they appear
>   Final play; learners look at transcript

(1) Pre-listening

1) Pre-teaching vocabulary

There are a number of reasons for not pre-teaching all the unknown vocabulary in a recording. It takes time — time which is much better spent listening. Very importantly, it also leaves students unprepared for what happens in a real-life listening encounter where, inevitably, there will be words which they do not know and have to work out for themselves. A third consideration is the effect upon the listening process. By pre-teaching all the new words in a recording, regardless of their importance, the teacher encourages the learner to listen out for those words. Result: the learner's attention is focused upon the language of the text rather than its meaning. It may also be misdirected to parts of the recording which are not strictly relevant to the main argument.

The current policy is to pre-teach only **critical words**. 'Critical' is taken to mean those words without which the recording could not be understood (for example, in a passage about jogging, we would want to be sure that learners knew the verb to *jog*). In any given listening text, there should be very few such critical items — at most, four or five.

2) Establishing context

It is important to compensate for the limitations of using an audio cassette by giving students a general idea of what they are going to hear. In a real-life situation, they would usually be aware of who the speakers were, where they were and so on. It is only fair to provide some of this information before the listening exercise.

However, the information does not need to be extensive. In fact, there is considerable danger in expounding too much on the context of the listening passage. The more we tell the learners, the less they will need to listen to the recording to extract the answers they need. The criterion should be: *what would the listener already know in real life before the speech event began?*

Here are typical pieces of contextualisation from the Cambridge First Certificate (FCE) exam:

> *You will hear part of a radio programme in which two women, Mary and Pat, will talk about their interest in being an amateur radio operator, or radio 'ham'.* (Paper 103, Part 3)
> *You will hear a man talking about how he jogs — runs — in order to keep fit.* (Paper 103, Part 2)

These introductions serve three different pre-listening purposes:

a. They establish 'context': including the situation, the topic and the genre of the recording.

b. They introduce critical vocabulary.

c. They mention names which help the listener to 'label' the speakers. A teacher might also include other proper nouns (e.g. names of cities) which would not be regarded as 'fair game', i.e. as part of any learner's normal vocabulary base.

3) Creating motivation

This is an important goal of pre-listening, and one that is sometimes neglected. We need to give listeners a purpose for listening. The quality and depth of listening is also enormously enhanced when the listener has the right **mental set** — in other words, when she has given some forethought to what the listening passage is likely to contain. How to create motivation? One way is to write a title for the listening passage on the board, and then to ask the learners to predict what they will hear (see panel below). Once they have created a set of expectations, the goal of the extensive listening phase is to check which of their predictions prove to be correct and which not. The process can even be competitive (*Anna thinks there will be* *something about noise pollution; Enrique doesn't agree. Let's see who is right.*). Note, by the way, that the interaction exemplified in the panel does more than just create a mental set. It also performs the pre-listening functions of outlining context and introducing critical vocabulary.

Creating motivation for listening

T: You're going to hear somebody talking about camels. He's a zoologist who's studied them. What do you think he'll talk about?

S1: Desert.

T: Yes, he might mention deserts [*writes DESERT on board*]. Anything else?

S2: Water. Water on the camel's back.

T: He might mention what the camel has on its back. Its hump. The word is 'hump' [*writes HUMP*]. Any other ideas?

S3: Hot temperature.

S4: Walking. Long distance.

T: He might talk about the heat in the desert [*writes HEAT*]. How do we measure that?

S1: Degree.

T: Yes, in degrees. Anything else?

S4: Walking. Camels walk a long distance, carry people.

T: Yes, he might mention how far the camel walks [*writes DISTANCE*]. Or ...?

S3: Very slowly.

S5: How fast is the camel.

T: Yes, how fast the camel walks [*writes SPEED*]. [*Other possibilities explored*]

T: Well, some of you guessed correctly and some of you are wrong. Let's listen and see who was right.

A similar guessing activity takes advantage of the lack of real-life context in an audio recording by playing a short uncontextualised extract and asking learners to work out what is happening. This is done to great effect by Maley and Duff (1978) with passages such as the one below. Conflicting interpretations lead to animated discussion in the classroom and (most importantly) to some very careful listening and re-listening to justify the conclusions that have been reached.

> **Contextual ambiguity**
>
> A: You know what this is, I'm sure ...
> B: Um ...
> C: Oh, isn't it, er ...
> A: Yes, I thought you might like something familiar.
> B: Oh, yes ...
> A: It's funny, it took me a long time to get to like it ...
> C: Oh?
> A: But now I'm very fond of it ... Of course, it's nothing special ...
> B: Oh no, it's ... very good.
> A: I thought you'd like it ...
>
> (Maley and Duff 1978)

(2) During listening

The goals of extensive listening remain unchanged — for the reasons outlined above. However, the approach to intensive listening has been greatly restructured.

1) Pre-set questions

If questions are not asked until after the recording has been heard, learners listen in a very untargeted way. They are unclear about where to direct their attention; and their ability to answer depends upon which parts of the recording they happen to have paid special heed to. Their responses also become heavily dependent upon memory — and their recall becomes unreliable as the teacher asks more and more questions and as time goes by.

A policy of setting questions ***before*** the second play of the cassette ensures that learners know in advance what they are listening for. They can write notes of their answers during listening, and their ability to respond will not be dependent upon their ability to remember what was said. Note the convention in both teaching and testing (a convention that has rarely been questioned) whereby the questions follow the same order as the passage.

2) Checking answers

The teacher allows learners time to write up their answers, and then checks them with the class as a whole. This is sometimes a difficult phase of the listening lesson. Learners may be slow to respond — partly because they need to switch psychologically from the receptive role of listener to the active one of class participant but often because of a lack of confidence in their replies. Some learners attribute their insecurity to the fact that they do not (as in reading) have the text before them in order to double-check before they commit themselves to an answer. One way of overcoming reluctance is for learners to compare answers in pairs before submitting them to the whole class.

(3) Post-listening

1) Functional language

The practice of replaying a listening passage in order to reinforce recently taught grammar has been abandoned, along with other structuralist notions. However, many of the dialogues which feature in published listening materials represent common types of human interaction. They therefore afford useful and well-contextualised examples of language **functions** such as refusing, apologising, threatening, offering, etc. These functions are relatively difficult to teach in isolation. It is worthwhile drawing attention to any which feature prominently in a listening passage, and even pausing briefly to practise them.

Drawing attention to functional language

T: What did George say about the damage?
S1: He wanted to pay.
T: Do you remember the words George used?
S2: 'I'll pay the damage.'
T: Yes. 'I'll pay for the damage.' So what was he doing?
S3: He promised.
T: Not quite promising …
S4: He offered.
T: That's right. He offered to pay for the damage. He *offered* … Offer to carry my bag.
S2: [*pause*] I'll carry your bag.
T: Offer to post the letter.
S5: I'll post the letter. *etc.*

---

2) Inferring vocabulary

If only minimal vocabulary is pre-taught, listeners have to learn to cope with unknown words in the passage. Here, they are gaining experience of exactly the kind of process that occurs in a real-life encounter, where there is no teacher or dictionary on hand to explain every word in an utterance. It is usually assumed (perhaps by analogy with L2 reading) that the way in which an L2 listener deals with an unknown word is to work out its meaning from the context in which it occurs. If one accepts the assumption, it is appropriate to give listeners some controlled practice in the process of inferring word meaning, similar to the practice given to readers. The teacher identifies a number of useful words in the recording which may be new to the class and whose meanings are relatively clearly illustrated by the context (one or two sentences) within which they occur. The teacher then writes the words on the board, and replays the sections of the listening passage which contain them. Students suggest possible meanings.

3) Paused play

Paused play has generally been dropped. It was often used as a way of practising intonation patterns — and was thus part of the unsatisfactory mixing of language and listening goals which has already been commented on. It was also criticised on the grounds that learners could repeat what they heard without necessarily understanding anything — the kind of parroting associated with behaviourist drilling. My personal belief is that paused play can still serve some purpose, as a way of checking whether learners can divide up short sections of connected speech into individual words. However, one has to recognise that it does not fit in well with current communicative approaches.

4) Final play

There is sometimes a final play during which, for the first time, the students are given a transcript of the listening passage. This is a valuable activity, since it allows learners, on an individual basis, to clarify sections of the recording which they have not so far succeeded in decoding. It may also enable them to notice, for example, the presence of short weak-quality function words which they would otherwise have overlooked.

One of the strengths of early approaches to listening was the insistence on separating the spoken and the written word. However, there is no reason why the latter should not be introduced at a late stage in the lesson in the form of a transcript that assists word recognition. It is important that learners take away with them some kind of permanent record of what they have covered in the listening lesson — and not just an echo in their heads of the voices of the speakers.

In addition to the above, two other major developments have occurred. Firstly, it has been recognised that it is very difficult to check understanding accurately through the use of conventional comprehension questions. Answering such questions often involves a great deal of reading or writing; and if a learner gives a wrong answer, it may not be due to a failure of listening at all. It may be because he/she has not understood the question properly (a reading problem) or because he/she lacks the language to formulate a written answer (a writing problem). There has therefore been a move towards checking understanding by setting **tasks** rather than questions. These tasks can be quite simple. Many involve the completion of simple grids. Others involve filling in forms. If the listening passage is a dialogue between a customer and a travel agent, then the task might require the learner to complete the kind of form that the agent would be using. The advantage of this kind of activity is not just that it reduces the amount and complexity of reading (and indeed writing) that has to be done. It also aligns the purposes and processes of listening more closely with what occurs in real-life encounters.

Task-based activities compare favourably with the practice of asking whole-class comprehension questions, where the strong listeners are often keen to respond while the weaker ones mask their failure of understanding behind bright smiles. All class members have to participate, and there is a tangible outcome in the form of a completed form or checklist which can be collected and marked.

Secondly, there has been a move towards using **authentic recordings** wherever possible. The term 'authentic' usually refers to listening items originally intended for the ears of a native listener rather than specially prepared for language learners. The arguments for using such materials are that they expose learners to the real sounds of the language (including the hesitations of spontaneous speech) and that they provide a listening experience more like that of real life, where students do not know every word and have to make guesses to fill in gaps in understanding. To summarise, the changes that have taken place reflect three developments in the way listening is viewed. Firstly, there has been a shift in perspective so that listening as a skill takes priority over details of language content. Secondly, there has been a wish to relate the nature of listening practised in the classroom to the kind of listening that takes place in real life. This is reflected in the way the teacher provides contextual background, gives practice in inferring the meaning of new words, uses recordings which are 'authentic' in origin and uses simulated tasks rather than formal exercises. Thirdly, we have become aware of the importance of providing motivation and a focus for listening. The listener is encouraged to develop expectations as to what will be heard in the recording, then to check them against what is actually said. By pre-setting questions and tasks, we ensure that learners are clear from the start about the purpose of the listening exercise and will not have to rely heavily on memory.

(F) Listening Exercises

(F1) Conversational Listening Activities

Listening, in the context of conversation, is clearly not just a psychoperceptual process. It is also a very social activity, in which both speaker and hearer affect the nature of the message and how it is to be interpreted. Grice's maxims are based on the assumption of mutual cooperation in conversation. Indeed, in analyzing conversation, it is not easy to talk about 'speaker' and 'listener', as both interlocutors (in a canonical dyadic exchange) take on both roles.

Concerning the specific listening roles in conversation, a number of activities can be distinguished, in addition to the psychoperceptual processing of the speaker's message. These are recognizing stages in the conversation, topic shift, back-channeling, reformula- tion, repair, turn-taking, and negotiating meaning and exploiting ambiguity (Clark 1996).

1) Recognizing Stages in the Conversation

One important activity that listeners perform is facilitating the mutual performance of the different sections in conversation. Conversations can be broken down into three major stages: ***openings***, ***closings***, and ***topics***.

In opening a conversation, there must be an initiator, or speaker, but there must also be an interlocutor, or listener. The initiator may begin with a ***summons***. The role of the listener is to respond to the summons. Let us take a hypothetical case of a speaker, Susan, and a listener, John. Susan begins with a summons, "John?" John's response, as the listener, to Susan's summons is crucial in deciding the direction the conversation will take. He may respond with a simple "Yes?" In that case, he will be signaling that the opening is successful and that Susan can now introduce a topic of her choice (although he will still be able to reject her chosen topic if he does not like it). On the other hand, he may ignore Susan's summons. Her opening will have been unsuccessful, and no conversation will ensue. As another alternative, he may signal a provisional acceptance of the opening, with something like "What do you want?" Continued conversation will then be conditional on the nature of the topic Susan introduces.

Closings are also important in conversations. A listener's inability to pick up when the speaker is wanting to close the conversation can lead to an embarrassing situation. For example:

> A: Well, nice talking to you.
> B: Yes, it's been lovely. We must do this again.
> A: Well, I really must go now.
> B: Where are you going?
> A: Oh, I have to get something from the supermarket.
> B: That's nice. I'll come with you.
> A: Oh, er ... well, actually, I have to go to the bank first.

2) Topic Shift

With respect to topics, which make up the main body of a conversation, the listener plays an important role in determining when the conversation will move from one topic to another, a process known as ***topic shift***. The role of the listener is to identify points in the discourse when it is appropriate to move on to a new topic. At various points in the ongoing discourse, listeners have the opportunity to take turns at speaking. At such points, they may decide to take a turn or allow the current speaker to continue. If they take a turn, they may choose between continuing with the current topic or switching to a new one. The important thing from the listener's point of view is that the shift must be appropriate. In the following example, A shifts the topic from newspapers to stamps when the transaction for the newspaper has been completed (at least partially).

> A: I'd like this newspaper, please.
> (pause)
> B: There you are. (hands over newspaper)
> A: Do you sell stamps?

Although it is not known exactly how listeners judge when a topic shift is appropriate, we may easily recognize when it is not appropriate. This explains why people are sometimes accused of 'changing the subject' when speakers consider that the current topic has not been completed, as in the following exchange:

> Mother: Have you done your homework?
> Child: I think I'll watch TV now.

3) Back-Channeling

Another listener activity that affects the structure of conversation is **back-channeling**. In order for speakers to continue with their message, they need signals, or **back-channel cues**, from their listeners to let the speakers know that they are attending. Without back-channel cues, a conversation would likely break down, as the speakers would not know whether the listeners were actively participating in the discourse. This is particularly true with regard to telephone conversations, as speakers may not even know that someone is on the line.

Back-channel cues may be verbal (***yeah, mm, um, ah, of course, oh dear,*** etc.) or nonverbal (head nodding, shoulder shrugging, facial gestures and eye gaze, laughter, etc.). Not only are back-channel cues needed to encourage speakers to continue speaking, but they also guide the direction of what is said. A head nod, indicating agreement, is likely to encourage speakers to continue in the same vein. But a shake of the head, indicating disagreement, may cause speakers to modify what they are saying and take a different direction. Back-channel cues may convey a range of attitudes of the listener, including empathy, agreement, disagreement, and indifference; in all cases, however, they affect what speakers say and how they say it.

4) Reformulation

Listeners may also guide a conversation by reformulating speakers' utterances. In this way, listeners clarify for speakers how they are interpreting what is being said. In the following exchange, for example, a professor uses a ***reformulation*** to interpret what a student is saying and check that his interpretation is in agreement with the intention of the student.

> Student: I can't come to see you tomorrow at 9:00 o'clock. I've got a lecture.
> Professor: So you want to make the appointment a bit later.
> Student: Yes. How about 11:30?

In this example, the professor uses a paraphrase to reformulate what he understands the student to have said. In some cases, however, reformulations may partially or exactly echo the statement they are reformulating. In the next exchange, which is part of a conversation between a university applicant and a professor, the professor repeats exactly the words used by the candidate (although the intonation pattern is different):

> Applicant: I got a distinction in my MA dissertation, and I want to go on to MPhil or PhD.
>
> Professor: You got a distinction in your dissertation, and you want to go on to MPhil or PhD. (pause) That would certainly be possible.

5) Repair

One way in which listeners may alter the direction a speaker is taking is by correcting misunderstandings, inaccuracies, or errors, referred to as ***repair***. In the following example, which took place in a restaurant, A asks to take a chair from an adjoining table, which is unoccupied. Perhaps because A uses the polite formula "Do you mind?" — which would require a negative to indicate agreement — he/she is taken aback at what is an apparent blunt refusal. Realizing that there is a misunderstanding, A clarifies by paraphrasing the original question without using the "Do you mind?" formula. The repair is successful, as this time there is no doubt that B is in agreement.

> A: Do you mind if I take this chair?
> B: Yes.
> A: Eh ... I mean, may I take it?
> B: Yes.

6) Turn-Taking

Successful performance of listener intervention strategies such as staging, back-channeling, reformulation, and repair depends on the ability of listeners to judge at what point to use them. To ascertain this, listeners need to be familiar with the conventions of ***turn-taking***: how interlocutors take turns at speaking and listening. Turn boundaries, rather obviously, are marked when one speaker stops talking and another takes over, although there may be some overlap. However, listeners do not wait until a speaker stops talking before deciding to take a turn. If this were the case, there would be pauses between turns, and studies have shown that speaker switches are usually accomplished with little or no pause at all. Listeners therefore must project forward to the completion of a speaker's turn, which will allow them to intervene. Sacks, Schegloff, and Jefferson (1974), who developed a system of rules for turn-taking, refer to the point at which it is possible for a turn switch to occur as a ***transition relevance point***. Listeners rely on a variety of cues to project forward to transition relevance points (Clark 1996). These include eye gaze, gestures, syntax, and intonation. Speakers usually tend to direct their gaze away from listeners during a turn and to refocus on the listeners as they finish the turn. (Listeners, in contrast, usually monitor speakers throughout their turns in order to pick up on the signals for the transition relevance point.) Gestures that speakers have been making to accompany their talk tend to be finished, and they tend to relax their bodies. At the end of a turn, the final syllable may be lengthened, accompanied by a falling intonation.

7) Negotiating Meaning and Exploiting Ambiguity

Finally, a listener influences the progress of a conversation by negotiating the meaning to be assigned to an utterance and exploiting ambiguity when it occurs. Although a speaker will usually have a particular intention in making an utterance, it is up to the listener to decide whether that intention, or meaning, is taken up. Thomas (1995) cites two exchanges that show how listeners may interpret the same statement in different ways and thereby influence the structure of the ongoing conversation:

< Example A >	< Example B >
David: Tea or coffee?	David: Tea or coffee?
Jenny: Coffee, please.	Jenny: Yes, please.
	David: Coffee?
	Jenny: Thank you.

In example A, the listener, Jenny, interprets David's utterance as an offer to provide her with whichever drink she chooses. In example B, she interprets it as a question as to whether she wants a drink or not (whether it be tea or coffee). In example A, the way Jenny interprets David's initial utterance results in just one exchange to resolve David's invitation. In example B, however, because Jenny interprets David's same statement differently, two exchanges are necessary.

In the following exchange, in which a wife enquires about what her husband would like as a dessert, the husband/listener reads perhaps more into the speaker's question than the latter intended (perhaps the honeydew melon was particularly good or perhaps it needed to be eaten).

Wife: Do you want honeydew melon?
Husband: Why?
Wife: No particular reason, I just thought you might like some.

What these examples show is that meaning is negotiable and that it may take a considerable stretch of discourse before a speaker's meaning becomes clear. Just how long a negotiation takes is dependent, to a great extent, on the role of the listener.

Conversation is one of the most important kinds of spoken text, and it is susceptible to cross-cultural and cross-linguistic variation. Back-channeling, reformulating, repairing, taking turns, negotiating meaning, recognizing sections, shifting topics, and exploiting ambiguity are doubtless universal to all languages and cultures. However, in the way they are applied, there is considerable variation. They are therefore features that merit particular attention as a part of second language listening pedagogy.

(G) Listening Techniques and Tasks

Dictation	Dicto-comp	Dictogloss
form-based, exact reproduction	meaning-based, approximate reconstruction	
during dictation	after dictation	
individual work	individual-based work	group-based work

Dictation with a difference	dictation (bottom-up processing) with top-down processing
Information Transfer	diagramming or drawing based on listening
Audio Motor Unit	TPR adaptation, T's command, Ss' listening and performing

⟨Dictogloss⟩

Dictogloss involves the teacher reading the passage at full speed several times. After a few readings, in which the students make notes, the task is to work in groups to reproduce a version of the passage that is written in good English and contains all the main ideas of the original. This involves much discussion and collaboration about areas of grammar, link words, sentence structure, etc. which tends to be very involving. At the end, they compare their version with the original.

The main point of dictogloss as a listening activity is to force our students to confront the difficulties of connected speech. The technique allows opportunities for the class to focus on features of pronunciation such as elision and assimilation. It also keeps the students focused on meaning and its relation to form (rather than on memory).

⟨Information Transfer⟩

A group of activities involving a small amount of written language is given the name **information transfer**. In these activities, learners reproduce the message they hear in a new form, for example when they listen and respond by ordering a set of pictures, completing a map, drawing a picture or completing a table. A key characteristic of such activities is that they involve a change in the form of the message but the message remains the same. Listen-and-draw techniques can thus be classified as information transfer techniques. We will now look in detail at information transfer activities.

There are good reasons for using information transfer activities to encourage meaning-focused listening and to support listening. The most obvious learning from information transfer relates to the information in the activity. In contrast to the use of comprehension questions, the visual structure of a well-designed diagram for information transfer provides a conceptual scaffold to assist comprehension. Put simply, the visual support makes listening easier.

Second, when used with listening, information transfer focuses learners' attention on listening without the extra burden of having to read a list of questions or write long answers. The principle here is that when the focus is on listening skills, the activity should not require learners to simultaneously read and/or write extensively.

Third, information transfer encourages deep processing of input. A key question that teachers should ask about an activity is, "What quality of thinking does this activity promote?" Information transfer requires learners to transform the input in some way, and this typically requires more mental effort than copying or responding to comprehension questions. In a sense then, information transfer activities are information transforming activities. It is likely that this deep processing provides good opportunities to learn new vocabulary and grammatical items contained in the spoken or written text, particularly those items that are focused on in the information transfer activity.

The above three reasons all focus on the role of information transfer in guiding understanding of input. In addition, information transfer also has a useful role in pushing learners' production. It does this by providing a simplified or diagrammatic representation of the original input which learners can use to 'reconstitute' the text in their own words. In this way, information transfer provides an intermediary bridge or link between input and output which discourages learners from relying too heavily on direct copying from the original text, but which still provides them with a conceptual scaffold for rebuilding the original text in their own words or for another purpose.

Finally, from a practical point of view, information transfer activities can be much easier to produce than sets of comprehension questions. A timeline related to a simple narrative, or a simple radio news item grid can easily be sketched onto a whiteboard for learners to copy. Alternatively, the diagram can be described to learners who then draw it, thus adding another valuable listening opportunity to the activity. The same diagram can become a template to be used regularly in lessons.

(H) Assessing Listening Comprehension - Dictation

Dictation can be a useful method of testing listening comprehension. Dictation tends to have a bad reputation among language learners and teachers because it has been used more as a spelling test than a test of listening comprehension, but Sandra Savignon has suggested that dictations can be graded based on the student's comprehension of specific ideas. For example, a student might write 'children laugh at song' when the sentence 'the children were laughing at the funny song' was dictated. According to Savignon's system, this response would be correct *on the basis of listening comprehension* because 'children laugh at song' captures the general meaning of the sentence. Of course, this response also demonstrates that the student missed several details and had not mastered the grammatical structures in the sentence.

최시원 **전공영어 영어교육학** PRACTICAL

Chapter 08 Mind Map

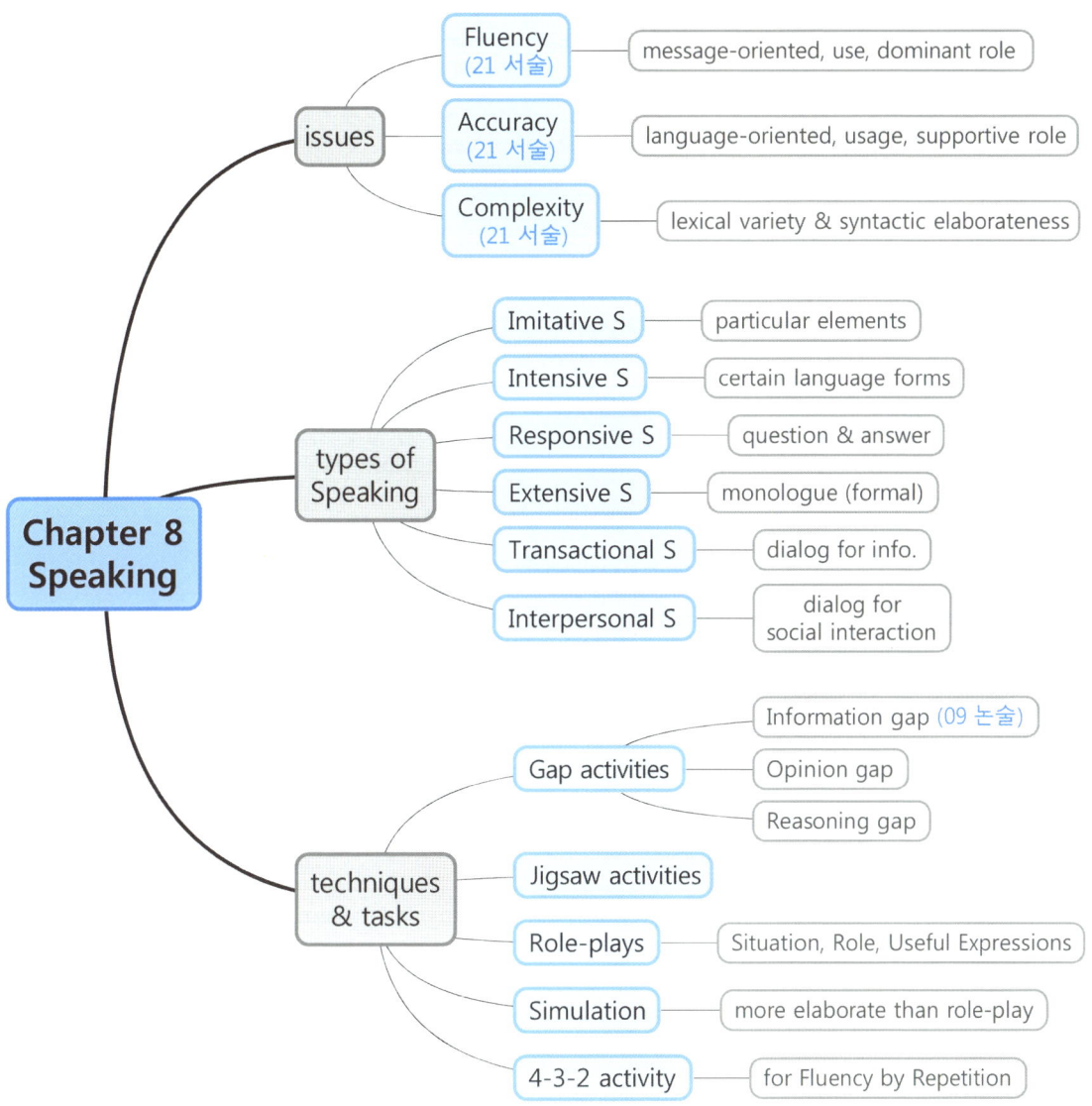

Chapter 08 — Teaching Speaking

(A) Accuracy vs. Fluency issues & Complexity

Accuracy	language-oriented; usage (supportive)
Fluency	message-oriented; use (dominant)
Complexity	lexical variety & syntactic elaborateness

(B) Types of Speaking Performance

Imitative S	particular elements of language form
Intensive S	beyond imitative S, certain language forms
Responsive S	question & answer, not into extensive
Extensive S	(monologue) extended, formal, deliberative
Transactional S	(dialogue) information, extended from responsive S
Interpersonal S	(dialogue) social interaction

(C) Speaking Techniques and Tasks

Gap activities	Information gap	the exchange of information among participants
	Opinion gap	sharing personal preferences, feelings, or attitudes
	Reasoning gap	deriving new info. by inferring from given info.
Jigsaw activities	bidirectional or multidirectional information gap	
Role-plays	situation, roles, useful expressions	
Simulations	more elaborate than role-play, props & documents	
4-3-2 activity	'fluency', automaticity, task repetition	

‹Gap activities›

1) Information gap activity

For genuine communication to occur in the language classroom, teacher-student (and student-student) exchanges must go beyond display questions and should be based on the gap that occurs between interlocutors when one does not know in advance what the other is going to say (Prabhu 1987). Teachers must thoughtfully prepare so that oral interaction involves a transfer of information from one person to another. The following role-play involves the teacher giving role cards to students for pair work. In the following role-play, paired students are asked to provide sustained speech for the specific purpose of persuading each other without causing offense.

Student A:	Student B:
You like dancing and going to discos. Suggest to your partner that you go out this evening. Try to persuade him/her to go where you prefer.	You don't like dancing and going to discos. You prefer going to the cinema or to a concert. Try to persuade your partner to go where you prefer.

2) Opinion gap activity

An **opinion gap activity** involves identifying and articulating a personal preference, feeling, or attitude. The activity may require using factual information, formulating arguments, and justifying one's opinions. For some topics, there may be no right or wrong responses and no reason to expect the same answers or responses from different individuals or different groups. For example, the teacher divides the class into several groups that will discuss or describe a common object from different perspectives. After all groups finish, the teacher asks the groups to report to the rest of the class.

> Example: Describe a television set from one of the following points of view:
> Group 1: prehistoric people
> Group 2: modern people
> Group 3: people from the future
> Group 4: people from another planet

3) Reasoning gap activity

A **reasoning gap activity** involves deriving some new information from given information through the process of inference or deduction and the perception of relationships or patterns. The activities necessarily involve comprehending and conveying information. Here is an ancient puzzle as an example:

> A man is standing by a river with a wolf, a sheep, and some vegetables. He wants to get everything across the river, but he has a small boat that cannot carry all three things at one time. The wolf will eat the sheep if the man goes away, and the sheep will eat the vegetables if the man goes away. Discuss how the man can get across the river without losing any of his belongings.

‹Role-play and Simulation›

Role-play minimally involves (a) giving a role to one or more members of a group and (b) assigning an objective or purpose that participants must accomplish. Examples:

> In pairs, student A is an employer and student B is a prospective employee. The objective is for A to interview B. In groups, similar dual roles could be assumed with assignments to others in the group to watch for certain grammatical or discourse elements as the roles are acted out.
>
> A group role-play might involve a discussion of a political issue, with each person assigned to represent a particular political point of view.

Simulations usually involve a more complex structure and often larger groups (of 6 to 20) where the entire group is working through an imaginary situation as a social unit, the object of which is to solve some specific problem.

> All members of the group are shipwrecked on a "desert island". Each person has been assigned an occupation (doctor, carpenter, garbage collector, etc.) and perhaps some other mitigating characteristic (a physical disability, an ex-convict, a millionaire, etc.). Only a specified subset of the group can survive on the remaining food supply, so the group must decide who will live and who will die.

(D) Assessing speaking

1) Using Rubrics

Many teachers find the use of rubrics helpful in the evaluation of speaking. Rubrics let you highlight the aspects of speaking that are most important to you and appropriate for the specific speaking task. They can also be modified for each student with different degrees of language proficiency or linguistic needs. Consider this example of a rubric for the assessment of an oral description.

Task: Students are shown a picture of a happy child with a tattered doll. They are first asked to tell what they see in the picture, and, second, to make up a story that led up to the picture they see. They are given up to two minutes to look at the picture and organize their thoughts before they are asked to start speaking.

Amount of Information Successfully Communicated	Virtually no information was conveyed.	*1 2 3 4 5*	The picture was described fully.
	Alternatively, you could make a hash mark for every piece of understandable information communicated: ///////		
Quality of Language Structure	One-word or L1 utterances.	*1 2 3 4 5*	A variety of sentence types used appropriately.
Flow	Many hesitations, false starts, and overly long pauses.	*1 2 3 4 5*	Language flows smoothly with appropriate pauses.
Pronunciation	Very nonnative-like. Incomprehensible to a native speaker.	*1 2 3 4 5*	Almost completely native-like. Only a few mispronunciations which do not interfere with comprehensibility.
Word Choice	Use of L1 and false cognates. Repetition of unspecific labels (this, that, thing).	*1 2 3 4 5*	Precise and accurate.
Overall Impression	Especially poor for a student at this level.	*1 2 3 4 5*	Especially good for a student at this level.

This rubric is just an example of the types of charts you can develop for your own purposes. This one is probably longer than one you would use in your class, but it includes examples of different types of judgments that can be used in speaking assessments. The assessment rubric can be different each time you test speaking, and it is a good idea to alert students in advance of the specific things you will be 'listening for'. For example, a speaking rubric associated with a social studies unit on the American Revolution could include vocabulary such as ***revolt***, ***taxation***, ***colony***, ***citizen***, and ***monarchy***.

2) Self-assessment

Self-assessment can also be very useful in the assessment of speaking, especially for older learners. Self-assessments are groups of statements that describe various ways a person might use the target language. Learners rate their ability to accomplish the specific task included in each statement. For example, the self-assessment item listed below concerns the individual's ability to order a pizza. The student responds on a scale from 1 to 5 indicating his or her ability to accomplish the task. You should notice that self-assessment statements are typically written in terms of the goal to be accomplished rather than whether specific grammatical structures were used correctly.

I can order pizza delivery by telephone in English	I am not usually able to order pizza.	1 2 3 4 5	I am always able to give the correct pizza order and directions to my house the first time I try.

Self-assessments can help students see their language ability more realistically and encourage them to set specific and reasonable goals.

Chapter 09 Mind Map

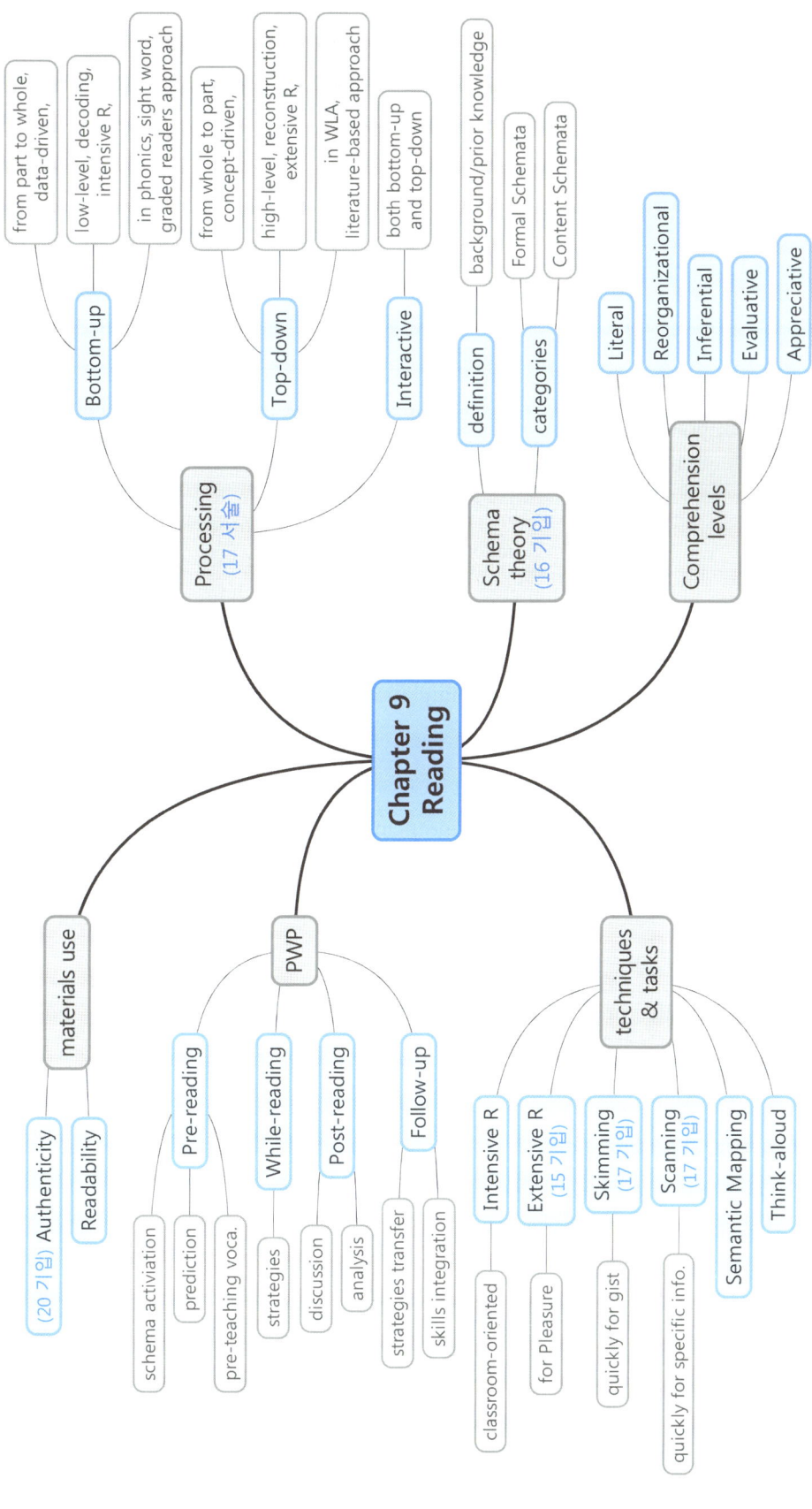

Chapter 09   Teaching Reading

(A) Bottom-up vs. Top-down process & Interactive process (interactive-compensatory model)

Bottom-up	Top-down
From part to whole, data-driven, low-level, decoding, intensive R, in phonics, sight word, graded reader approach	From whole to part, concept-driven, high-level, reconstruction, extensive R, in WLA, literature-based approach
Interactive	
bottom-up & top-down	

(A1) Bottom-up Model

A **bottom-up** reading model is a reading model that emphasizes the written or printed text. It says that reading is driven by a process that results in meaning (or, in other words, reading is driven by text) and that reading proceeds from part to whole. To elaborate, Gough (1972) proposes a phonics-based or bottom-up model of the reading process which portrays processing in reading as proceeding in serial fashion, from letter to sound, to words, to meaning, in the progression. Stated in Gough's terms the reading system, from a bottom-up perspective, functions in sequences as follows.

First, the graphemic information enters through the visual system and is transformed at the first level from a letter character to a sound, that is, from a graphemic representation to a phonemic representation. Second, the phonemic representation is converted, at level two, into a word. The meaning units or words then pass on to the third level and meaning is assimilated into the knowledge system. Input is thus transformed from low-level sensory information to meaning through a series of successively higher-level encodings, with information flow that is entirely bottom-up, no higher level processing having influence on any lower level processing. This process is also referred to as **data-driven**.

However, some researchers have already noticed the weaknesses of the bottom-up model in which processing is seen as proceeding only in one direction, so this implies that no higher level information ever modifies or changes lower level analysis. In some cases, readers are able to identify a word correctly only by employing higher level semantic and syntactic processing.

(A2) Top-down Model

A **top-down** reading model is a reading approach that emphasizes what the reader brings to the text. It contends that reading is driven by meaning and proceeds from whole to part. It is also known as **concept-driven** model.

To these theorists, efficient reading doesn't result from the precise perception and identification of all the elements in a word, but from skills in selecting the fewest, most productive cues necessary. They contend that readers have a prior sense of what could be meaningful in the text, based upon their previous experiences and their knowledge about language. Readers are not, in their view, confined only to one source of information — the letters before their eyes, but have at their disposal two other important kinds of information which are available at the same time: semantic cues (meaning), and syntactic cues (grammatical or sentence sense). Thus, what readers bring to the text separately in terms of both their prior knowledge of the topic and their knowledge about the language assists them in predicting what the upcoming words will be. Readers sample the print, assign a tentative hypothesis about the identity of the upcoming word and use meaning to confirm their prediction. If meaning is constructed, readers resample the text and form a new hypothesis. Thus, readers need to only briefly sample the marks on the page in order to confirm word identity. In this model it is evident that the flow of information proceeds from the top downward so that the process of word identification is dependent upon meaning first. Thus, the higher level processes embodied in past experiences and the reader's knowledge of the language pattern interact with and direct the flow of information, just as listeners may anticipate what the upcoming words of speakers might be. This view identifies reading as a kind of 'psycholinguistic guessing game' (Goodman 1967).

The top-down model centers upon the assumption that good readers bypass the letter sound correspondence when they read because they read so quickly. That is, because good readers read at a faster speed, they do not depend upon the phonemic code. However, this view is also challenged. Recent evidence presented by Stanovich (1980) discredits this assumption. A lot of research suggests that instead of depending on meaning only, good readers may well markedly attend to graphic information, especially when they are uncertain about a word. Contrary to the view of the top-down theorists, good readers do rely on graphic information, which may be more efficient than endeavouring to predict words based only upon context and language structure. Moreover, the fact that good readers make better use of contextual clues than poor readers is not evidence that they actually do so in reading. Good readers use context only when orthographic and phonemic cues are minimal. Despite the view of top-down theorists then, it would appear that even as readers become more accomplished they still employ data-driven strategies to unlock words.

(A3) Interactive Model

Since neither the bottom-up nor top-down model of the reading process totally accounts for what occurs during the reading process, Rumelhart (1977) proposes an **interactive** model in which both letter features or data-driven sensory information and non-sensory information come together at one place. Using a computer analogy, Rumelhart labels this place a 'message board'. In this model, reading is not viewed simply as either a bottom-up or top-down process, but instead as a synthesizing of patterns, calling for the application or integration of all of the previously identified knowledge sources. Reading, according to Rumelhart, is thus neither a bottom-up nor top-down process, but a synthesis of the two.

Moreover, Stanovich (1980) proposes an **interactive-compensatory** model, which adds a new feature to the interactive Rumelhart Model by suggesting that strength in one processing stage can compensate for weakness in another. According to Stanovich, problems in both the bottom-up and top-down models can be reduced with his model. That is, bottom-up models do not allow for higher-level processing strategies to influence lower-level processing, and top-down models do not account for the situation in which a reader has little knowledge of a text topic and, therefore, cannot form predictions. In Stanovich's words, "Interactive models assume that a pattern is synthesized based on information provided simultaneously from several knowledge sources. The compensatory assumption states that a deficit in any knowledge source results in a heavier reliance on other knowledge sources, regardless of their level in the processing hierarchy." (1980) Stanovich's theory explains the apparent anomaly found in many experiments in which poor readers sometimes show greater sensitivity to contextual constraints than do good readers. Poor readers may be thus using strong syntactic or semantic knowledge to compensate for less knowledge of orthography or lexicon.

(A4) Approaches for teaching to read

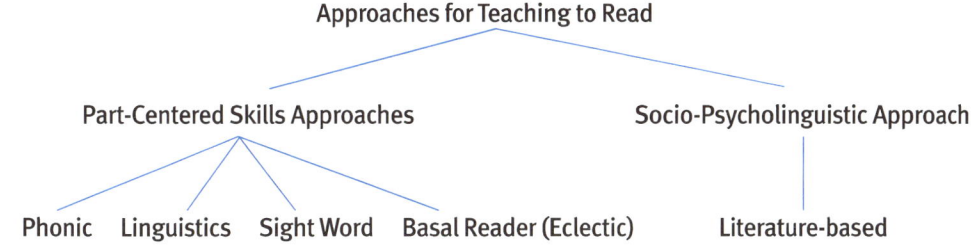

1) A phonics approach

Advocates of a phonics approach are concerned about helping beginners become independent readers as soon as possible. They feel the best way to do this is to help children learn letter/sound correspondences so that they can sound out, or 'decode', words. Often, children are taught not only basic letter/sound correspondences but rules for pronouncing letters and combinations of letters and for sounding out words.

A phonics approach was especially popular from about 1890 through the 1920s, when it was gradually superseded by a sight word approach. Phonics began a revival in the mid-1960s, with increased incorporation of phonics lessons and activities into basal reading programs (see 'A Basal Reader Approach' below). The current existence of so many programs for teaching phonics extensively and intensively suggests that this revival has reached a new high.

2) A 'linguistic' approach

The so-called linguistic approach is based upon the tenets of structural linguists, whose view of language and language learning was prominent in the 1950s. Those who advocate this particular approach are generally concerned with helping children internalize regular patterns of spelling/sound correspondence, on the assumption that this will enable them to read unfamiliar words without actually stopping to sound them out.

The linguistic approach is like a phonics approach in its emphasis on learning letter/sound patterns, with no specific attention to comprehension. But in another respect, the linguistic approach differs sharply from a phonics approach. Whereas a phonics approach emphasizes the direct teaching of patterns and often conscious learning of rules, the linguistic approach advocates exposing children to regularly spelled words from which children can unconsciously infer common spelling/sound patterns.

3) A sight word, or 'look-say', approach

Those who advocate a sight word approach, in contrast to phonics, claim to be concerned that meaning be emphasized from the very outset of reading instruction. They stress helping children develop a stock of words that the children can recognize on sight. Thus instead of stressing letter/sound correspondences and phonics rules, teachers might use flash cards and other devices to help children learn to recognize basic words like *I*, *and*, and *the*. Advocates of a sight word, or 'look-say', approach argue that if children can begin with a stock of about one hundred basic sight words, they will be able to read about half the words in any text they might ordinarily encounter.

This approach was widely used from about 1930 until about the mid-1960s, when it became increasingly intertwined with (or permeated by) a phonics approach. Although advocates of the sight word approach commonly expressed concern with meaning, during the heyday of this approach actual classroom instruction came to focus heavily on the identification of words, and this emphasis continues implicitly in many of today's basal readers. Thus, like advocates of phonics, practitioners of sight word instruction as well as the general public reflect the 'commonsense' assumption that once words are identified, meaning will take care of itself. The sight word approach differs from a phonics approach in that it focuses on whole words rather than on parts of words, but in practice, both are concerned more with word identification than with meaning.

Today, the sight word approach survives primarily as part of or supplement to a basal reader program. A whole language approach is sometimes claimed to be nothing more than a new name for the sight word approach, which is simply untrue. Whole language theorists lump phonics and sight words together as a 'bottom-up', 'bits and pieces' method of learning to read. They prefer a 'top down' meaning approach in which children get meaning from larger units of print without first learning how to read the words.

4) A Basal Reader Approach

Basal reading approach is a technique used to teach children reading skills. Commonly called 'reading books' or 'readers', **basal readers** are short stories, including individual books for learners, a teacher's edition, workbooks, assessments and activities for a specific reading level.

Most of today's basal programs contain both narrative and expository text that encompass a variety of genres. They now feature anthologies and journals while providing a scope and sequence of skills and strategies to be taught at various levels and grades. Depending on your beliefs, basal instruction could be considered a bottom-up approach, presenting skills to be taught in a sequence, or an interactive program, featuring unedited children's literature selections, strategy instruction, and writing opportunities. Basal reading, frequently described as eclectic, runs the gamut from word recognition skills to extended and meaningful reading, discussing, and writing.

5) A Literature-Based Instruction

Literature-based instruction approaches accommodate individual student differences in reading abilities and at the same time focus on meaning, interest, and enjoyment. In literature-based instruction, teachers encourage their students to select their own trade books (another name for popular books). Self-selection of trade books or literature books is part of personalizing reading through the individualized approach. Reading instruction delivered in this way emanates from assumptions about the reading process that are interactive and top-down. Literature-based approaches depend on teachers who know children's literature and classroom organization.

(B) Schema Theory

Schema(ta)	
background/previous/prior knowledge	
Content schema(ta)	Formal schema(ta)
our knowledge about people, the world, culture, and the universe	our knowledge about language and discourse structure

(C) Comprehension Level: Types of Questions

Literal	focusing on information explicitly stated in the text
Reorganizational	organizing information explicitly stated in the text
Inferential	going beyond the immediate text
Evaluative	making judgements
Appreciative	responding emotionally and aesthetically

It is possible to classify questions according to the skills they require from the reader; for the reading teacher, this is much more important than their grammatical form. The classification presented here is intended as a checklist; by checking your questions against it, you can find out whether you are omitting any important types of question, and thus failing to give practice in some important skills.

> ### Sample Text: A Son to be Proud of
> Last week, Rahman's wife Leila had an accident. Rahman's youngest child, Yusof, was at home when it happened. He was playing with his new toy car. Rahman had given it to him the week before, for his third birthday.
>
> Suddenly Yusof heard his mother calling 'Help! Help!' He ran to the kitchen. His mother had burned herself with some hot cooking oil. She was crying with pain and the pan was on fire.
>
> Rahman had gone to his office. Both the other children had gone to school. Yusof was too small to help his mother, and she was too frightened to speak sensibly to him. But he ran to the neighbour's house and asked her to come and help his mother. She soon put out the fire and took Yusof's mother to the clinic.
>
> When Rahman came home, Leila told him what had happened. He was very proud of his son. 'When you are a man, you will be just like your father,' he said.

1) Questions of literal comprehension

These are questions whose answers are directly and explicitly available in the text. Questions of this kind could often be answered in the words of the text itself. Such questions are essential preliminaries to serious work on a text, because until you are sure that the plain meaning of the text has been grasped, there is no point attempting more sophisticated exercises. Look at the sample text. Some literal comprehension questions on this might include the following:

> a) When did Rahman's wife have an accident?
> b) What was Yusof doing when the accident happened?
> c) Why didn't Yusof help his mother?

2) Questions involving reorganization or reinterpretation

Slightly more difficult than Type 1 are questions which require the student to obtain literal information from various parts of the text and put it together, or to reinterpret information. Such questions are valuable in making the student consider the text as a whole rather than thinking of each sentence on its own; or in making him assimilate fully the information he obtains; for example:

> a) How old was Yusof? (Reinterpretation)
> b) How many children had Rahman? (Reorganization)
> c) Was Yusof playing in the kitchen? (Reinterpretation)

3) Questions of inference

These are questions that oblige the student to 'read between the lines', to consider what is implied but not explicitly stated. Questions of this kind are considerably more difficult than either of the former types, because they require the student to understand the text well enough to work out its implications. The difficulty is intellectual rather than linguistic in most cases. Like Type 2, they often require the reader to put together in his mind pieces of information that are scattered in the text, so that their joint implications can be recognized. Some examples of inferential questions follow:

> a) Which people were in Rahman's house when the accident happened?
> b) Why was Rahman proud of his son?

4) Questions of evaluation

Evaluation questions involve the reader in making a considered judgment about the text in terms of what the writer is trying to do, and how far he has achieved it. The reader may be asked to judge, for example, the writer's honesty or bias (e.g. in newspaper reporting or advertising copy), the force of his argument (e.g. citing of evidence), or the effectiveness of his narrative power (e.g. in a novel).

Questions of this kind are the most sophisticated of all, since they ask the reader not merely to respond, but to analyse his response and discover the objective reasons for it, as well as measuring it against the presumed intention of the writer. We should include here questions of literary appreciation as the most sophisticated representatives of the type, since the central concern is to find out how the writer has produced his effects and how far he has succeeded in his aim. This is an activity for advanced students, and many will never need to deal with questions of this kind.

5) Questions of personal response

Of all the types of question, the answer to this depends most on the reader and least on the writer. The reader is not asked to assess the techniques by means of which the writer influences him, but simply to record his reaction to the content of the text. This may range from 'I'm convinced' or 'I'm not interested' to 'I'm moved' or 'I'm horrified'.

If the text is suitable, into this category will fall such questions as 'What is your opinion of X's behaviour?' 'Would you like to live in Y?' 'How would you have felt if you had been Z?' Personal response is naturally most often invoked in relation to creative writing, but it is sometimes appropriate to other kind of writing too, for example, 'What does this writer contribute to our understanding of the field?' 'Do you sympathize with the writer's arguments?' 'How far does your own experience agree with that described?'

Nevertheless, such responses cannot ignore the textual evidence; they do not rely only on the reader, but essentially involve him with the writer. So we need to ask the student to explain why the text makes him feel as he does, and we must make sure that his response is at least based on correct understanding of the text.

To divide questions into types like this is not particularly helpful in itself, except for evaluating the questions you find in textbooks, and for helping you to develop your own. You will find that many questions in textbooks fall into Type 1, with perhaps a few Types 2 and 5. Of course literal comprehension is an essential preliminary to any work on the text. But in fact it is Types 2, 3 and 4 that ought to concern us most, since it is questions of these types that force the reader to think about not just what writer has written, but how he has written it. And unless our students think about that, they are not likely to become as competent as we would like in tracking difficult texts.

(C1) Signpost questions

A signpost stands at a crossroads to show travellers the way. Its function is to direct them along the right road, making the journey quicker and saving them from getting lost. A **signpost question** (SPQ) has a similar function: its purpose is not to test but to guide the readers, directing their attention to the important points in the text, preventing them from going off along a false track.

Questions of this kind are particularly useful when the reading lesson is based (as I suggest it usually should be) mainly on silent reading. It is helpful to give the students a question or task (it does not have to be an actual question) **before** they read. This gives a specific reason for reading: they read more purposefully in order to find the answer or complete the task.

An obvious danger is that students will look only for the answer to the SPQ and not read the rest of the text carefully. To avoid this:

- Make sure students know there will be a lot more questions when they have finished reading. (Most of the work, of course, follows the reading.)
- Make sure the SPQ cannot be answered until the whole (or most) of the section has been read.
- Devise SPQs that require students to think about the meaning, not just locate information.

1) Devising signpost questions

Writing good SPQs requires some skill, which you can acquire by practice coupled with constructive criticism from colleagues. You may like to begin by criticizing somebody else's SPQs in the following Activity.

Activity *Signpost questions*

Read the following text, *A Son to be Proud of*. Then decide which of the following would be the best SPQ for the whole text. If possible discuss your choice, and your reasons for rejecting the others, with your colleagues.

> the same text as in (C) "A Son to be Proud of"

Possible SPQs for *A Son to be Proud of*

1. How old was Yusof when this story happened?
2. Why did Yusof run to the neighbour's house?
3. What did Leila tell Rahman?
4. Why was Rahman proud of his son?
5. Who put out the fire?
6. Why did Yusof run to the kitchen?

Comment

1. important but too early in the text / 2. better, but comes rather early / 3. too easy (literal)

4. the best SPQ since it cannot be answered without understanding the whole text.

5. not really important / 6. too early and not important

If you have tried the activity and checked the key, you will realize that the best SPQs relate either to the whole section (the whole text, in this case) or its final part, so that they cannot be answered until the whole section has been read and understood. Did you also keep in mind the function of the SPQ? — not to test but to help the reader to understand by directing attention to things that might otherwise be missed (particularly potential sources of misunderstanding) and by focusing on the main point.

You can of course ask more than one SPQ if you think this would be helpful, but the fewer the better, otherwise the signposting becomes less clear.

2) Using signpost questions

You can ask an easy SPQ on the whole text, as an initial top-down activity; and/or you can ask one for each section. Write the SPQ on the board or OHP. Ask the class to read the text silently and find the answer. After silent reading, perhaps followed by group discussion, check whether they have been able to do this. If a fair number have not, leave it open and explain that you will return to it later and that, as they read more closely, people should be looking for evidence to improve their answers. Turn to the other questions and tasks and return to the SPQ later, when the text is better understood. Avoid giving an answer yourself if you possibly can.

(C2) Developing Comprehension Ability through Strategy Instruction

Traditional views of reading comprehension conceive effective understanding as mastering a number of distinct skills such as finding the main idea, drawing inferences, and remembering details from a script. Some skills, according to these views, are deemed necessary for others; comprehending and recalling explicit knowledge in a text (literal comprehension), for instance, is regarded as a prerequisite for making inferences.

An alternative approach, based on a very different conception of comprehension, however, stresses the strategic nature of skilled reading. This approach emphasizes the necessity of adopting comprehension curricula founded on the teaching of a set of basic strategies applicable to a variety of texts. Comprehension strategies are 'specific cognitive procedures that guide readers to become aware of how well they are comprehending as they attempt to read or write'. The major strategies are: comprehension monitoring, cooperative learning, graphic and semantic organizers, question answering, question generation, summarization, and multiple strategy.

1) Comprehension Monitoring

This strategy is intended to develop metacognitive abilities in readers; that is, to help them think about their own comprehension processes. It involves teaching the learners certain strategies that enable them to be aware of their understanding when they read, to know when they understand, what they do not understand, and to take steps to overcome their comprehension difficulties.

2) Cooperative Learning

Cooperative learning involves learners to work together on strategies and to be engaged in intellectual discussions to sustain their reading comprehension.

3) Using Graphic and Semantic Organizers and Recognizing Story Structures

Graphic organizers are diagrams or charts that are drawn to represent the relationship of ideas and information in a print. Different texts take different structures; history texts, for instance, present events in chronological order, an article may be organized around a main thesis whereby supporting details are matched to make a persuasive argument, and a story, on the other hand, is organized around a series of events. Recognizing a story structure or the way its events are organized into a plot enables the readers to become aware of the important story elements (setting, characters, events, etc.) and facilitates their understanding and recall. Graphic organizers, thus, help readers be familiar with different text structures and hence enable them to grasp the flow of information within a particular selection.

4) Question Answering

Question answering strategy involves showing the learners how to find and use information from a text to answer teacher's questions in order to get more from their reading.

5) Question Generation

Question generation involves learners' asking and answering of questions about their reading. This improves their understanding and retention. Activating and using background knowledge is often used as part of question answering and question generating strategies. Prior knowledge activation implies the elicitation of students pre-existing knowledge of the world that they can use to understand what they read. This may be achieved through pre-reading activities which are conceived as a 'bridge between readers' knowledge base and the text'; they are viewed as 'a preparatory step in which purpose setting and concept development are primary goals'. One way to fulfil this aim is to ask students to predict text content relying on their prior knowledge, often in response to pre-reading questions.

6) Summarization

Summarization requires from the learner to recognize the important ideas of a text. This strategy helps learners to know about the organization of a text, to identify its main ideas and to connect them together.

7) Multiple Strategy Instruction

Multiple strategy instruction entails the use of two or more strategies involved in a teacher-learners interaction, usually in small groups. Readers have to be flexible in choosing among the wide range of strategies according to text demands.

(D) Authenticity vs. Readability issues in choosing texts

Suitability of content	A text interesting, enjoyable, challenging, and appropriate for Ss' goals
Exploitability	A text that facilitates the achievement and integratable with other skills
Readability	A text with lexical and structural difficulty that will challenge students

(D1) Input Modification (Modified Input)

Modifications to input can be divided into two types: **simplification**, in the form of less complex vocabulary and syntax, and **elaboration**, in which unfamiliar linguistic items are offset with redundancy and explicitness (Yano, Long, & Ross 1994). More specifically, typical features of linguistic simplification include the use of shorter utterances, simpler syntax, simpler lexis (smaller type-token ratios and avoidance of low-frequency vocabulary), deletion of sentence elements or morphological inflections, and preference for canonical word order. On the other hand, elaboration of input involves increasing redundancy and actualizing underlying thematic relations straightforwardly.

A baseline text and the corresponding simplified text follows.

> **Baseline text:**
>
> We are less credulous than we used to be. In the nineteenth century, a novelist would bring his story to a conclusion by presenting his readers with a series of coincidences — most of them wildly improbable. Readers happily accepted the fact that an obscure maid-servant was really the hero's mother....

> **Simplified version:**
>
> We are less believing than we were. In the nineteenth century, a novelist would end his story by many accidental events. Most of the events are not likely to happen in reality. Readers happily believed that a humble servant was really the hero's mother....

In the simplified version, low-frequency words (***credulous, coincidences,*** and ***obscure***) were replaced by higher frequency words (***believing, accidental events,*** and ***humble***). In addition, the multiword expressions ***used to be, bring ... to a conclusion,*** and ***accept the fact*** were replaced by one-word items with similar meanings (***were, end,*** and ***believe***), thereby reducing the length of sentences as well. As it was difficult to find an appropriate higher frequency word that corresponded to ***wildly improbable***, an explanatory verbal phrase, ***are not likely to happen in reality***, was added, although it increased the sentence length.

To construct the elaborated texts, I added redundancy and clearer signaling of thematic structure in the form of examples, paraphrases and repetition of original information, and synonyms and definitions of low frequency words contained in the baseline passages. The elaborated version of the sample text above follows.

> **Elaborated version:**
>
> We are less credulous than we used to be in the past. We don't easily believe coincidences, or accidental happenings. In the nineteenth century, a novelist would bring his story to a conclusion by presenting his readers with a series of such coincidences, though most of them were wildly improbable. That's why so many nineteenth century novels end by some accidental events which are never likely to happen in real life. But, readers in the nineteenth century happily accepted the fact that an obscure, humble maid-servant was really the hero's mother....

In the past (in the first sentence) and ***in the nineteenth century*** (in the last sentence) were added to clarify ***used to be*** and ***readers***, respectively, and the second and fourth sentences were inserted to paraphrase the respective preceding sentences. The conjunctions ***though*** and ***but*** were supplied to clarify the relationships between the preceding and the following information. Although the elaborated passage retains low-frequency lexical items such as ***credulous, coincidences, obscure,*** and ***wildly improbable***, supplementary definitions, synonyms, and paraphrases (i.e., ***don't easily believe, accidental happenings / some accidental events, humble,*** and ***never likely to happen in real life***) provide cues to their meanings.

Unlike the simplified passages, the baseline and elaborated passages contained a symmetrical distribution of low-frequency vocabulary, relative clauses, sentential complements, and compound and complex sentences. The elaborated passages were much more linguistically complex than the simplified ones. They had more words per passage. The elaborated passages were longer than even the baseline texts but were of approximately the same complexity. Of the three forms of the passages, therefore, the objective linguistic counts showed the simplified versions to be the simplest, and the elaborated and baseline versions were more comparable on these linguistic variables.

To the question raised by several ESL/EFL researchers — What factors make input more comprehensible to second/foreign language learners? — the findings of the present study suggest one possible answer: The provision of elaborative information in written input enhances the reading comprehension of even low-proficiency learners while exposing them to native-like features that are usually absent in simplified input. Although elaboration often produces texts that are longer and linguistically more complex than the simplified versions, elaborative amplification of pivotal terms and concepts can compensate for the greater linguistic complexity and length. Elaborative modification, by multiplying opportunities for dealing with text information through redundancy and clearly signaled thematic structure, seems to improve the comprehensibility of written input.

(E) PWP

Pre-reading tasks	drawing Ss' attention, making predictions by schema activation
While-reading tasks	reading with strategies by focusing on decoding skills
Post-reading tasks	expanding the knowledge by discussion and analysis of the text content
Follow-up	transferring strategies to other texts & integrating with other skills

(F) Reading Techniques and Tasks

Intensive R	classroom-oriented activity (shorter text)
Extensive R	pleasure reading (longer text)
Skimming	quick reading to get the gist (main idea)
Scanning	quick reading to locate specific information
Semantic Mapping	grouping ideas into meaningful clusters
Think-aloud	verbalizing the thinking to make inferences

(F1) Intensive reading

> ### Intensive reading activity sample "What Sparkle!"
>
> Select a short authentic text such as a nursery rhyme, an accessible poem, or even a popular song. Include a gloss for important vocabulary words that would be difficult to infer from the text. Here is an example; "Twinkle Twinkle Little Star". First, lead a discussion designed to activate students' background knowledge. For example, you could ask about celestial objects or wishing customs in different countries. Ask students if they have ever wondered what stars are made of or what they would look like if they were up close. Play a tape of the song and have students read along with the text. Have students read the text again, and ask inference questions to make sure that they have understood it. After you are confident that students have understood the song, it is time to discuss its structure. For example, you could ask students about the rhyming pattern, the words that create a sense of a personal relationship between the singer and the star, or the song's use of repetition. This could be expanded into a writing activity by having students write a poem about stars or a paragraph describing their perceptions of stars.

(F1a) Reading Fluency

Anderson defines reading fluency as 'reading at an appropriate rate with adequate comprehension' (Anderson 2009). Appropriate rates will depend on the age of the reader, whether the reader is reading orally or silently, and what our reading purpose is. Adequate comprehension also is dependent on a variety of factors. The key to this definition of reading fluency is the combination of both reading rate and reading comprehension. Fluency is not one of these elements alone, but the combination of both.

Anderson outlines five different in-class instructional activities that can be applied to the classroom: (1) shadow reading, (2) rate build-up reading, (3) repeated reading, (4) class-paced reading, and (5) self-paced reading. The point that he wants to emphasize is that we cannot expect readers to improve their reading fluency by simply telling them to read faster. We must provide guided classroom practice so that learners know what to do to increase their reading fluency.

1) Shadow Reading

Shadow reading has five steps. First, students listen to the reading passage. Second, students listen and follow the text with their eyes. Next, students listen and speak the text. Fourth, students read the text silently. Finally, students read the text aloud. After each of the above steps, the teacher engages the students in a comprehension check so that the focus is not just on reading rate. Also, any of these steps may be repeated as many times as is necessary to achieve fluent reading.

2) Rate-Building Reading

Students are assigned a printed text and are asked to read as much material as they can in 60 seconds period of time. They then start reading again from the beginning of the text and are given an additional sixty seconds. They are to read more material during the second sixty second period than in the first. The activity is repeated a third and fourth time. The purpose of this drill is to reread 'old' material quickly moving smoothly into the new. As their eyes move quickly over the 'old' material, students actually learn to read faster. This activity is not intended to move the eyes quickly; it aims, however, at joining the twin goals: quick reading and efficient understanding.

3) Repeated Reading

Repeated reading is somewhat similar to rate-building reading in its purpose but not in how it is carried out. Students to read a short passage over and over again until they achieve criterion levels of reading rate and comprehension. For example, they may try to read a short 100-word paragraph four times in two minutes. The criterion levels may vary from class to class, but reasonable goals to work toward are criterion levels of 200 wpm and 70% comprehension.

4) Class-Paced Reading

Anderson (1999) states: "The class-paced reading activity allows the class to set a goal for a minimal reading rate." In other words, the class establishes a push speed or pacing speed which is beyond or above their normal reading speed. In paced-reading exercises, the teacher controls the time allowed for the readings. Concerning the passages to be read, a mark is placed in the margin of the text next to the line containing each 100th word. The teacher then tells the students, with a tap on the desk, to move to the next mark, according to the speed the teacher is pacing. For instance, if students are pacing at 150 words per minute, the tap would be every 45 seconds to read 100 words.

5) Self-Paced Reading

Like class-paced reading where the teacher establishes the speed goal to pace for, self-paced reading allows students to read at a specified pace they determine on their own. In this vein, students establish their own objective speed (eg 180 wpm) and according to it, they determine the amount of material to be read in one minute to meet their speed goal. These activities do not require specially developed texts; they can be implemented by teachers using class texts.

(F2) Extensive reading & readers

There is a great deal of evidence that **extensive reading** (ie reading longer texts, such as a novel, over time) has a powerful impact on language learning. The more someone reads, the more they pick up items of vocabulary and grammar from the texts, often without realising it and this widening language knowledge seems to increase their overall linguistic confidence, which then influences and improves their skills in other language areas, too (though this is probably only true in cases where the material they read is self-chosen and is genuinely relevant and interesting to them).

So, there are strong arguments for actively encouraging students to read a lot in the target language, both in and outside the classroom. We can help by:

- providing a library of readers (see below), magazines, newspapers, leaflets, etc:
- training learners how to select suitable reading material and in ways to read it;
- creating a 'book club' environment that encourages learners to choose what books to purchase, talk about favourite books, share them with each other, write brief recommendations, etc;
- allowing sections of classroom time purely for students to read; some teachers who have five or six lessons a week set aside one of these lessons as quiet reading time.

Readers are books of stories (or other content) published specifically for learners to get extended exposure to English. They often have their grammar and vocabulary 'graded' to named levels (eg Elementary) so that learners at that level should stand a reasonable chance of successfully reading them. Many state the size of vocabulary used and have footnotes or glossaries of words outside their stated word limit. The main aim of readers is to provide opportunities for extensive reading for pleasure. For this reason, be careful about integrating comprehension checks, tests and exercises into your teaching. As far as possible, let students read, enjoy and move on, rather than read and then have to do lots of exercises afterwards.

Extensive reading activity sample "Plain Vanilla"

Have students select books or magazines *of their choice* from the class or school library. This is not a time to be snobby! Extensive reading is about interesting reading, *not* the development of a sophisticated taste in reading materials. Direct students to materials that you think would be particularly interesting to them. Have them keep a log of the materials they have read. (Note: Neither this activity nor other extensive reading activities include discussions or comprehension-checks of the content of the reading materials. Extensive reading is typically individualized, with students choosing their own materials, so a whole-class discussion is generally impossible. Extensive reading activities typically have students make a simple report on their reading such as making a reading log or drawing descriptive pictures.)

(F3&4) Skimming and scanning

Skimming is reading quickly to get the gist of a passage (eg to discover key topics, main ideas, overall theme, basic structure, etc). A typical skimming task would be a general question from the teacher, such as *Is this passage about Jill's memories of summer or winter?* Or *Is this story set in a school or a restaurant?* The learners would attempt to find the answer quickly, without reading every word of the passage, by 'speed-reading' through some portions of the text.

Scanning is moving eyes quickly over the text to locate a specific piece of information (eg a name, address, fact, price, number, date, etc) without reading the whole text or unpacking any subtleties of meaning. A common scanning activity is searching for information in a leaflet or directory, and a typical scanning task would be *What time does the Birmingham train leave?* Or *What does Cathy take with her to the meeting?*

Skimming and scanning are both 'top-down' skills. Although scanning is involved with finding individual points from the text without reading carefully through every word of the text, the way that a reader finds that information involves some degree of processing of the overall shape and structure of the text, moving her eyes quickly over the whole page, searching for key words or clues from the textual layout and the content that will enable her to focus in on smaller sections of text that she is likely to get answers from.

Skimming activity sample "Celebrity Matching?"

Give students paragraph descriptions of four celebrities who they would be familiar with (You could also use the names of people who work at your school.) at the bottom of the page, list the names of six celebrities (the four described in the paragraphs and two distracters). Have students match the descriptions with the names. Students should work quickly to encourage skimming.

> **Scanning activity sample "Treasure Hunt"**
>
> Divide the class into small groups, and give each group an instruction sheet for a math project. Place the needed materials (counters, Cuisenaire rods, M & M's, or whatever) in various places in your room. Have groups race to see which one can assemble the required materials first. Have groups check off each material from the list as they obtain it.

(G) Assessing reading comprehension - Cloze tests

Cloze tests are often mentioned as a good way to test reading comprehension. **Cloze tests** are written passages in the target language that have had words deleted. Students read along and anticipate what should be put in each blank. Since students only use one word to fill in each blank, problems resulting from writing difficulties are minimized. Even so, it is still difficult to entirely separate reading comprehension and content knowledge in this type of test.

According to John Oller, cloze tests tap into the student's **expectancy grammar**. As students read, they come to expect what will come next. These intuitions include guesses both about content and about sentence structure. For example, students may not know which noun to put in a blank, but if the cloze passage is at an appropriate reading level, they seldom try to put a verb in a blank requiring a noun or pronoun.

Teachers sometimes use **fixed-ratio deletion** cloze passages, which means that the words were deleted in a regular pattern, for example, every ninth word. Several scholars suggest an alternative type of cloze test called **rational deletion** cloze passage, in which words are deleted intentionally in order to assess the student's knowledge of a specific grammatical structure or set of vocabulary words. Although students still must read to complete a rational deletion cloze test, many scholars classify them as grammar or vocabulary tests rather than reading tests because students are required to use a particular part of speech. These scholars believe that rational deletion cloze does not tap into a student's expectancy grammar in the same way a reading task does. On the other hand, many scholars believe that rational deletion cloze passages are preferable to traditional fill-in-the-blank grammar tests because the items are more authentic and include more text.

Since it is more difficult to read a passage with deleted words than it is to read a passage of intact text, cloze passages for students should be based on reading materials at or even below their current reading levels. It is also a good idea to use longer texts and to delete every eleventh, thirteenth or even fifteenth word to maintain the flow of the text.

차시원 **전공영어 영어교육학** PRACTICAL

Chapter 10 Mind Map

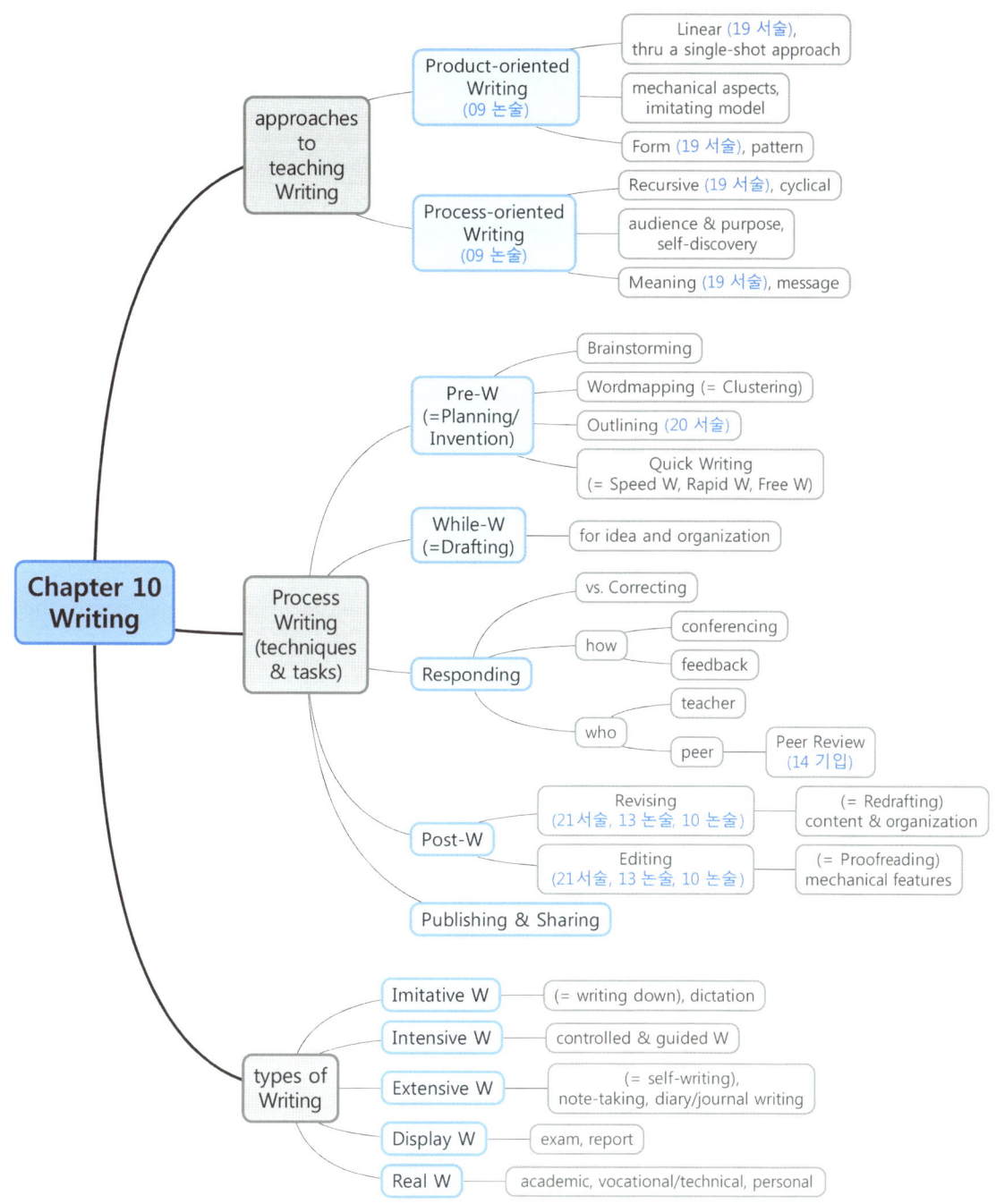

Chapter 10 Teaching Writing

(A) Product- vs. Process-oriented Writing

Product-oriented Writing	Process-oriented Writing
linear, thru a single-shot approach mechanical aspects, imitating model form, pattern	cyclical, recursive audience & purpose, self-discovery meaning, message

(A1) A Genre-Based Approach to Writing

Genre-based approach is a relative newcomer to ELT. It shares some similarity with **product approach**. It emphasizes that writing varies with the social context in which it is produced. The central aspect is purpose and audience in addition to the subject matter, the relationships between the writer and the audience, and the pattern of organization.

It is widely recognized that if students are expected to write in a particular genre, they first need to become familiar with its purpose and features through immersion in the genre and the explanation of sample texts. The familiarization and immersion will lay a solid basis for the students to develop into next stage in the cycle. At the stage of deconstruction in the cycle, the students will be instructed to do **genre analysis** so that they will be familiar with language features and procedural stages of a typical genre.

1) Benefits of Genre Analysis in Pre-writing

Studies of the role of examples in learning other cognitive skills have shown that the major benefits of examples accrue to students who invest more time in analysing them. In genre teaching, active analysis of a model before taking on a specific writing task may help students construct new textual patterns or enrich the patterns they know. Student writers are able to infer linguistic and procedural features from models. And those who actively look for and contemplate such features in the models they read are more likely to construct reliable new structures.

Second, consulting models actively before the writing process may provide the students with a database for testing whether a candidate idea should be included. The students may infer that the practice of the writer who produced the model is typical and may include or exclude information on the basis of whether or not it shows up in the model.

Genre analysis can also help students consciously structure their texts and develop effective control over different writing tasks for different purposes. As Swales (1987) claimed: genre analysis promoted 'more effective negotiations and consultations as well as providing each child with their own individual scaffolding that can be developed to produce successful texts'.

Genre analysis can therefore provide the vocabulary and concepts to explicitly teach the text structures the students are expected to produce. It places language at the centre of writing development by allowing shared understanding and explicit guidance. Actually, control over the conventions of a genre is a prerequisite for creativity, and students simply require more information on the features that constitute good texts in order to improve their own writing skills. It can thus provide a methodological environment that develops writing skills and encourages creativity. It can provide opportunities for students to reflect on and discuss how language works in a given context and how it can most effectively be employed to meet particular goals.

2) Application in classroom teaching: A LESSON PLAN

The lesson plan is designed in the light of genre-based approach, which focuses attention on the purpose and the audience of a writing text. Genre analysis will be the main task, which is expected to be accomplished by students following different steps instructed by the teacher. The reason for this arrangement is that the students will be enlightened and exposed to a new way of development in writing skills. The way is quite different from a conventional one and is supported by an established theory.

<Stage 1: Introduction>

This is a preparatory stage before the students are introduced into more specific analysis of genre. The aim of this stage is to create general impression on the students for what they are expected to do in the class. The focus is on the general explanation of the organization of a genre. The following steps will be included in this stage.

Step 1: Teacher's general introduction of the topic. It is necessary because an explicit introduction about what the students are going to do in the class will help to release their pressure and protect them from the shock of encountering with an unfamiliar topic.

Step 2: Ask students to discuss questions which are intended to make sure how much they already know about the genre they're going to study.

Step 3: Observation on model genre text. Students are expected to do a brief observation of the model text by themselves.

Step 4: Presentation of the students on the results of their investigation.

Step 5: Teacher's comment and brief summary.

HOW DO HEARING-IMPAIRED PEOPLE TALK?

Hearing-impaired people cannot hear sounds well. How do they "hear words and talk?

Many hearing impaired people use American Sign Language (ASL). They talk with their hands. Sometimes two hearing-impaired people talk to each other. They both use ASL. Sometimes a person who can hear interprets for hearing-impaired people. The person listens to someone talking, and then he or she makes hand signs.

There are two kinds of sign language. One kind has a sign for every letter in the alphabet. The person spells words. This is finger spelling. The other kind has a sign for whole words. There are signs for verbs, things, and ideas.

Some of the signs are very easy, for example, *eat, milk,* and *house*. You can see what they mean. Others are more difficult, for example, *star, egg,* or *week*.

People from any country can learn ASL. They don't speak words. They use signs, so they can understand people from other countries.

ASL is almost like a dance. The whole body talks. American Sign Language is a beautiful language.

QUESTIONS:

1. What is the purpose of this text? Is it to entertain? To inform? Or to explain?
2. Who do you think is the audience of this piece of writing?
3. Do you think the author successfully achieve the intended purpose? How?
4. What are the striking features in the structure of the text? Try to explain in detail about how these features affect the effects of the text.
5. What is the specific language characteristics represented by this text? Try to find out the words that you think can effectively achieve the intended purpose of the author.

\<Stage 2: Familiarization\>

At this stage, students will be instructed to do a specific reading and detailed analysis on the features of the target genre. Although linguistic features are also expected to be observed by the students, the main task will be on the organizational features of the genre. This will enable the students to be more familiar with the genre they encountered in the first stage.

Step 1: Individual reading of a model text. Students are asked to read while preparing for questions proposed by the teacher on organizational features of the genre.

Step 2: Group discussion and evaluation. The students will collaboratively work together with group members in order to add sufficient information about the genre into mind.

Step 3: Representative presentation. The student representative of each group is invited to report their ideas on the observation of the genre.

Step 4: Evaluation on the proposed ideas of representative students. This will enable the students to pool into mind as much information about the model genre as they can.

Step 5: Teacher's comment and summary. The teacher shows the students transparency of a model analysis so that they may deepen their understanding in the discussion. (the material in step 1, transparency)

\<Stage 3: Reinforcing\>

The concept of the genre established in the first two stages may be loosely laid. And the students would easily forget new information unless they can restructure or reinforce in the mind so as to select and store in the Long Term Memory. Thus, this stage will require the students to rethink and reinforce through all kinds of activities.

Step 1: Reordering activity. The students are expected to do a reordering exercise delivered by the teacher for the purpose that they can use what they have learned in the previous stages to do a genre analysis by themselves. Each group should be given a differently ordered version of a same text.

(Student's Handouts)

Directions: The following sentences are disorderly arranged. You are expected to rearrange them according to the structure of explanation. You are allowed to do the work in groups. Each group may include no more than 4 persons. And each group will be asked to present your result to the class.

1. People all over the world eat rice.
2. Farmers grow rice in many countries, even in the southern part of the United States and in eastern Australia.
3. No one really knows where rice came from.
4. Some people eat almost nothing but rice.
5. Rice is a kind of grass. (and so on)

(Note: Some more versions of rearrangement exercise may be designed basing on the original text. And group work is especially encouraged.)

Step 2: Presentation. A selected member of each group is allowed to present their reasoning on the order of the text.

Step 3: Checking. The teacher will show the original text and ask the students to check their own results.

(Teacher's Copy)
RICE

People all over the world eat rice. Millions of people in Asia, Africa, and South America eat it every day of their lives. Some people eat almost nothing but rice.

Rice is a kind of grass. There are more than seven thousand (7,000) kinds of rice. Most kinds are water plants. Farmers grow rice in many countries, even in the southern part of the United States and in eastern Australia.

No one really knows where rice came from. Some scientists think it started to grow in two places. They think that one kind of rice grew in southern Asia thousands of years ago. Someone in China wrote about it almost five thousand (5,000) years ago. Another kind probably grew in West Africa. Other scientists think rice came from India, and Indian travellers took it to other parts of the world. ⋯

Step 4: Teacher's analysis and explanation on the model text.

(B) Process Writing (Writing Techniques and Tasks)

Pre-W	(= Planning / Invention)	Brainstorming
		Wordmapping (Clustering, Outlining)
		Quick Writing (= Speed W, Rapid W, Free W)
While-W	(= Drafting)	for idea and organization
Responding (vs. Correcting) - conferencing & feedback / teacher & peer		
Post-W	Revising	(= Redrafting) for content & organization
	Editing	(= Proofreading) for mechanical features
Publishing & Sharing		

(B1) Techniques in Process Writing

Process writing as a classroom activity incorporates the four basic writing stages — planning, drafting (writing), revising (redrafting) and editing — and three other stages externally imposed on students by the teacher, namely, responding (sharing), evaluating and post-writing. Process writing in the classroom is highly structured as it necessitates the orderly teaching of process skills, and thus it may not, at least initially, give way to a free variation of writing stages cited earlier. Teachers often plan appropriate classroom activities that support the learning of specific writing skills at every stage. The planned learning experiences for students may be described as follows.

1) PLANNING (PRE-WRITING)

Pre-writing is any activity in the classroom that encourages students to write. It stimulates thoughts for getting started. In fact, it moves students away from having to face a blank page toward generating tentative ideas and gathering information for writing. The following activities provide the learning experiences for students at this stage:

① **Listing**

Try jotting down all the ideas that pop into your head about your topic. Free-associate; don't hold back anything. Try to brainstorm for at least ten minutes.

② **Freewriting**

Some people simply need to start writing to find a focus. Take out several sheets of blank paper, give yourself at least ten to fifteen minutes, and begin writing whatever comes to mind on your subject. Don't worry about spelling, punctuation, or even complete sentences. Don't change, correct, or delete anything. If you run out of things to say, write "I can't think of anything to say" until you can find a new thought. At the end of the time period you may discover that by continuously writing you will have written yourself into an interesting topic.

③ **Looping**

Looping is a variation on freewriting that works amazingly well for many people, including those who are frustrated rather than helped by freewriting. Looping involves writing freely for a short time, reading and selecting the 'centre of gravity sentence' (i.e. the most important idea) then using it as the topic of other pieces, which are also written freely by the learner. For example:

> <The first loop>
> This week has been one of those weeks when nothing goes right. I had an exam on Monday, but because we had a party the day before, I couldn't study at all, so I failed the exam. I felt awful. On Tuesday, I lost my calculator in my math class. <u>On Wednesday, I had an argument with my best friend</u>, and the next day I had my mobile phone stolen. On my way to school on Friday, I fell off my bike and broke my arm. I will have to stay in the hospital for a week or so until my arm gets better. I'm so glad that at least I won't be going to school next week.
>
> <The second loop>
> On Wednesday, I had an argument with my best friend. He wanted to borrow my mobile phone to play the game in it during the history class. I didn't think it was a good idea and didn't give him the phone, but he insisted and insisted. When I refused, he kicked me, but when I wanted to get back at him for it, the teacher saw me and <u>sent me to the school office</u>. My friend told her nothing, and I just had to leave the class. I felt miserable.

In this example, the underlined section in the first loop is the centre of gravity, which comprises the topic of the second loop. The centre of gravity in the second loop has also been underlined and can be the topic of the next loop, and in this way learners can continue choosing the centre of gravity sentences and keep looping. Of course, this technique does not always result in neat and cohesive paragraphs as in the example above. Redundancies, inaccuracies and disorganized ideas are to be tolerated and do not have to be monitored or corrected by the teacher. Indeed, the teacher has to be more 'responsive' than 'authoritative' (Murray 1985).

④ **The Boomerang**

Still another variation on freewriting is the technique called the boomerang, named appropriately because, like the Australian stick, it invites your mind to travel over a subject from opposite directions to produce new ideas. Suppose, for example, members of your class have been asked to write about their major field of study, which in your case is Liberal Arts. Begin by writing a statement that comes into your mind about majoring in the Liberal Arts and then freewrite on that statement for five minutes. Then write a second statement that approaches the subject from an opposing point of view, and freewrite again for five minutes. Continue this pattern several times. Boomeranging, like looping, can help writers see their subject in a new way and consequently help them find an idea to write about. Here's an abbreviated sample of boomeranging:

> 1. Majoring in the Liberal Arts is impractical in today's world. [Freewrite for five minutes.]
> 2. Majoring in the Liberal Arts is practical in today's world. [Freewrite for five minutes.]
> 3. Liberal Arts is a particularly enjoyable major for me. [Freewrite for five minutes.]
> 4. Liberal Arts is not always an enjoyable major for me. [Freewrite for five minutes.] and so on.

By continuing to 'throw the boomerang' across your subject, you may not only find your focus but also gain insight into other people's views of your topic, which can be especially valuable if your paper will address a controversial issue or one that you feel is often misunderstood.

⑤ **Clustering**

Another excellent technique is **clustering** (sometimes called '**mapping**'). Place your general subject in a circle in the middle of a blank sheet of paper and begin to draw other lines and circles that radiate from the original subject.

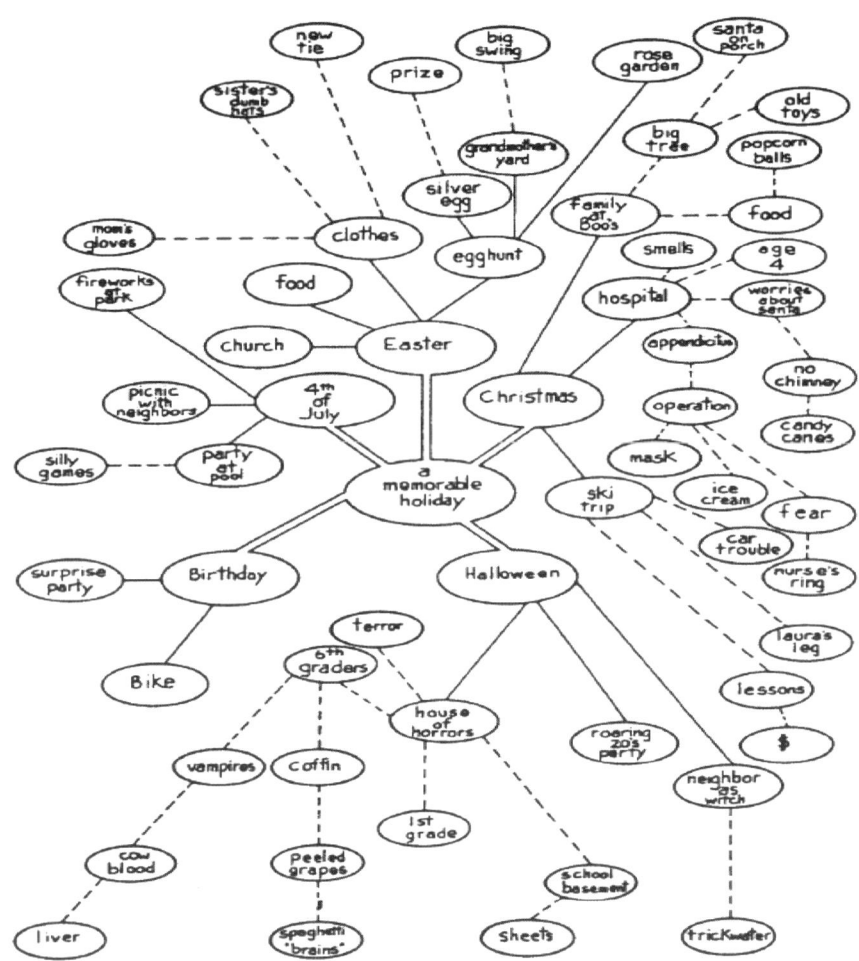

Cluster those ideas that seem to fall together. At the end of ten minutes see if a topic emerges from any of your groups of ideas. Ten minutes of clustering on the subject of *A Memorable Holiday* might look like the drawing above. This student may wish to brainstorm further on the Christmas he spent in the hospital with a case of appendicitis or perhaps the Halloween he first experienced a house of horrors. By using clustering, he has recollected some important details about a number of holidays that may help him focus on an occasion he wants to describe in his paper.

⑥ **Cubing**

Still another way to generate ideas is cubing. Imagine a six-sided cube that looks something like the figure below. Mentally, roll your subject around the cube and freewrite the answers to the questions that follow. Write whatever comes to mind for ten or fifteen minutes; don't concern yourself with the 'correctness' of what you write.

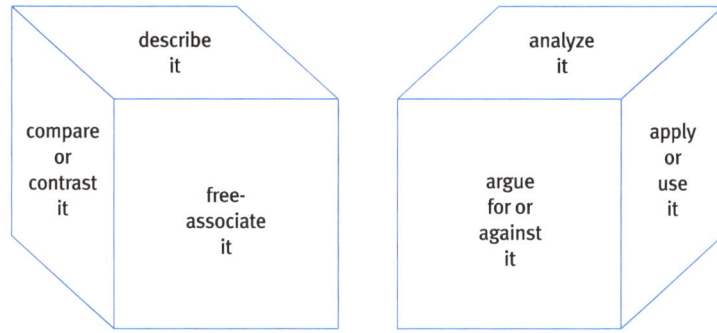

a. ***Describe it***: What does your subject look like? What size, colors, textures does it have? Any special features worth noting?

b. ***Compare or contrast it***: What is your subject similar to? What is your subject different from? In what ways?

c. ***Free-associate it***: What does this subject remind you of? What does it call to mind? What memories does it conjure up?

d. ***Analyze it***: How does it work? How are the parts connected? What is its significance?

e. ***Argue for or against it***: What arguments can you make for or against your subject? What advantages or disadvantages does it have? What changes or improvements should be made?

f. ***Apply it***: What are the uses of your subject? What can you do with it?

⑦ **Interviewing**

Another way to find a direction for your paper is through interviewing. Ask a classmate or friend to discuss your subject with you. Let your thoughts range over your subject as your friend asks you questions that arise naturally in the conversation. Or your friend might try asking what are called 'reporter's questions' as she or he 'interviews' you on your subject: **Who? When? What? Why? Where? How?** Listen to what you have to say about your subject. What were you most interested in talking about? What did your friend want to know? Why? By talking about your subject, you may find that you have talked your way into an interesting focus for your paper. If, after the interview, you are still stumped, question your friend: if he or she had to publish an essay based on the information from your interview, what would that essay focus on? Why?

2) DRAFTING

Once sufficient ideas are gathered at the planning stage, the first attempt at writing — that is, drafting — may proceed quickly. At the drafting stage, the writers are focused on the fluency of writing and are not preoccupied with grammatical accuracy or the neatness of the draft. One dimension of good writing is the writer's ability to visualise an audience. Although writing in the classroom is almost always for the teacher, the students may also be encouraged to write for different audiences, among whom are peers, other classmates, pen-friends and family members. A conscious sense of audience can dictate a certain style to be used. Students should also have in mind a central idea that they want to communicate to the audience in order to give direction to their writing.

Depending on the genre of writing (narrative, expository or argumentative), an introduction to the subject of writing may be a startling statement to arrest the reader's attention, a short summary of the rest of the writing, an apt quotation, a provocative question, a general statement, an analogy, a statement of purpose, and so on. Such a strategy may provide the lead at the drafting stage. Once a start is made, the writing task is simplified 'as the writers let go and disappear into the act of writing' (D'Aoust 1986).

3) RESPONDING

Responding to student writing by the teacher (or by peers) has a central role to play in the successful implementation of process writing. Responding intervenes between drafting and revising. It is the teacher's quick initial reaction to students' drafts. Response can be oral or in writing, after the students have produced the first draft and just before they proceed to revise. The failure of many writing programmes in schools today may be ascribed to the fact that responding is done in the final stage when the teacher simultaneously responds and evaluates, and even edits students' finished texts, thus giving students the impression that nothing more needs to be done.

Text-specific responses in the form of helpful suggestions and questions rather than 'rubber-stamped' comments (such as 'organisation is OK', 'ideas are too vague' etc.) by the teacher will help students rediscover meanings and facilitate the revision of initial drafts. Such responses may be provided in the margin, between sentence lines or at the end of students' texts. Peer responding can be effectively carried out by having students respond to each other's texts in small groups or in pairs, with the aid of the checklist in the following table (adapted from Reinking & Hart 1991).

TABLE. PEER RESPONDING CHECKLIST
When responding to your peer's draft, ask yourself these questions: • What is the greatest strength of this composition? • What is its greatest weakness? • What is the central idea of this composition? • Which are the ideas which need more elaboration? • Where should more details or examples be added? Why? • What are some of the questions that the writer has not answered? • At which point does this composition fail to hold the reader's interest? Why? • Where is the organisation confusing? • Where is the writing unclear or vague?

4) REVISING

When students revise, they review their texts on the basis of the feedback given in the responding stage. They reexamine what was written to see how effectively they have communicated their meanings to the reader. Revising is not merely checking for language errors (i.e., editing). It is done to improve global content and the organisation of ideas so that the writer's intent is made clearer to the reader.

To ensure that rewriting does not mean recopying, Beck (1986) suggests that the teacher collect and keep the students' drafts and ask them for rewrites. 'When the students are forced to act without their original drafts, they become more familiar with their purposes and their unique messages. ... The writers move more ably within their topics, and their writing develops tones of confidence and authority'.

Another activity for revising may have the students working in pairs to read aloud each other's drafts before they revise. As students listen intently to their own writing, they are brought to a more conscious level of rethinking and reseeing what they have written. Meanings which are vague become more apparent when the writers actually hear their own texts read out to them. Revision often becomes more voluntary and motivating. An alternative to this would be to have individual students read their own texts into a tape recorder and take a dictation of their own writing later. Students can replay the tape as often as necessary and activate the pause button at points where they need to make productive revision of their texts.

5) EDITING

At this stage, students are engaged in tidying up their texts as they prepare the final draft for evaluation by the teacher. They edit their own or their peer's work for grammar, spelling, punctuation, diction, sentence structure and accuracy of supportive textual material such as quotations, examples and the like. Formal editing is deferred till this phase in order that its application not disrupt the free flow of ideas during the drafting and revising stages.

A simple checklist might be issued to students to alert them to some of the common surface errors found in students' writing. For instance:

- Have you used your verbs in the correct tense?
- Are the verb forms correct?
- Have you checked for subject-verb agreement?
- Have you used the correct prepositions?
- Have you left out the articles where they are required?
- Have you used all your pronouns correctly?
- Is your choice of adjectives and adverbs appropriate?
- Have you written in complete sentences?

The students are, however, not always expected to know where and how to correct every error, but editing to the best of their ability should be done as a matter of course, prior to submitting their work for evaluation each time. Editing within process writing is meaningful because students can see the connection between such an exercise and their own writing in that correction is not done for its own sake but as part of the process of making communication as clear and unambiguous as possible to an audience.

6) EVALUATING

Very often, teachers pleading lack of time have compressed responding, editing and evaluating all into one. This would, in effect, deprive students of that vital link between drafting and revision — that is, responding — which often makes a big difference to the kind of writing that will eventually be produced.

In evaluating student writing, the scoring may be **analytical** (i.e., based on specific aspects of writing ability) or **holistic** (i.e., based on a global interpretation of the effectiveness of that piece of writing). In order to be effective, the criteria for evaluation should be made known to students in advance. They should include overall interpretation of the task, sense of audience, relevance, development and organisation of ideas, format or layout, grammar and structure, spelling and punctuation, range and appropriateness of vocabulary, and clarity of communication. Depending on the purpose of evaluation, a numerical score or grade may be assigned.

Students may be encouraged to evaluate their own and each other's texts once they have been properly taught how to do it. In this way, they are made to be more responsible for their own writing.

7) POST-WRITING

Post-writing constitutes any classroom activity that the teacher and students can do with the completed pieces of writing. This includes publishing, sharing, reading aloud, transforming texts for stage performances, or merely displaying texts on notice-boards. The post-writing stage is a platform for recognising students' work as important and worthwhile. It may be used as a motivation for writing as well as to hedge against students finding excuses for not writing. Students must be made to feel that they are writing for a very real purpose.

(C) Responding & Correcting

Responding	concerned with the content and design	conferencing: face to face
		feedback: thru paper
Correcting	concerned with the accuracy	

(C1) Responses to Writing – Marking

Getting back a piece of work with a teacher's comments and corrections on it can be helpful. It can also be discouraging, especially if there is too much information, if the information is inappropriate or hard to interpret, or if the general tone is negative rather than positive. The red pen particularly has associations for many people with insensitive and discouraging correction and judgement. Some alternatives are listed below.

- Use a green or a blue pen!
- Discuss the marking criteria with students. Agree on a mark or grade.
- Write the correct answers in the margin.
- Use correction codes in the margin.
- Underline all errors of one type. (eg all verb tense mistakes, all spelling mistakes)
- Write a letter in reply.
- Write nothing. Discuss the work with the individual students.
- Only write a comment about the meaning and message of the piece.
- Create a composite essay using good bits and problematic bits from a number of students' work. Photocopy it and hand it out for students to discuss and correct, together or in groups or individually, perhaps for homework.

In all of these options, there is one important guideline to bear in mind: tell students (or agree) before the writing what will happen afterwards (eg ***I'll be marking tense mistakes only***).

(C1a) Correction codes

Codes can indicate where an error is and what type of error it is. However, they leave the learners to do some work in order to find the corrections for themselves. This may seem preferable to handing them the correction 'ready made'. It is, of course, essential that the students understand your own set of codes.

Code	Error Indicated	Code	Error Indicated
∧	A word is missing	C / Cap	Capitalization error
/	Start a new sentence	c/unc	Countable/uncountable error
//	Start a new paragraph	Wo	Wrong word order
Gr	Grammar error	Ww	Wrong word
S / Sp	Spelling error	Wt	Wrong tense
P	Punctuation error	Wf	Wrong form
Agr	Agreement error	Irreg	Irregular verb
Art	Error with articles	? / ???	Unclear

It often seems inappropriate to point out every error; it can be dispiriting to get back to work with a large quantity of marks on it. You probably need to decide which errors you think are most important or useful for the student to work on at the moment and then to draw attention to these.

(D) Types of writing performance

Imitative W	(= writing down), dictation
Intensive W	controlled & guided W, dicto-comp
Extensive W	(= self-writing), note-taking, diary/journal writing
Display W	exam, report
Real W	academic, vocational/technical, personal

‹Dialogue Journals (in Self-writing)›

Dialogue journals are a worthwhile addition to any classroom, especially for ESL students. ESL students need more help on an individual basis because of their unique situation which involves not only learning a new language, but learning a new culture. Dialogue journals provide a caring audience, give the students a chance to choose their own topic, supply students with conversation practice, allow students to write freely without being evaluated, and permit students to write at their own level of proficiency. Because of these features, dialogue journals provide an ideal, non-threatening environment for the students to explore and experiment with the English language.

With encouragement and the aid of dialogue journals, teachers can open a way for their students to explore and discover ideas and topics in the world of writing. Students are encouraged to write clearly when they know that someone will be reading their entry and responding to what they write. Dialogue journals also give shy students the opportunity to take a private spotlight in voicing their opinion to a caring audience. An added benefit of dialogue journals lies in the close ties that can be formed between student and teacher. In addition, the students can develop a sense of ownership of the entry because the dialogue journal entries are entirely of the students' creation. Dialogue journals also provide teachers with the chance to monitor individual progress on a daily basis.

(E) Assessing writing - Portfolios

Portfolios are also an excellent approach for evaluating student writing, with the added advantage of involving learners in the evaluation process. Some teachers have students include all their written work over a given period of time, while others ask students to choose representative works for their portfolio. At certain times throughout the year, students are asked to review their portfolios in preparation for a conference with their teacher. Some teachers give students a rubric to include with their portfolios.

최지원 **전공영어 영어교육학** PRACTICAL

Chapter 11 Mind Map

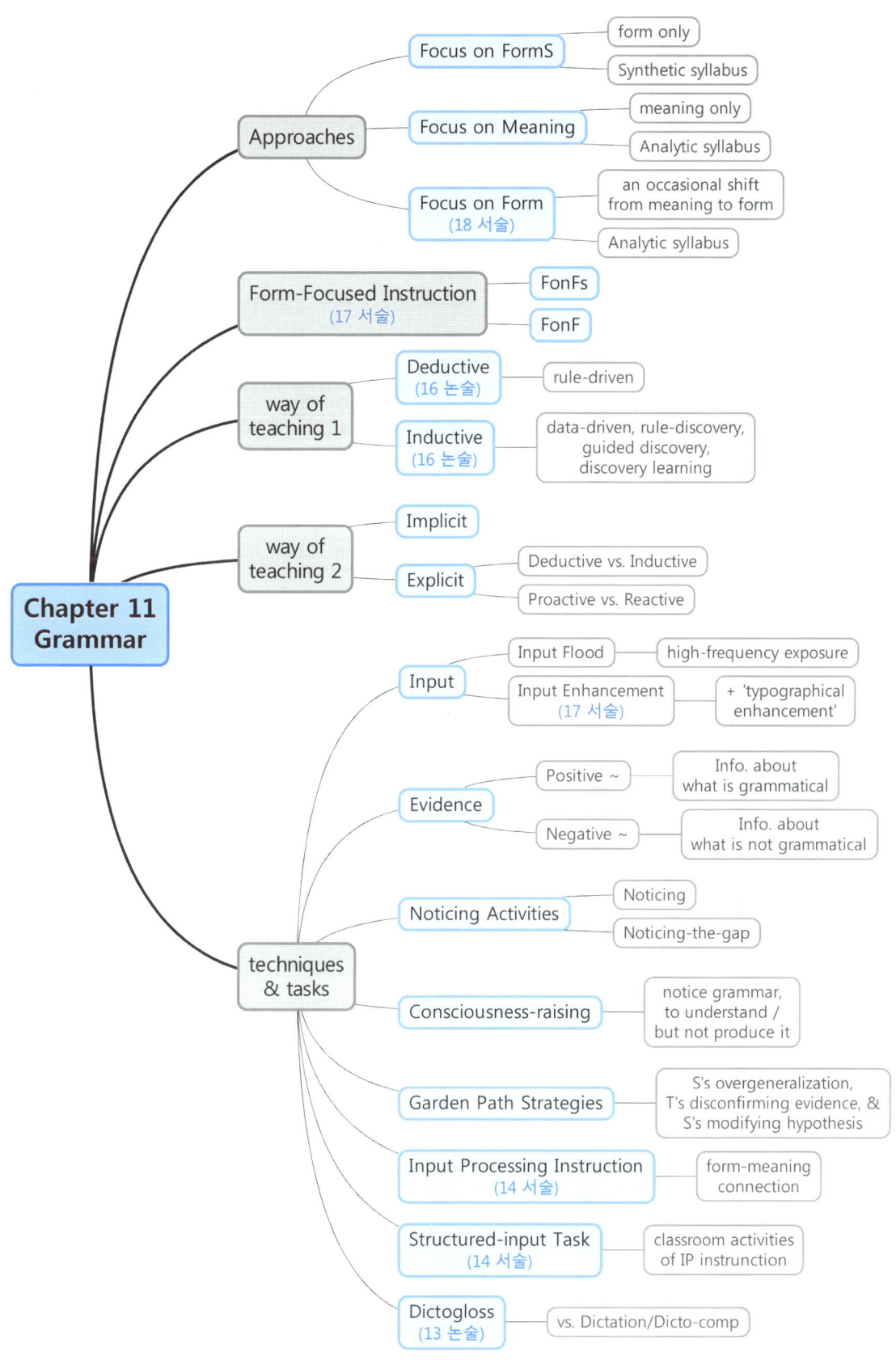

Chapter 11   Teaching Grammar

(A) Approaches to Teaching Grammar & FFI

Focus on Forms	form only	
Focus on Meaning	meaning only	FFI
Focus on Form	an occasional shift from meaning to form	

    The purpose of this section is to show you some of the ways that the concepts and techniques of teaching grammar in the second language classrooms are realized in the classroom. In the following two sequences, Teacher A and B were using the same task. It is interesting to notice the very different ways in which a set of materials can be exploited by different teachers.

Teacher A	Teacher B
T: OK, now, look at the picture and the words. Can you see the people?	T: Right everybody! Remember these words? Siu Ming?
Ss: Yes, yes.	S: Yes.
T: So, now we're going to practice the words. Listen to me and repeat. "Erik is tall.", "Erik is tall."	T: Tan?
	S: Yes.
Ss: Erik is tall.	T: OK. I'm going to say a word, and I want you to make a statement. And NOT one you can see on the page, OK? Um … George. Siu Ming?
T: Again.	
Ss: Erik is tall.	
T: Good! Amy.	S: George has a mustache.
Ss: Amy is tall.	T: (laughs) Well, yes, that's true, but NOT one that you can see on the page. Try again.
T: Good! Glasses. Jun?	
S: Amy is glasses.	S: Um … George is middle-aged.
T: Is?	T: George is middle-aged. Yes, right. Short hair. Tania.
S: Has.	
T: Yes …?	S: Kathi has short hair.
S: Amy has glasses.	T: She does? (shakes head)
T: Amy HAS glasses. Yes, right. Everyone.	S: Oh … Um … Tony has short hair.
Ss: Amy HAS glasses.	T: That's good. Tony has short hair. Repeat everybody! Tony has short hair.
T: George.	
Ss: George HAS glasses.	Ss: Tony has short hair.
	T: Good. Tony's almost bald! (laughs)

Both teachers are getting students to learn key vocabulary that they will need later in the lesson and to practice making statements about appearance using the simple present tense with **be** and **have**. Teacher A is using a classical audiolingual substitution drill. Unfortunately, the teacher is only concerned with grammatical accuracy, not with meaning. When a student makes the grammatically correct, but semantically incorrect statement "Amy is tall", (Amy is NOT tall, she's short!) the teacher responds by saying "Good!"

Teacher B achieves the same goals, but within a communicative context. The students have to make statements that are grammatically correct and semantically true. The exercise is also slightly more creative, in that the students have a choice over who to describe and what aspect of their appearance to focus on.

(A1) Options in Language Teaching

Option 2	Option 3	Option 1
analytic	*analytic*	*synthetic*
focus on **meaning**	focus on **form**	focus on **formS**
←		→
Natural Approach, Immersion Procedural Syllabus etc.	TBLT, Content-Based LT (?) Process Syllabus (?) etc.	GT, ALM, Silent Way, TPR Structural / N-F Syllabuses etc.

<Figure> Options in language teaching

1) Focus on forms

Although by no means the only important issue underlying debate over approaches to language teaching down the years, implicit or explicit choice of the learner or the language to be taught as the starting point in course design remains one of the most critical. The popular position has long been that teacher's or syllabus designer's first task is to analyze the target language (or more commonly to adopt an existing analysis, usually in the form of a pedagogical grammar or a textbook), that is, what Wilkins (1976) termed the synthetic approach (Figure - Option 1).

Depending on the analyst's linguistic preferences, the L2 is broken down into words and collocations, grammar rules, phonemes, intonation and stress patterns, structures, notions, or functions. The items in the resulting list(s) are then sequenced for presentation as ***models*** to learners in linear, additive fashion according to such criteria as (usually intuitively assessed) frequency, valence, or difficulty. Synthetic syllabi, still used in the vast majority of classrooms the world over, with the structural syllabus being the most common, are those in which:

> parts of the language are taught separately and step by step so that acquisition is a process of gradual accumulation of parts until the whole structure of language has been built up ···. At any one time the learner is being exposed to a deliberately limited sample of language. (Wilkins 1976)

The learner's role is to synthesize the pieces for use in communication. Synthetic syllabi, together with the corresponding materials, methodology, and classroom pedagogy, lead to lessons with a **focus on formS**. The syllabus consists of inductively or deductively presented information about the L2. Pedagogical materials and accompanying classroom procedures are designed to present and practice a series of linguistic items, or forms. They have no independent reason for existence.

Synthetic syllabi — lexical, structural, notional-functional, and in practice to date, topical and situational — and the synthetic 'methods' and classroom practices (repetition of models, transformation exercises, display questions, explicit negative feedback, i.e., error 'correction', etc.) commonly associated with them are generally produced and used, although they need not be, before a ***needs analysis*** is conducted for a particular group of learners. Moreover, synthetic syllabi, 'methods', and classroom practices either largely ignore language learning processes or tacitly assume a discredited behaviorist model. Of the scores of detailed studies of naturalistic and classroom language learning reported over the past 30 years, none suggest, for example, that presentation of discrete points of grammar one at a time (albeit in 'spiral' fashion), as dictated by a synthetic syllabus of some kind, bears any resemblance except an accidental one to either the order or the manner in which naturalistic or classroom acquirers learn those items. As Rutherford (1988) noted, SLA is not a process of accumulating entities.

2) Focus on meaning

A growing sense that something was wrong, recognition that traditional synthetic syllabi and teaching procedures were not working as they were supposed to, and familiarity with the findings of studies of instructed interlanguage development have, over the years, led a small minority of experienced teachers and syllabus designers, and several SLA theorists, to advocate abandonment of a focus on formS in the L2 classroom in favor of an equally single-minded **focus on meaning** (Figure - Option 2). Although the terminology has varied, some have gone so far as to claim that learning an L2 ***incidentally*** (i.e., without intention, while doing something else) or ***implicitly*** (i.e., without awareness) from exposure to comprehensible target language samples is ***sufficient*** for successful second or foreign language acquisition (L2A) by adolescents and adults, just as is it appears to be for first language acquisition (L1A) by young children. Others have suggested that harnessing L1A learning processes is adequate or even optimal as the basis for teaching a second or foreign language. In fact, although the rationales have differed considerably, variants of the 'noninterventionist' position go back hundreds of years, if not longer. The essential claim is that people of all ages learn languages best, inside or outside a classroom, not by treating the languages as an object of study, but by experiencing them as a medium of communication. Language teaching syllabi of this second kind are what Wilkins (1976) termed ***analytic***:

[P]rior analysis of the total language system into a set of discrete pieces of language that is a necessary precondition for the adoption of a synthetic approach is largely superfluous. Analytic approaches ... are organized in terms of the purposes for which people are learning language and the kinds of language performance that are necessary to meet those purposes. (Wilkins 1976)

Although Wilkins's distinction focused on treatment of the language to be taught and said little about related learning processes, analytic syllabi assume, in current terminology, that adolescent and adult L2 learners are still capable, like young children, of (1) subconsciously analyzing linguistic input and inducing rules and/or forming new neural networks underlying what looks like rule-governed behavior, and/or (2) accessing, partially or completely, innate knowledge of linguistic universals and the way languages can vary. The emphasis, therefore, is on the provision of sufficient quantities of ***positive evidence*** about what is possible in the L2.

3) Focus on form

As indicated in the above table, the syllabus for Option 3 is analytic, employing a nonlinguistic unit of analysis, such as task. Syllabus content is a series of ***pedagogical tasks*** (or, in some content-based approaches, curricular subject matter), the justification for which is that the content or tasks are related to the current or future needs of the particular group of learners to be served. As described elsewhere, pedagogical tasks are designed, with no specific linguistic focus, as successively more complex approximations to the target tasks that a task-based needs analysis has identified as facing the learner, such as attending a job interview, making an airline reservation, reading a restaurant menu or a journal abstract, writing a lab report, or taking a driving test. Attempts by the materials designer and teacher to make students notice the sorts of linguistic problems identified by L. White and others are not scheduled in advance by means of an external synthetic syllabus of some kind but, instead, exploit opportunities that arise naturally from the interaction of learners and tasks.

Focus on form refers to how focal attentional resources are allocated. Although there are degrees of attention, and although attention to forms and attention to meaning are not always mutually exclusive, during an otherwise meaning-focused classroom lesson, focus on form often consists of an occasional shift of attention to linguistic code features — by the teacher and/or one or more students — triggered by perceived problems with comprehension or production. This is similar to what happens when native speakers who are good writers pause to consider the appropriate form of address to use when composing a letter to a stranger, or when efficient readers suddenly 'disconfirm a hypothesis' while reading and are momentarily obliged to retrace their steps in a text until they locate the item — perhaps a little *not* they had missed earlier in the sentence — which caused the semantic surprise. The usual and fundamental orientation is to meaning and communication, but factors arise that lead even the fluent language user temporarily to attend to the language itself.

Focus on form is sometimes used to describe teacher's behavior of the use of some devices to increase the perceptual salience of target items, which is what Sharwood Smith calls ***input enhancement***. What it is hoped that a pedagogical activity will achieve and what it actually achieves are not necessarily the same, however. Clearly, a more important sense of focus on form than the teacher's external behavior or its intended result is the learner's internal mental state. That is to say, how focal attention is allocated is something that is negotiated by the teacher and students and not directly observable. The intended outcome of focus on form is what Schmidt calls ***noticing***:

> I use ***noticing*** to mean registering the simple occurrence of some event, whereas ***understanding*** implies recognition of a general principle, rule, or pattern. For example, a second language learner might simply notice that a native speaker used a particular form of address on a particular occasion, or at a deeper level the learner might understand the significance of such a form, realizing that the form used was appropriate because of status differences between speaker or hearer. Noticing is crucially related to the question of what linguistic material is stored in memory ⋯ understanding relates to questions concerning how that material is organized into a linguistic system.

(B) Deductive vs. Inductive teaching

Deductive teaching	rule-driven
Inductive teaching	data-driven, rule-discovery, guided discovery, discovery learning

In the **deductive** classroom, the teacher gives a grammatical explanation or rule followed by a set of exercises designed to clarify the grammatical point and help the learners master the point. In deductive teaching, you work from principles to examples. Inductive procedures reverse this process. In **inductive** teaching, you present the learners with samples of language and through a process of **guided discovery**, get them to work out the principle or rule for themselves.

So, which is better, deductive or inductive teaching? The answer is — it depends. It depends on the grammar point being taught, and the learning style of the student. In my (Nunan's) own teaching, I try and combine both approaches. I prefer induction because I believe learning in the longer term. The disadvantage of an inductive approach is that it takes more time for learners to come to an understanding of the grammatical point in question than with a deductive approach. Study the following teaching sequences in which two different teachers are using the book *Expressions 1*.

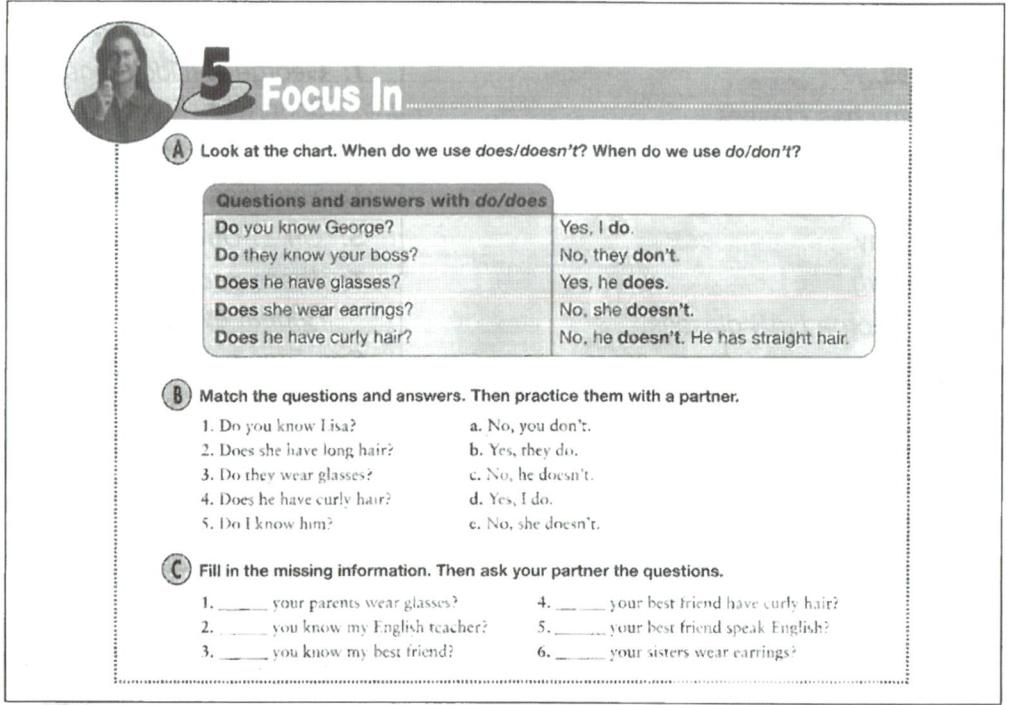

Teacher A

T: OK, then I want you to work in your pairs. Kevin, who's your partner? Jackie, is it?
S: (nods)
T: Good. OK, look at the questions and answers in the, um, yellow box. I want you to practice the questions and answers in your pairs. OK? Kevin — Can you and Jackie do the first one for the class?
S: Do … do you know George?
S: Yes, I do.
T: OK. Excellent. … So — off you go.
(Ss practice the questions and answers in pairs).
T: Everyone finished? … That sounded pretty good. Now, I'm going to ask you some questions, and I want you to answer me. OK? Sharmy, do you know Kevin?
S: Yes, I do.
T: Of course you do! (laughs) Kevin, do you wear earrings?
S: No, I don't.
T: How about Sharmy, does she wear earrings?
S: Yes, she does.
T: Yes, she has great earrings, doesn't she? Um, Lillian, do you have curly hair?
S: Yes, I am.
T: Yes, I … ?
S: Does … sorry … do.
T: Yes, I do. Yes, I do. Good. OK, so … when do we use *do/don't* and when do we use *does/doesn't*? (Puts the following table on the board.)

do/don't	does/doesn't
I, Sandra, you, we, your best friend	he, Erik and Amy, your boss, they

T: Some of these words are in the wrong box. Understand? Yes?
Ss: (nod)
T: OK, I want you to work with your partner. Copy the table, but put the words in the right box. Then see if you can add two more items to each box.

Teacher B

T: I want you all to look at the grammar box. What … what does it show us? … Anyone? Alice?
S: About *do/does*.
T: OK, good. It shows us when we use the verb *do/don't, does/doesn't* in questions. Look at this table. (Puts the following table on the board.)

do/don't	does/doesn't
I, you, we, they, George and Kathi	he, she, Erik

T: Understand?
Ss: (nod)
T: OK, now I want you to look at Exercise B — matching the questions and answers. I want you to put a circle around all of the *do* and *don't* words you can find, and underline all of the *does* and *doesn't* words. OK, Fan? Understand?
S: (nods)
T: All right. And I want you to notice the pronouns they go with — I, you, he, she — maybe you can highlight them. OK? Right. Then I want you to match the questions with the right answers, and when you've done that, practice the questions and answers with your partner.

Teacher A begins by getting the students to practice the target language (yes/no questions with do/does; asking and answering questions about appearance). She then personalizes the exercise by getting students to answer questions about the appearance of their classmates. She then tries an inductive activity designed to focus students on the appropriate pronouns and noun phrases to match with do/don't and does/doesn't. She does this through a ***spot-the-mistake*** exercise. This is a good exercise to introduce in a review/recycling lesson, but probably unwise if the grammar point is being introduced for the first time.

Teacher B has the same pedagogical objectives as Teacher A. However, she tackles the task somewhat differently. She focuses the students on the grammar point to be studied, presents the grammar box deductively, and then gets students to find examples of the grammar item. Only after students have studied the grammar point does she get them practicing questions and answers using the point.

(B1) Explicit vs. Implicit instruction

To understand what is meant by 'explicit instruction' it is first necessary to consider how it differs from 'implicit instruction'. Ellis (2008) explained the difference as follows:

① **Explicit instruction** involves 'some sort of rule being thought about during the learning process (DeKeyser 1995). In other words, learners are encouraged to develop metalinguistic awareness of the rule. This can be achieved deductively as when a rule is given to the learners, or inductively as when the learners are asked to work out a rule for themselves from an array of data illustrating the rule.

② **Implicit instruction** is directed at enabling learners to infer rules without awareness. Thus it contrasts with explicit instruction in that there is no intention to develop any understanding of what is being learned.

It should be noted, however, that implicit instruction need not be entirely devoid of attempts to induce learners to attend to form. As Housen and Pierrard (2006) point out, the key difference lies in whether the instruction 'directs' or 'attracts' attention to form. Explicit instruction directs learners to not just attend to grammatical forms but also to develop conscious mental representations of them. Learners know what they are supposed to be learning. However, implicit instruction aims to attract learners' attention to exemplars of linguistic forms as these occur in communicative input but does not seek to develop any awareness or understanding of the 'rules' that describe these forms.

(B1a) Types of explicit grammar instruction

Ellis (2008) distinguished four types by referring to two dimensions of explicit instruction. The first is the deductive/inductive dimension. Deductive explicit instruction involves providing learners with explicit information about a grammatical feature. Inductive explicit instruction provides learners with the data and guidance that they need to derive their own understanding of the grammatical feature. It entails the use of what I have called 'consciousness-raising tasks'. It can also take the form of practice exercises designed to develop learners' awareness of how a grammatical structure works. The second dimension concerns whether the explicit instruction is proactive (i.e. involves planned interventions designed to prevent error from occurring) or reactive (i.e. involves responding explicitly to errors that learners make). Proactive explicit instruction is based on a structural syllabus (i.e. a graded list of the grammatical structures to be taught). Reactive explicit instruction can occur in lessons based on a structural syllabus or in lessons based on focused tasks (i.e. tasks that have been designed to elicit the use of a specific target feature in a communicative context). The four types of explicit instruction that result from juxtaposing these two dimensions are shown in the following table.

	Deductive	Inductive
Proactive	Metalinguistic explanation	Consciousness-raising tasks, Production- & comprehension-based practice exercises
Reactive	Explicit correction, Metalinguistic feedback	Repetition, Corrective recasts

These four types of explicit instruction are often combined in a single lesson. For example, proactive deductive explicit instruction in the form of metalinguistic explanation of a grammatical feature is often followed by practice exercises (proactive inductive explicit instruction) and, if learners make errors, by explicit correction (deductive reactive explicit instruction) and/or corrective recasts (inductive reactive explicit instruction). Indeed this is probably many teachers' prototypical idea of what explicit instruction entails. Nevertheless, there is merit in separating out the components of such instruction as it allows us to consider exactly what each consists of. I will now draw on Ellis (2008) to provide a more detailed description of each type.

① Proactive/deductive explicit instruction

This type is realised by means of metalinguistic explanations. These typically consist of information about a specific linguistic property supported by examples. Metalinguistic explanations can be provided orally by the teacher or in written form in a text book or reference grammar.

② Proactive/inductive explicit instruction

Proactive/inductive explicit FFI involves either practice exercises or consciousness-raising tasks. In Ellis (1991), I defined a **CR task** as 'a pedagogic activity where the learners are provided with L2 data in some form and required to perform some operation on or with it, the purpose of which is to arrive at an explicit understanding of some regularity in the data. Thus, CR tasks constitute a form of discovery learning. Practice activities are sometimes viewed as a form of implicit instruction if learners are not told what structure they are practising. But, in fact, intensive practice, even when there is no accompanying metalinguistic explanation, will almost certainly involve awareness of the target structure on the part of the learners and for this reason I have classified practice as a kind of explicit instruction. Only when the learners view an activity as requiring them to 'communicate' rather than to 'practise' (as with 'focused tasks') does the practice become implicit.

③ Reactive/deductive explicit instruction

There are two types of reactive/deductive explicit instruction — explicit correction and metalinguistic feedback. Lyster and Ranta (1997) define explicit correction 'as the explicit provision of the correct form' accompanied by a clear indication that what the learner said was incorrect. They define metalinguistic feedback as follows: Metalinguistic feedback contains either comments, information, or questions related to the well-formedness of the student's utterance, without explicitly providing the correct form. Often these two types are combined when teachers correct learner errors.

④ Reactive/inductive explicit instruction

The key characteristic of this type of explicit instruction is that learners are provided with feedback that is unambiguously corrective in force by indicating that an error has been committed. Two kinds of corrective feedback manifest this characteristic — repetition and corrective recasts. The former involves the repetition of the student's erroneous utterance with the location of the error signalled by means of emphatic stress. A corrective recast reformulates the learner's erroneous utterance with the correct form highlighted intonationally, as in this example from Doughty and Varela (1998):

> L: I think that the worm will go under the soil.
> T: I *think* that the worm *will* go under the soil?
> L: (no response)
> T: I *thought* that the worm *would* go under the soil.
> L: I *thought* that the worm *would* go under the soil.

Such feedback can be considered inductive because learners are required to carry out a cognitive comparison of their original and reformulated utterances. I have chosen to consider repetition and corrective recasts as explicit (see Ellis and Sheen 2006). However, other researchers (e.g. Long 2006) view them as implicit. (Corrective feedback can be implicit, in which case the corrective force is disguised. Many recasts are implicit in nature. Explicit and implicit corrective feedback are best seen as poles on a continuum rather than dichotomous.) I argue that they are explicit because the intention is to make learners aware that they have made an error.

(C) Techniques and tasks in teaching grammar

(C1) Input Flood vs. Input Enhancement & Positive vs. Negative Evidence

Input Flood	high-frequency exposure to a particular form w/o grammar teaching
Input Enhancement	'typographical enhancement' added to input flood
Positive evidence	information about what is grammatical in the L2
Negative evidence	information about what is not grammatical in the L2

(C1a) Positive evidence vs. Negative evidence

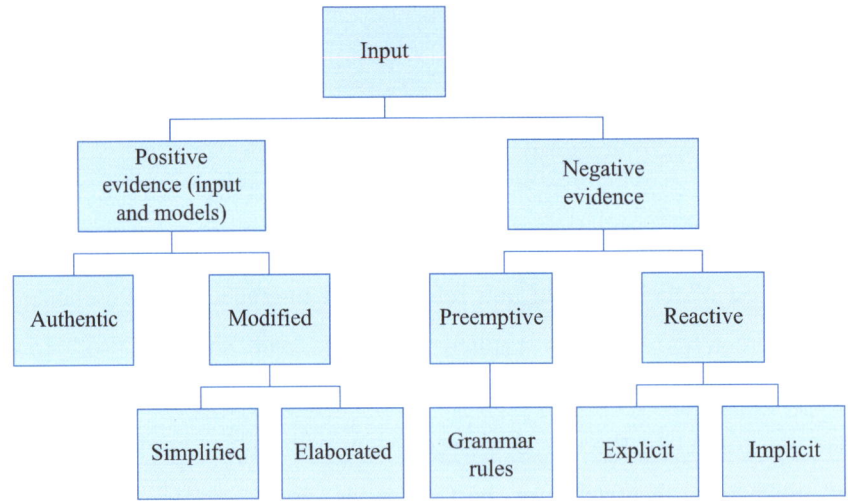

<Types of evidence for second language acquisition (Doughty 1998)>

As illustrated above, **exposure**, more commonly referred to in the literature as **target language input**, can take the form of **positive evidence**, understood as information about what is accurate and therefore possible and acceptable in a second language, or 'language used, that is utterances in context' (Gregg 2001), and **negative evidence**, defined as information that certain utterances are incorrect and thus impossible in that language, or 'language mentioned' (Gregg 2001). Positive evidence contains exemplars of accurate utterances in the ambient input as well as models of such utterances deliberately presented by the teacher in the classroom environment, and it can be **authentic** (e.g. a newspaper article intended for native speakers or a movie with an original soundtrack) and **modified** with the adjustments made in the latter involving either **simplification** (e.g. a coursebook text which contains a limited number of tokens and types of vocabulary items, and is written with the help of relatively simple grammatical structures) or **elaboration** (e.g. difficult words are defined and exemplified when the teacher is telling a story). When it comes to negative evidence, it can be *preemptive*, when pertinent rules are provided and grammatical explanations offered before the learner has a chance to make a mistake, or *reactive*, in which case it represents various options in error correction or negative feedback. Although the graphical representation suggests that such evidence can only be explicit (i.e. overt or direct, as in the provision of the correct version) or implicit (i.e. covert or indirect, as in a recast or a clarification request), it can also differ along other dimensions, the most important of which concerns whether a particular corrective move is input-providing or output-inducing.

Commenting on the significance of these two types of data, Gass (2003) writes that "[p]ositive evidence is the most obvious necessary requirement for learning. One must have exposure to the set of grammatical sentences in order for learning to take place. However, the role of negative evidence is less clear". Indeed, even a total layperson would be very unlikely to even contemplate the possibility that successful second language acquisition could ever occur without adequate access to utterances in the target language, be they spoken or written. By the same token, although influential SLA theories may differ with respect to a number of issues, such as the role of form-focused instruction, the requirement for comprehension and production, or the characteristics of input that would make it the most conducive to language development, all of them consider the presence of a sufficient amount of language data to be indispensable for learning. The situation is entirely different when it comes to various types of negative evidence, both preemptive and reactive, since its utility is called into question by the proponents of theoretical positions based on nativist accounts of language acquisition, such as Krashen's Monitor Model, which have provided an impetus for the advent of non-interventionist approaches embracing the zero grammar option (i.e. deep-end variants of CLT).

Leaving such theoretical considerations aside, it should be clarified that opportunities to engage in output production also play such an essential role in language acquisition because oral and written interactions are bound to generate more positive and negative evidence that learners can make use of in restructuring their developing interlanguage systems. This is because, for example, active participation in conversational exchanges with more proficient interlocutors inevitably results in increased exposure to well-formed utterances in the target language as students listen to their questions and responses. On the other hand, the very act of language production creates numerous contexts in which errors are likely to be committed, which can provide a stimulus for the occurrence of negative evidence, as the use of incorrect forms provokes the provision of corrective feedback by native speakers, teachers, or more proficient peers. As mentioned above, such correction may in itself constitute positive evidence as well, let alone the fact that it can be accompanied by additional models when brief grammatical explanations are given.

(C2) Noticing activities

The noticing hypothesis suggests that unless learners notice the way language is used, their grammatical proficiency will not develop. An example of taking a noticing activity outside the classroom is when students act as 'language detectives':

> Students can be asked to observe and notice target forms in use in the 'real world', such as by watching interviews and other speech events on the internet or on television and documenting the use of particular grammatical features they have been asked to focus on. This can serve to reinforce vocabulary or particular forms, but it can also be used to help more advanced students become aware of how grammar works together at a textual level instead of focusing only on vocabulary or on sentence-level structures. Students can use a notebook or mobile device for recording examples and can bring these to class for further discussion or clarification.

(C3) Consciousness-raising tasks

Consciousness-raising (CR) tasks requires learners to communicate directly about grammar structures, perhaps by generating a rule for their use. Although learners' attention is drawn to the nature of the target structure, the tasks are communicative, since learners are engaged in meaning-focused interaction. The 'taskness' of a CR-task lies not in the linguistic point that is the focus of the task but rather in the talk learners must engage in in order to achieve an outcome to the task. (Ellis 2001) R. Ellis (1993) made a distinction between grammar consciousness-raising tasks and practice tasks. In the latter, learners practice the use of grammatical structures through production activities. The former involves "activities that will seek to get a learner to understand a particular grammatical feature, how it works, what it consists of, and so on, but not require that learner to actually produce sentences manifesting that particular structure". This particular use of the term "consciousness raising" emphasizes the fact that it leads to noticing. Once noticing has occurred, task performance can be followed by other communicative activities containing the target structure to further enhance noticing. R. Ellis (2002) discusses the general concept of consciousness raising as follows: "Consciousness-raising … involves an attempt to equip the learner with an understanding of a specific grammatical feature — to develop declarative rather than procedural knowledge of it".

The main characteristics of CR tasks, according to Ellis, are the following:

1. There is an attempt to isolate a specific linguistic feature for focused attention.

2. The learners are provided with data which illustrate the targeted feature and they may also be supplied with an explicit rule describing or explaining the feature.

3. The learners are expected to utilize intellectual effort to understand the targeted feature.

4. Misunderstanding or incomplete understanding of the grammatical structure by the learners leads to clarification in the form of further data and description or explanation.

5. Learners may be required (although this is not obligatory) to articulate the rule describing the grammatical structure.

The following example of a CR task is provided by Fotos and Ellis (1991).

A. What is the difference between verbs like 'give' and 'explain'?
   She gave a book to her father. (= grammatical)
   She gave her father a book. (= grammatical)
   The policeman explained the law to Mary. (= grammatical)
   The policeman explained Mary the law. (= ungrammatical)

B. Indicate whether the following sentences are grammatical or ungrammatical.
   1. They saved Mark a seat.
   2. His father read Kim a story.
   3. She donated the hospital some money.
   4. They suggested Mary a trip on the river.
   5. They reported the police the accident.
   6. They threw Mary a party.
   7. The bank lent Mr. Thatcher some money.
   8. He indicated Mary the right turning.
   9. The festival generated the college a lot of money.
   10. He cooked his girlfriend a cake.

C. Work out a rule for verbs like 'give' and 'explain'.
   1. List the verbs in B that are like 'give' (i.e. permit both sentence patterns) and those that are like 'explain' (i.e. allow only one sentence pattern).
   2. What is the difference between the verbs in your two lists?

(C4) Garden Path Strategies

Garden Path Strategies	inductive, overgeneralize → present disconfirming evidence → modify Ss' hypothesis

(C5) Input Processing Instruction

Processing instruction is a particular approach to teaching grammar that is based on how learners interpret and process input for meaning. This approach rests on the assumption that the role of input is central to language acquisition and that grammar can best be learned when learners attend to it in input-rich environments. Theoretically, the approach draws on a model of input processing developed by VanPatten and his colleagues. In this approach, an initial exposure to explicit instruction is combined with a series of input-processing activities that aim to help learners create form-meaning connections as they process grammar for meaning. Due to the explicit grammar component of processing instruction, some researchers have equated it with a focus on forms approach. However, VanPatten (2002) has argued that since the aim of this approach is "to assist the learner in making form-meaning connection during IP [input processing]; it is more appropriate to view it as a type of focus on form".

This approach can be a useful technique in helping learners to attend to form in the context of understanding message content. However, like any other instructional strategy, it has its own shortcomings and limitations. One of the limitations, for example, is that processing instruction can address only certain linguistic forms or constructions that have transparent form-meaning relationships. For example, it would be difficult to see how input processing tasks can be designed so that they can help learners to correctly process articles in English. Such forms have complex form-meaning relationships and also their understanding always depends on the context in which the form is used. Another limitation is that it does not require learners to produce output. This, of course, does not mean output is not essential or less important than input. VanPatten has warned that although processing instruction emphasizes the role of input, this does not negate the importance of output. Production may play a crucial role in the development of fluency, accuracy and automatization of various aspects of language. This suggests that to be fully effective, teaching grammar should involve learners with ample opportunities for both input and output. Therefore, we recommend that teachers should view processing instruction as only one of the options in their tool kit for teaching grammar. To increase its effectiveness, teachers should combine structured input activities with other classroom activities, including output and interactive tasks and corrective feedback on learner errors.

(C5a) Structured Input Activities

Classroom activities that are used in input-processing instruction are called **structured input**. They are so called because they are specifically designed to contain input that facilitates form-meaning connections. They are designed to force students to focus on the target structure and to process it for meaning. They are also designed to discourage learners from using processing strategies that negatively affect comprehension.

Structured input activities are of two main types: referential and affective (VanPatten 1996). Referential activities are activities for which there is always a right or wrong answer. For example, learners can be asked to choose between two noun phrases that have been associated with a drawing (e.g., a singular and a plural). In these activities there is a right or wrong answer, and the learners' right answers reveal that they have understood the meaning correctly. Affective activities are those that do not have any right or wrong answer. These activities require learners to provide an affective response by indicating their agreements or opinions about a set of events. For example, these could involve tasks that require learners to respond to what they have heard or read by checking boxes labeled 'agree' or 'disagree'. Classroom teachers can use these activities separately or in combination. Structured input activities can involve both oral and written activities.

1) Referential Activities

The following three activities provide examples of referential activities. The aim of the first two activities is to help learners with the acquisition of English past and future tenses, respectively. The third activity facilitates learning causative constructions. According to the input-processing model, learners prefer processing lexical items to morphological items. Since tenses in English can be marked both morphologically and lexically, learners may not process the morphological marker if the tense is also marked lexically with a time reference, such as an adverb of time. The goal of activity 1 is to push learners to process the morphological marker -ed, which they may not otherwise notice if the past adverbial is provided.

<Activity 1>

	Now	Before
1. The teacher corrected the essays.	☐	☐
2. The man cleaned the table.	☐	☐
3. I wake up at 5 in the morning.	☐	☐
4. The train leaves the station at 8 am.	☐	☐
5. The writer finished writing the book.	☐	☐
6. The trees go green in the spring.	☐	☐

Instruction: Listen to the following sentences and decide whether they describe an action that was done before or is usually done.

Activity 2 focuses on the English future tense. In this activity, the time referent has been omitted from the statements. Therefore, to process the tense of the sentence, the learner must pay attention to the morphological marker. Similar activities can be designed with a focus on other tenses.

<Activity 2>

Instruction: Read the following statements and decide whether the person is talking about what he currently does or what he will do when he retires.

	Now	Retirement
1. I meet new people.	☐	☐
2. I will travel a lot.	☐	☐
3. I will work hard.	☐	☐
4. I give money to charities.	☐	☐
5. I will be happy.	☐	☐
6. I am a role model.	☐	☐
7. I play soccer.	☐	☐
8. I will hold many parties.	☐	☐

One of the grammatical forms that may be difficult for English language learners is causative construction, sentences in which someone is caused to do something. Examples of such constructions include: "I had my students write an essay" and "I made the man clean the room." Since these sentences include two agents, according to the input processing model, students may always assign the role of the person who did the activity to the first noun. Therefore, they may have problems interpreting the statements accurately. For example, in the sentence "John had his student write an essay," students may incorrectly interpret it as "John wrote the essay." A structured input activity such as the following can be designed to help learners to interpret such statements accurately.

<Activity 3>

Students' instruction: Listen to each of the following sentences and then decide who is performing the action by checking the box.

The teacher's instructions: Read each sentence only once and then, after each sentence, ask for an answer. Do not wait until the end to review answers. Students do not repeat or otherwise produce the structure.

1. The girl made the man check the house for mice.
2. My dad made my brother babysit the children all night.
3. Mom let the boys go to three different circuses in one week.
4. The boss had the chef prepare several roast geese for the wedding dinner.
5. Jack let Joe collect some of the data required for our project.
6. The professor had the students create hypotheses for their science experiment.

1. Who checked the house for mice?	The girl ☐	The man ☐
2. Who babysat the children all night?	My dad ☐	My brother ☐
3. Who went to three different circuses in one week?	Mom ☐	The boys ☐
4. Who prepared several roast geese for the wedding dinner?	The boss ☐	The chef ☐
5. Who collected some of the data required for our project?	Jack ☐	Joe ☐
6. Who had the students create hypotheses for their science experiment?	The professor ☐	The students ☐

2) Affective Activities

The following two activities provide examples of affective activities. The aim of the first activity is to push students to process the present and past participle adjectives. The aim of the second activity is to help learners process the simple past tense. The activities can be conducted orally or in written forms.

<Activity 4>

Instruction: Read the following sentences and decide whether you agree with the statement.	Agree	Disagree
1. The book was boring.	☐	☐
2. I am bored when someone tells a joke.	☐	☐
3. People who gossip a lot are very irritating.	☐	☐
4. I get irritated with small talk.	☐	☐
5. It is interesting to talk about yourself.	☐	☐
6. The book was interesting.	☐	☐

<Activity 5>

Step 1: Read the following activities and indicate whether you did the same things over the weekend.

	Yes	No
1. I did my homework.	☐	☐
2. I watched TV.	☐	☐
3. I wrote a letter to my friend.	☐	☐
4. I had a birthday party.	☐	☐
5. I walked to the beach.	☐	☐
6. I cleaned my room.	☐	☐
7. I went downtown.	☐	☐
8. I rode my bike.	☐	☐

Step 2: Now form pairs and compare your responses with your classmate to see whether he or she did the same activities.

(C6) Dictation, Dicto-comp, & Dictogloss

Dictation	Dicto-comp	Dictogloss
form-based, exact reproduction	meaning-based, approximate reconstruction	
during dictation	after dictation	
individual work	individual-based work	group-based work

Before turning to the specific techniques, I would like to briefly consider the question of rationale: why might dictation, as a ***general method,*** be useful for teaching grammatical structures?

Oller's notion of a 'grammar of expectancy', which includes syntactic, semantic, and pragmatic knowledge, comes to mind immediately as one theoretical construct bearing directly on this question. A learner's expectancy grammar, according to Oller, is the nucleus of his or her predictive capacity, the ability to make sense of speech by 'continually formulating, modifying, and reformulating hypotheses about the underlying structure and meaning of input signals' (Oller 1978). Dictation obviously provides an excellent means of practising and improving this general capacity, as it encourages the learner to attend not only to the forms but also to the meanings — both semantic and pragmatic — of grammatical structures. Dictation thus promotes grammatical competence in a holistic fashion, not as an isolated component of the learner's overall proficiency. This approach accords with the modern view that the learning of grammatical forms must always occur in association with semantic and/or pragmatic factors, the latter including both sociolinguistic and discourse-related meanings (Larsen-Freeman 1991).

Other practical advantages could easily be added to this argument, but it is time to turn our attention to the two specific techniques promised earlier.

(C6a) Dicto-comp

The innovative procedure I would like to describe, called **dicto-comp**, introduces a radically different pattern: students must try to reproduce the passage on their own, ***after dictation is completed.*** This technique was first suggested by Wishon and Burks (1968). It can be used to provide practice in any structure, from simple to complex.

As a first step, the teacher selects (or makes up) a passage containing a number of instances of the structure to be practiced (e.g., any tense or combination of tenses; the passive voice; relative clauses). Students must already have been made aware, through previous instruction, of the form and meaning of the target structure, and in fact it is probably a good idea for the teacher to review the structure prior to the dictation and point out that it will be contained in the text.

The teacher then reads the dicto-comp three times, at a normal speed. The students listen but do not write until after the last dictation. After each of the first two readings, the students are allowed to ask questions about words or phrases that confuse them, and they can discuss the meaning of the passage. During these clarification sessions, the students should be allowed to jot down unfamiliar words, idioms, or expressions. The teacher should encourage as much communication as possible during the clarification phases, since complete understanding is crucial to the students' success in replicating the text. After the third and final reading, the students try to reproduce the original as accurately as possible. When they cannot remember the exact wording of a sentence, they should produce their best approximation. The teacher should remind them at this point to pay particular attention to reproducing all occurrences of the target structure. As a last step, some version of the correction phase can be carried out. Collaboration would certainly be a useful experience here, as students could compare and modify their individual versions of the text.

As a simple example, consider the following text, a modification of a passage in Wajnryb (1990), which is intended to provide practice in using the passive voice.

> Man is an enemy to many animals. Raccoons and foxes are trapped for their furs. Alligators are killed and their skins are used for purses and shoes. Elephants are destroyed for their ivory, which is used for jewelry. Whales are hunted for their oil. Whole species are being endangered for fashion!

An advantage to dicto-comp is that students are required to reproduce the target structure as part of a ***whole text*** which they ***understand.*** The meaning of this structure is therefore reinforced and internalized as a natural by-product of the task, as are discourse-related conditions on use.

(C6b) Dictogloss

The technique, called dictogloss, is the most sophisticated dictation variant and specifically designed to teach grammar. It resembles dicto-comp in that students are required to recreate the text following the dictation phase rather than during it, though the two techniques differ in a number of important respects. The dictogloss procedure contains four stages.

1. ***preparation***

    The teacher introduces the topic of the passage in some imaginative and interesting manner. This activates the students' background schema and promotes receptivity and comprehension. The teacher also pre-teaches any unfamiliar vocabulary items necessary in the text, and then organizes the students into groups of 3 or 4.

2. *dictation*

A short text containing a number of instances of the target structure (or structures) is read to the students twice at normal speed. During the first reading, the students do not write — they simply listen for meaning. On the second reading, they jot down important words and phrases that will ultimately help them to reconstruct the text. Content words are best for this purpose; function words should generally be ignored, as students will not have time to copy everything. (T should pause 2 or 3 seconds between sentences in the second reading.)

3. *reconstruction*

The students work in their small groups to produce their own written versions of the text. They pool the information they have written down and try to 'reconstruct a version of the text from their shared resources' (Wajnryb 1990). One student in each group acts a scribe, writing down the group's text as it emerges from discussion and negotiation. Both text interpretation and text reconstruction depend heavily on intragroup cooperation, and it is this collaborative aspect which most obviously distinguishes dictogloss from dicto-comp.

4. *analysis and correction*

The different group versions are examined and compared during the stage, with special attention devoted to the target structure(s). There are many ways of conducting this final phase. But whatever method is chosen by T, the students should be encouraged to *compare* the various versions and *discuss* the language choices made. By doing this, they will be led to understand the source of their errors, and (ideally at least) the resulting 'consciousness raising' will help to promote the internalization of the correct rules.

Before giving an example of this method, I must emphasize one crucial point about the students' task: the aim of a dictogloss activity is ***not*** for the students to reproduce the original text exactly. As Wajnryb observes, the objective is for each group of students to produce 'its own reconstructed version, aiming at grammatical accuracy and textual cohesion but not at replicating the original text'. Clearly, the dictation task under these conditions becomes an exercise in creative language production rather than a matter of mere imitation.

As an example of dictogloss, I offer the following intermediate level passage entitled "Koala Suicide" (Wajnryb 1990). The obvious target structure here is the past perfect tense, though other structures (e.g., past tense) are practised as well.

> A zoo-keeper in Japan has killed himself. His wife said that he had always taken his job very seriously. She told the police that he had recently been looking after four koalas in the zoo and that this responsibility had made him very anxious. She said he had been worried that the koalas might get sick, as this had happened at other zoos. The police statement said that the man hanged himself from a tree in the zoo.

Chapter 12 Mind Map

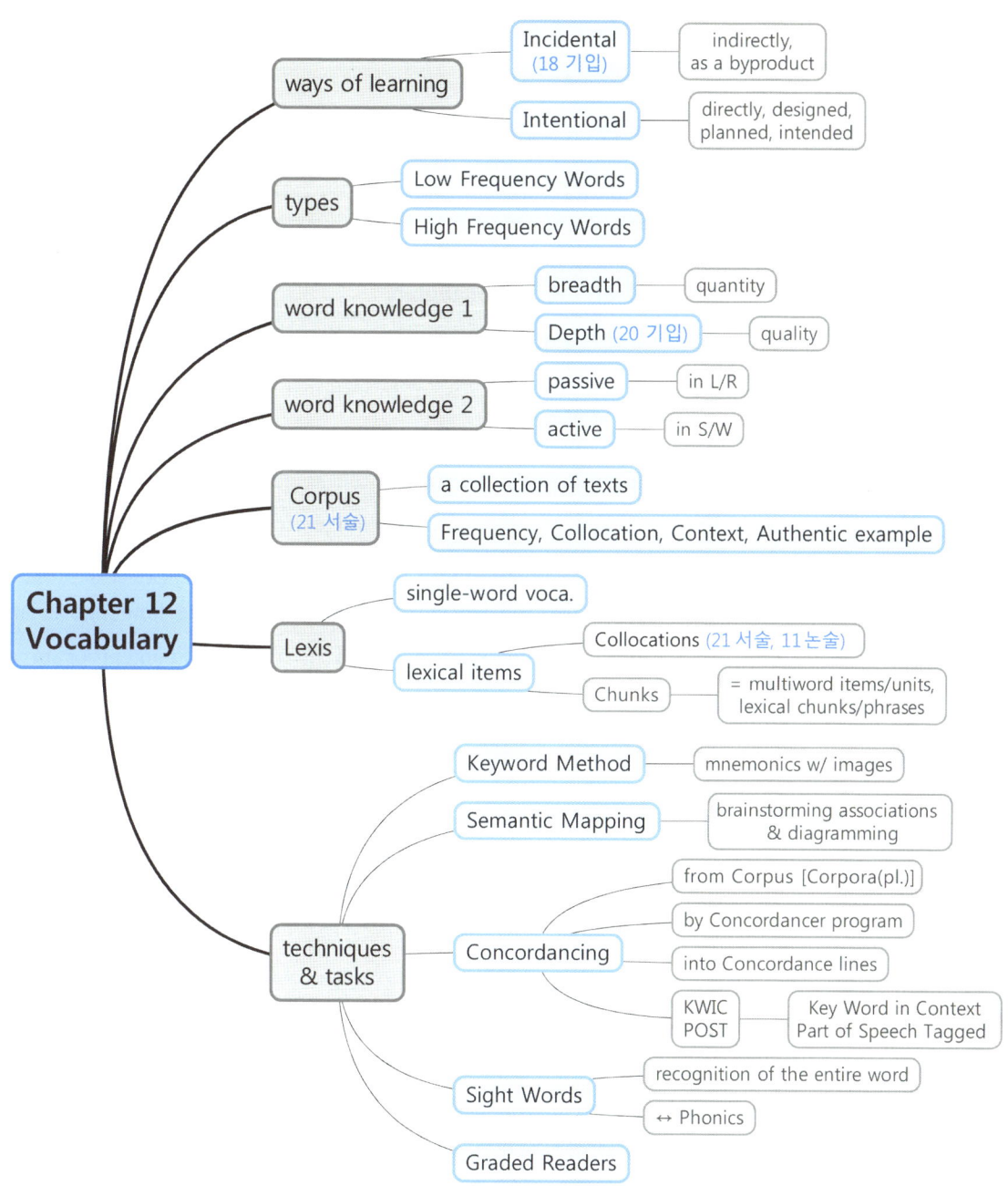

Chapter 12   Teaching Vocabulary

(A) Incidental vs. Intentional learning

Incidental learning	indirectly / as a byproduct
Intentional learning	directly / designed, planned, or intended

(A1) Implicit learning vs. Explicit learning of vocabulary

In support of the implicit learning of language, Wode (1999) states that in general, "A language is learned not for its own sake but as a by-product of a given individual's socialization process. That is, children acquire the language(s) of their environment as part of learning to cognize the world around them. Moreover, the socialization process is never completed because people need to adapt continuously to changes in their environment, even as adults. Such adaptation includes the acquisition and development of whatever language(s) the individual may be challenged to learn, regardless of whether or not the language is an L1, L2, or reacquisition, or whether a language is acquired in a natural context or in a classroom in which the language is the instructional medium. In this sense the acquisition of a language is incidental with respect to the situation in which it occurs because the language is not the primary object of the activity or process.".

Explicit learning is the specifically planned learning of a clearly specified form of knowledge in which the subject is overtly advised or even guided to strive and commit the specified element to memory. Intentional learning becomes explicit when the learners are clearly informed about what activity they are to perform and what objective(s) they are supposed to attain by the end of the activity, without any essential part whatsoever hidden or obscured. According to Hulstijn (2003), intentional learning occurs when the learner is clearly informed that he will be tested at the end of an activity (e.g. vocabulary), and it 'involves awareness at the point of learning by trying to understand what the function of a certain language form is'. DeKeyser (2003) defines it as a more explicit [overt] process whereby various mnemonics, heuristics and strategies are engaged to induce a representational system.

Both implicit and explicit modalities need to be balanced in teaching in general and in teaching vocabulary in particular. Ellis (1994) suggested that "diverse areas of research reveal that vocabulary acquisition neither depends solely on implicit learning, nor does it purely reflect explicit learning". The explicit mode consists of the study of decontextualized lexis for acquiring, consolidating and elaborating vocabulary, with the use of dictionaries and inferencing meaning from the local context. The implicit mode consists of meaning-focused reading that engages the development of vocabulary size and fluency from extensive reading and why not intensive reading as well! Researchers argue that, in teaching vocabulary, implicit teaching helps to maintain the target items over a longer period of time while the explicit teaching modality appears to negligibly favor immediate vocabulary retention without the advantage of maintaining the retained items longer over time.

(A2) Vocabulary Knowledge

(A2a) Depth of Vocabulary Knowledge

Vocabulary depth can be defined as how well a learner knows a word. Comparing with vocabulary breadth, we view vocabulary depth as the quality of words rather than quantity. Qian (1998) refined the theoretical frameworks of Richard's and Nation's to clarify the vital components of vocabulary depth including pronunciation and spelling, morphological properties, syntactic properties, meaning, register, and frequency as follows.

Firstly, phonetically and phonologically, to be familiar with phonemes and their combination in words meant the ability to master the pronunciation of words. The concept of places of articulation, manners of articulation, the permissible combinations of phonetic inventory, and supra-segmental factors were all involved in this domain.

Secondly, morphology was to explore the formation of a word. The concept relative to word root, derivational and inflectional morphemes, and part of speech all belonged to morphological properties. Besides, the word coinages such as compounds, abbreviations, acronyms, blending, and conversion were related to the derivational combination of a single word.

Thirdly, a syntax domain was to discuss the internal structure of a sentence including word's collectability, its possible position in a sentence, and its syntagmatic relations with other words in a given context, so the concept of lexical constituent and grammatical category were the main focus.

Fourthly, the concept of word meaning contains both semantic and pragmatic knowledge. For example, the concept of polysemy, synonym and antonym were categorized in lexical semantics, while in the pragmatic aspect, the focus was on how to appropriately use a word with respect to its appearing context, which could be discussed from both a linguistic context and situational context.

Fifthly, register and discourse features were to discuss the social and regional differences of language use and the application of a word. Hence, the social appropriateness of using a word was the main focus in this aspect.

Finally, the concept of word frequency was to analyze the use of common and uncommon words in given contexts. That is, it was to concern the popularity of given words.

To sum up, we could know that vocabulary can be examined from micro to macro continuum. When we use a word, we exercise our knowledge of each aspect to reach a particular purpose. Furthermore, an examination of the theoretical foundations mentioned enables us to recognize that the dimension of vocabulary was multifaceted, and that each dimension was closely interrelated.

(A2b) Dimension of Vocabulary Knowledge

Knowing a word could mean being capable of recognizing and using these factors and applying words to meet different purposes. Using the ideas of partial precise knowledge, depth of vocabulary knowledge, and receptive and productive knowledge, Henriksen (1999) generated three underlying assumptions to define vocabulary knowledge, and she also believed these three dimensions demonstrated an upgrading status of vocabulary learning. The first assumption was that lexical knowledge of a person should function as a competence to provide translation equivalents, to find the correct explanation in multiple-choice tasks, and to paraphrase target words. The second assumption indicated that the components of vocabulary depth should cover both **paradigmatic** and **syntagmatic** knowledge. The former involved a shift of the word meaning in an antonymy, synonymy, hyponymy, and gradation, and the latter dealt with collocation restrictions of words. The third assumption suggested that word knowledge should consist of a receptive and productive aspect. Receptive performance stood for reading and listening ability while productive ability meant writing and speaking.

(A2c) Procedural vocabulary

Procedural vocabulary refers to vocabulary used to explain other words, to structure and organize their meaning. Robinson (1988) gives an excellent example in two dictionary entries (Longman Dictionary of Contemporary English 1978):

> **ver·mic·u·lite** /vɜːˈmɪkjʊlaɪt‖vɜrˈmɪkjə-/ *n* [U] a type of MICA that is a very light material made up of threadlike parts, that can be used for keeping heat inside buildings, growing seeds in, etc.
> **ver·mi·form** /ˈvɜːmɪfɔːm‖ˈvɜrmɪfɔrm/ *adj* shaped rather like a worm

The key vocabulary here is 'type', 'material', 'made up', 'parts', 'used', 'keep', 'shaped', and 'like'. These words, we may note, are ***core words*** and are higher order superordinates; these, and many other superordinate and general words like them, are highly useful not only in ***talking about*** specific words like 'vermiculite' but also in the cognitive process of categorizing and organizing features of meaning relative to other, known entities. Thus 'vermiculite' is crucially ***a material, made up*** of ***a, b, c, used*** for ***x, y, z***; it is a ***type*** of something too. All our key words in these definitions are part of the procedural vocabulary enabling us to talk about and conceptualize the relationships between items and between fields, and to locate items within fields as we acquire them.

Classroom data provides us with good examples of how students and teachers interact when new words and meanings are being discussed. Note how in this example from Pender's (1988) data, core items ('spare time', 'free time') are used by the teacher and a student to establish the meaning of the non-core 'leisure':

> T: Leisure is what?
> S: Spare time
> S: Leisure are some activities that we do with leisure, no? For example, for use, for example, for me dancing is a leisure activity, no?
> T: Well it would be. It would be an activity that you do in your leisure time or your free time at your leisure
> S: And that you like, no?
> T: Well, when you speak of leisure you're, you're speaking of free time away from your work, when you want to do something that you like ...

The use of procedural vocabulary is fundamental to the strategies of definition and paraphrase; procedural words establish basic cognitive categories for words (type, size, colour, material, dimensions, intensity, etc.), and those used in dictionaries for this purpose are also found in the class. Learners at all levels will need to confront the procedural lexicon of the language they are learning.

(B) Corpora

A **corpus** (pl. **corpora**) is a database of real language as it has been said or written by people in conversations or other genres. You can use this to research how language is really used (as opposed to how we might think it is used) by typing in word or phrase and seeing lots of examples from the database. There are many corpora available. At the time of writing, the British National Corpus was freely available for research at: http://corpus.byu.edu/bnc/. I wanted to find out whether ***different from*** was more common than ***different to***. Entering each of these phrases into the BNC told me that ***different from*** had 3,278 entries while ***different to*** had only 483. I was, of course, then able to examine all those entries to find out more about how each was used. A 'dirty', instant, free corpus-like experience can be gained by simply entering a search term into Google! ***Different from*** = 81,500,000 entries. ***Different to*** = 5,240,000 entries.

(C) Lexis

Lexis	single-word voca.	ex) dog, green, wash	lexical items
	Collocations	ex) pass the exam	
	Chunks	(= multiword items/units, lexical chunks/phrases) ex) it's up to you	

(C1) Multi-word Units

When words are not joined to form compounds, we have seen that groups of more than one word, such as 'bits and pieces, do up, look for', can function as a meaningful unit with a fixed or semi-fixed form. Technically these are known as **multi-word units**, but they are often called simply **lexical chunks**. For example, in the following extract (in which two workers are discussing the Australian car industry — a Holden is an Australian car) the lexical chunks are in italics:

> Keith: *It's amazing how* the bleeding car industry's *swung round.* It's Holdens *for years* and now Fords have got it. *Well and truly.* [...] *Year after year* they're *laying* more *off* towards *the end of the year* so they knew this was coming — it wasn't *out of the blue*.
>
> Jo: I think that they shipped *a lot of* the accessory overseas too. Before they did *a lot of the bits and pieces* themselves.

The chunks vary in terms of how fixed, and how idiomatic, they are. For example, **out of the blue** is both idiomatic (that is to say, its meaning is not easily recoverable from its individual components) and fixed — you can't say **from the blue** or **out of the green**, for example. **Well and truly** and **bits and pieces** are also fixed, but less idiomatic. **Year after year**, on the other hand, is only semi-fixed. It allows a limited amount of manipulations: we can say **month after month** and **day after day**. Note that both **a lot of** and **for years** are typical of the enormous number of chunks that are used to express vague quantities and qualities: **loads of, that sort of thing, more or less, now and again**.

To handle the fact that there are multi-word items that behave like single words, the term **lexeme** was coined. A lexeme is a word or group of words that function as a single meaning unit. For example, in the sentence "I like looking for bits and pieces like old second-hand record players and doing them up to look like new.", we could count **looking for, bits and pieces, record players, doing ... up**, and **to look** as single lexemes, along with **I, like, old, them**, etc.

(C2) Collocations

Unlike compounds or multi-word units, there is a looser kind of association called **collocation**. Two words are collocates if they occur together with more than chance frequency, such that, when we see one, we can make a fairly safe bet that the other is in the neighborhood. The availability of corpus data now allows us to check the statistical probability of two words co-occurring. The most frequent collocate of **record**, for example, is **world**. Another is **set**.

Collocation is not as frozen a relationship as that of compounds or multi-word units, and two collocates may not even occur next to each other — they may be separated by one or more other words. **Set**, for example, is the second most frequent collocate of **record** but it seldom occurs right next to it: ***He set the junior record in 1990.*** Notice that ***set*** and ***record*** can also collocate in quite a different sense: ***Just to set the record straight*** .... In fact ***set the record straight*** is such a strong collocation that it almost has the status of a chunk, and indeed it gets a separate entry (under ***record***) in dictionaries, as do some other strong collocates with ***record***, such as ***for the record, off the record*** and ***on record***.

Collocation, then, is best seen as part of a continuum of strength of association: a continuum that moves from compound words (***second-hand, record player***), through multi-word units — or lexical chunks — (***bits and pieces***), including idioms (***out of the blue***) and phrasal verbs (***do up***), to collocations of more or less fixedness (***set the record straight, set a new world record***).

Here is a text with some of its more frequent collocations underlined, while the more fixed multi-word units are in italics:

> A record number of 54 teams will be competing in three sections as the Bryants Carpets Intermediate Snooker League *gets underway* this week. Once again all three sections *are likely to* be very closely contested. In Section A, defending champions Mariner Automatics, captained once again by the most successful skipper in the league, John Stevens, will be *the team to beat*.

It should be clear from this passage the extent to which word choice is heavily constrained by what comes before and after. This is perhaps the single most elusive aspect of the lexical system and the hardest, therefore, for learners to acquire. Even the slightest adjustments to the collocations — by substituting one of its components for a near synonym (underlined) — turns the text into non-standard English:

> A record lot of 54 teams will be competing in three sections as the Bryants Carpets Intermediate Snooker League reaches underway that week. One time again all three sections are possibly to be very nearly contested...

(D) Techniques and Tasks in teaching vocabulary

keyword method	a mnemonic technique using pronunciation and image
semantic mapping	brainstorming association & diagramming the results
concordancing	a process of looking at relationships among words, KWIC/POST
sight words	bottom-up, recognizing an entire word (↔ phonics: sounding out the word)
graded readers	with limited vocabulary, for extensive R, R for pleasure

⟨Keyword Method⟩

The **keyword method** of vocabulary acquisition is a two-step mnemo-technic for learning vocabulary terms. The first step, the acoustic link, generates a keyword based on the sound of the foreign word. The second step, the imagery link, ties the keyword to the meaning of the item to be learned, via an interactive visual image or other association. Say, for example, that the keyword method is used to learn the Korean term, 'p'osu', meaning gunner. The first step is to generate a keyword, for example 'poor Sue'. The second step is to link this keyword to the memory by an image, say a mental picture of poor Sue, the gunner. Although this technique may seem involved, other research has indicated it is effective.

⟨Concordancing⟩

The term **corpus** refers to a computerized database consisting of hundreds of millions of words of authentic texts and spoken transcripts, usually with the **parts of speech tagged** (**POST**). It is searched by a **concordancer**, a software program designed to analyze corpora for every occurrence of a key word or phrase, and to display the results either alphabetically or on the basis of frequency. This display is known as a **concordance** and it is usually presented in **KWIC** (**key word in context**) format in which every instance of the target structure is centered and bolded on a separate line with a number of words displayed before and after the item. The following concordance-based activity from Thornbury (1999) shows an example of how to use concordances to help learners understand the correct uses of lexical items such as *remember, forget,* and *stop*. The number of examples shown has been cut to three each, but at least 12 is recommended to show the variety of usages. The sample activity 'Using Corpora to Encourage Learners to Focus on Grammar' follows.

Instructions

The teacher divides the class into three groups (A, B, and C), and gives each group a different set of concordance lines as shown below. The groups are told to study their lines, and divide them into two patterns. If they find this difficult, they should be told to look at the form of the verb that immediately follows the word in the central column of each set of lines and try to discover the differences. If possible, they should formulate a grammar rule.

Group A: Remember

Yanto, thoughtfully. On the other hand, **remember** seeing them dancing together at a ball shortly before the month's Top to Tail if you own a poodle. **Remember** to listen out for Katie and friends on Radio 2. Should you there wasn't anyone to see me go. **remember** thinking how white and cold her face looked, with

Group B: Forget

the United States government last year announced that those who **forget** to flush public toilets will be fined up to US dollars. Results frothy fronds lit up by evening sun. I'll never **forget** seeing your Grandfather for the first time. I couldn't believe acting inspector over the weekend. I'll never **forget** being in hospital.

Group C: Stop

probably tense, listening. At the age of twelve, Bailey **stopped** eating meat. Although he had already taken his mouthful though Anna was sure her mother had not **stopped** having baths or using perfume. Annabel was determined asthma? And it was two o'clock when they **stopped** talking, they stopped having their break! Results

Chapter 13 Mind Map

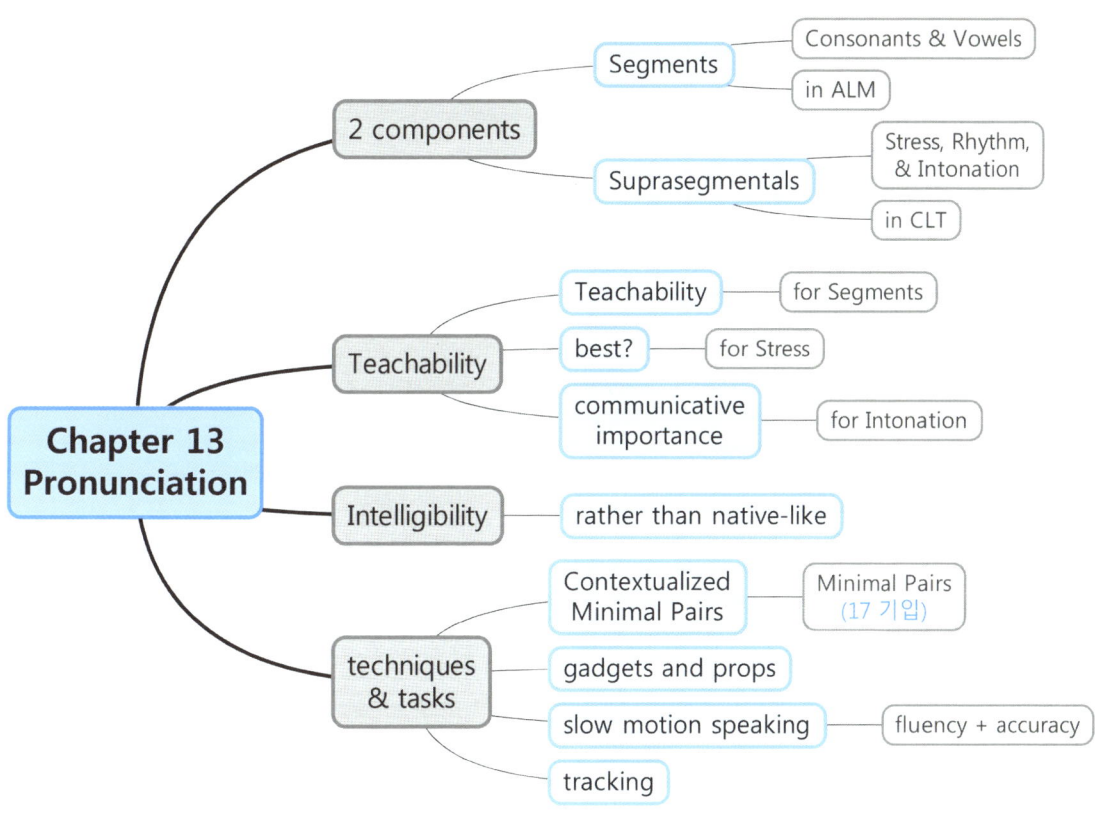

Chapter 13 Teaching Pronunciation

(A) Segments & Suprasegmentals

segments	consonants & vowels
suprasegmentals	stress, rhythm, & intonation

(B) Teachability issues in pronunciation

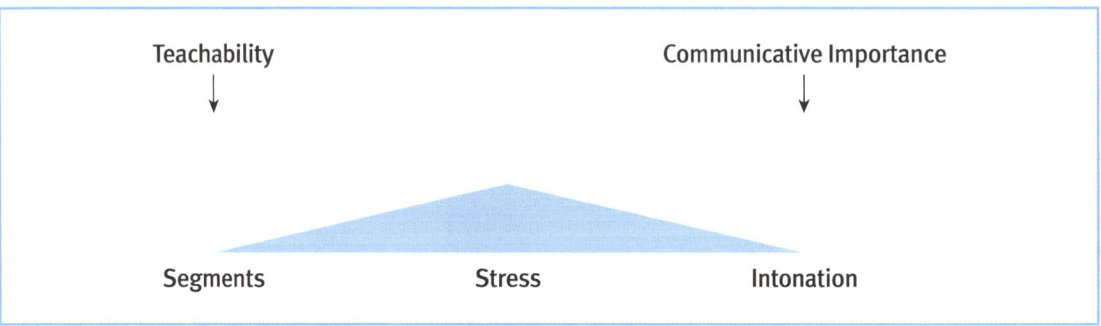

(C) Intelligibility issues in pronunciation

intelligibility	understandability rather than native-like pronunciation

(C1) Integrated pronunciation teaching

Of all the skills that complement listening, pronunciation has arguably the closest link. Every focus on every aspect of pronunciation is also a focus on listening. Students need to know the way sounds change in connected speech — elision, assimilation — in order to improve their listening as well as their speaking. Sensitivity to rhythm and stress patterns — traditionally seen as aspects of pronunciation — is vital for listeners. Approximately 80 per cent of multisyllable content words in English are stressed on the first syllable. Native listeners use this knowledge subconsciously to perceive word boundaries — where words begin and end. This perception may not be available to non-native listeners unless they have a strong affinity with the rhythms of English. From before we are born, we hear, and possibly feel, the rhythms of our native language. Thereafter, we often subconsciously assume that this rhythm fits all languages. It doesn't. In English, the stressed syllables are up to three times as long as the unstressed syllables. In Italian and Spanish, the stressed syllables are only 1.5 times as long as the unstressed. For this reason, much early teaching of listening and pronunciation needs to be concerned with getting native speakers experience in understanding speakers whose first language is not English.

In addition to these two points — rhythm, and the way sounds change in connected speech — intonation is also a listening issue. It affects the meaning of an utterance. For example, intonation alerts us to the mood or attitude of the speaker, and also tells us, via a falling pitch when the speaker has finished.

In summary, the many facets of pronunciation affect our ability to listen and comprehend. It follows logically that the teaching of pronunciation and listening needs to be integrated.

(D) Techniques and tasks in teaching pronunciation

Contextualized Minimal Pairs	minimal pairs w/ pictures or drawing
Gadgets and Props	e.g. rubber bands and balls for teaching suprasegmentals
Slow Motion Speaking	imitating T' slowed-down pronunciation
Tracking	speaking concurrently with the voices of the recording

최지현 **전공영어 영어교육학 PRACTICAL**

Chapter 14 Mind Map

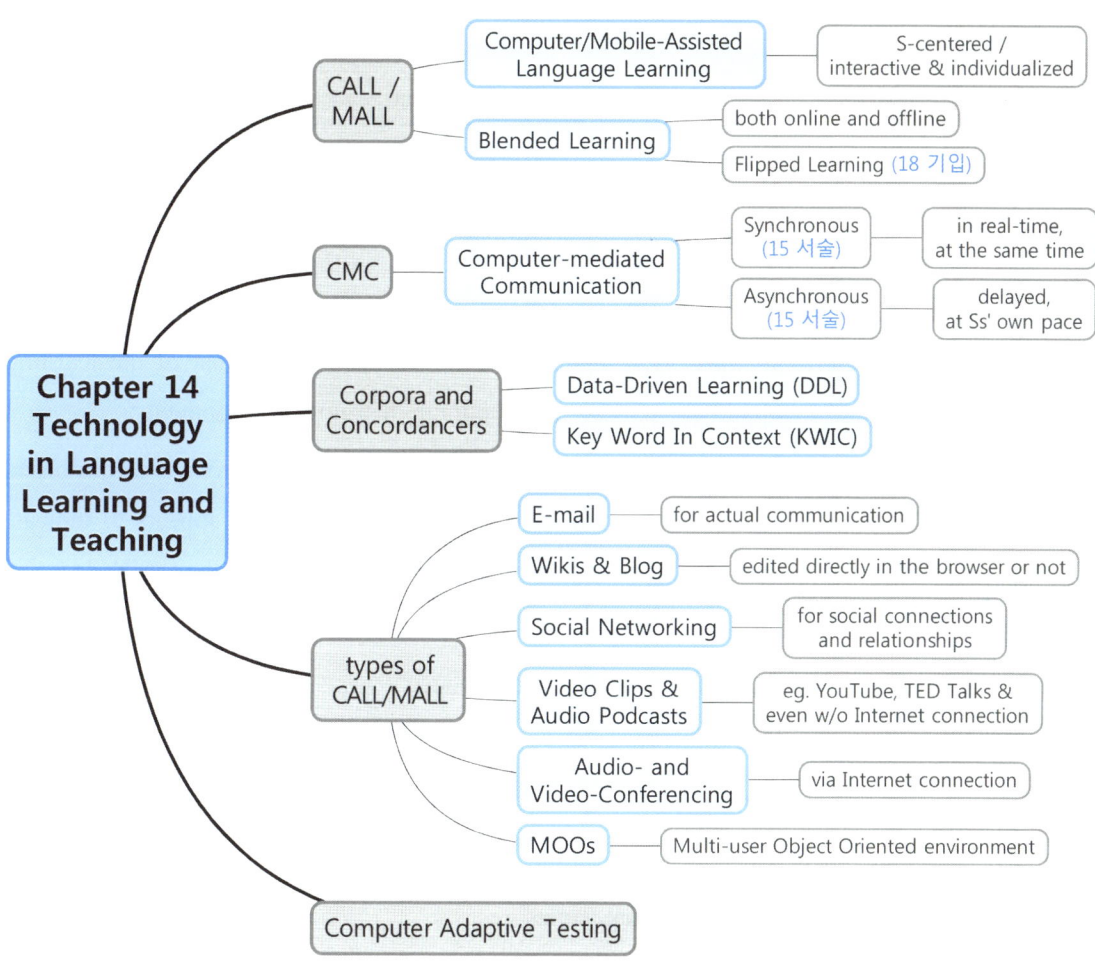

Chapter 14: Technology in Language Learning and Teaching

(A) CALL & MALL

CALL / MALL	S-centered / interactive & individualized (↔ CALI)
Blended Learning	CALL/MALL + face-to-face learning
Flipped Learning	a model of blended learning

‹Blended Learning›

Today **blended learning** can refer to any combination of different methods of learning, different learning environments, different learning styles. In short, the effective implementation of blended learning is essentially all about making the most of the learning opportunities and tools available to achieve the 'optimal' learning environment.

Blended language learning (i.e., integrating the use of technology into classroom-based learning and teaching) is still a relatively new concept, but recent research appears to indicate that when 'appropriately' implemented, blended learning can significantly improve the learning experience. The following strengths of blended language learning have been identified.

- provides a more individualized learning experience
- provides more personalized learning support
- supports and encourages independent and collaborative learning
- increases student engagement in learning
- accommodates a variety of learning styles
- provides a place to practice the target language beyond the classroom
- provides a less stressful practice environment for the target language
- provides flexible study, anytime or anywhere, to meet learners' needs
- helps students develop valuable and necessary twenty-first century learning skills

<Flipped Learning>

Most ELT classes are not teacher centered. Students are often working in groups and pairs and teachers are aware of the need to get students to communicate and use the language. This is largely due to the impact of Communicative Language Teaching. In other classes teachers may even be using discovery techniques and inductive/deductive approaches to learning as well as task based approaches. In reality then, in ELT we already flip our classes to a certain degree.

That doesn't mean that the Flipped Classroom doesn't have a place in ELT. We don't have to flip all our classes, but the model could be useful for certain lessons or certain part of the syllabus. For example, we often need to teach grammar, explain different writing genres, or focus on the construction of paragraphs. A lot of this 'teaching stuff' could be put on-line so that the teacher is able to spend more time in the class getting the students to use what has been taught via the homework.

For example, let's imagine that we are looking at the construction of paragraphs. We could make a video/screen cast that explains to students how a paragraph is normally made up. It might include an explanation of what a subject sentence is and how it should be supported by the rest of the paragraph. Perhaps there is also a simple quiz that the students have to do to check understanding after they watch the video. In class, the students are giving a series of paragraphs where the sentences have all been mixed up. The students work in groups and order the sentences, making sure the topic sentence is at the start of the paragraph. They then have a second exercise where they have been provided with a topic sentence but are asked to write the rest of the paragraph in groups. The different groups could then present their answers to the second exercise to the rest of the group. The idea is that in the class time the students are applying and using their knowledge. The teacher's role would be to move around providing support, making sure the students clearly understand the task, etc. The lesson may even include time for reflection on the task itself.

<Data-driven learning>

Computer Assisted Language Learning (CALL), among many other applications, includes the use of language corpora, where learners get hands-on experience of using a corpus through guided tasks or through materials based on corpus evidence, such as concordance lines on handouts. Here an inductive approach relies on an 'ability to see patterning in the target language and to form generalisations' about language form and use. This activity is commonly referred to as 'data-driven learning' (DDL) after Johns. Johns sees DDL as a process which 'confront(s) the learner as directly as possible with the data', 'to make the learner a linguistic researcher' where 'every student is Sherlock Holmes'. Over the years Johns, among others, has developed the idea and contributed many teaching materials based on the DDL approach.

Empirical studies on the learning benefits of DDL are relatively few, but they do show positive results. Cobb reports on his longitudinal study of vocabulary acquisition using concordance line tasks (see for example Cobb 1997). This study provides interesting examples (with screen shots) of a variety of sequential DDL activities which draw on a specially designed corpus of 10,000 words (comprised of 20 texts of about 500 words each, assembled from the students' reading materials). The following figure shows the opening task:

<Example of DDL task from Cobb (1997)>

Part 1: Choosing a meaning. The learner is presented with a small concordance of four to seven lines, in KWIC format with the to-be-learned word at the centre, and uses this information to select a suitable short definition for the word from one correct and three randomly generated choices.

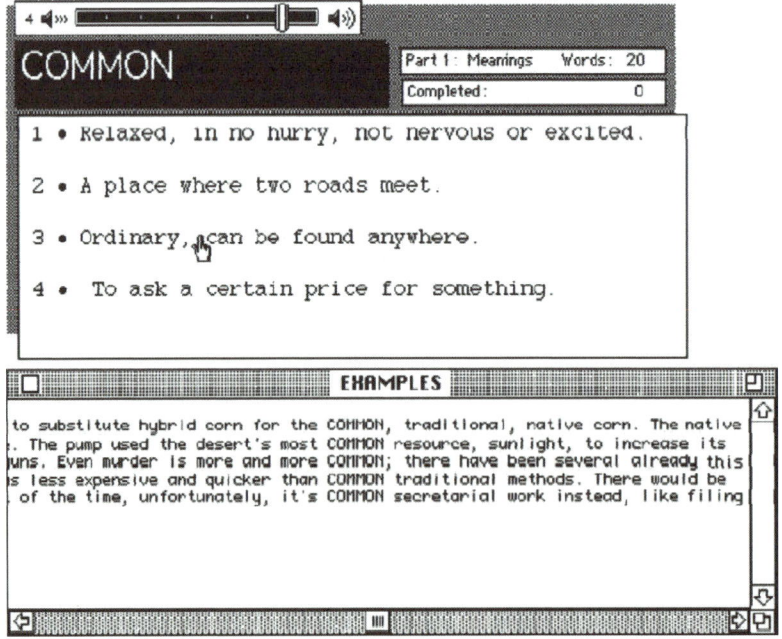

(B) CMC (= Computer-mediated Communication)

(B1) Synchronous vs. Asynchronous communication

Synchronous	in real-time, at the same time	web conferencing, MOOs ...
Asynchronous	delayed, at students' own pace	e-mail, Wikis, Blog ...

(C) Types of CALL Activities

E-mail	for actual communication with individuals around the world
Wikis	websites with multiple hyperlinked pages, edited directly in the browser
Blog	websites with multiple hyperlinked pages, constructed by an individual
Social Networking	for social connections and relationships both online and offline
Video Clips	e.g. YouTube, TED Talks
Audio Podcast	used as authentic listening materials w/o Internet connection
Web Conferencing	(= Audio- and Video-Conferencing) via Internet connection
MOOs	(= Multi-User Object Oriented Environment) text-based Virtual Reality

(D) Corpora and Concordancers

Corpus (pl. Corpora)	authentic discourse data
Concordancing	searching for words in context and collocations
Concordancer	a computer program that automatically constructs a concordance
Concordance (line)	a comprehensive index of the words used in a corpus
KWIC (= key word in context)	the keyword is shown highlighted in the middle of the display, with the text forming its context on either side
POST (= part of speech tagged)	a special label assigned to each word in a corpus to indicate the part of speech and other grammatical categories

Concordancing is a core tool in corpus linguistics and it simply means using corpus software to find every occurrence of a particular word or phrase. This idea is not a new one and many scholars over the years have manually concordanced the Christian Bible, for example, painstakingly finding and recording every example of certain words. With a computer, we can now search millions of words in seconds. The search word or phrase is often referred to as the 'node' and concordance lines are usually presented with the node word/phrase in the centre of the line with seven or eight words presented at either side. These are known as **Key-Word-In-Context** displays (or **KWIC** concordances). Concordance lines are usually scanned vertically at first glance, that is, looked at up or down the central pattern, along the line of the node word or phrase. Initially, this may be disconcerting because we are accustomed, in Western cultures, to reading from left to right. Concordance lines challenge us to read in an entirely new way, vertically, or even from the centre outwards in both directions. Here are some sample lines from a concordance of the word ***way*** using the Limerick Corpus of Irish English (LCIE):

```
ether in northern Ireland is no different in a way then em what they were desperately
           you see it? Some of you anyhow? Now in a way 'What Dreams may come' it's not
           subject to study in college in fact it's a way of life and you find this right
        and how could he present things in such a way that he would persuade people.
ul and the purpose of life is to live in such a way that when you die your soul is
    t he was obviously he obviously lived a certain way of live and they wanted to know
    lem that they had to deal with in a different way they couldn't deal with it by
    asically in football stadium that's the easiest way to describe it. There is a large
        sking for you ok I find this the most effective way. Ok now today em you have as well
        speculative because there is no evidence either way. You can't have evidence about
        e theologian starts from the top and works his way down. The theologian will have
        rts from the ground so it speaks and works its way up. The theologian starts from
```

<Concordance lines for *way* from LCIE>

Most software allows the number of words at either side of the node word or phrase to be adjusted to allow more of the context to be viewed and you can usually go back very easily and quickly to the source file containing the full text or transcript. Software normally facilitates the sorting of the concordance lines so that we can examine the lexico- grammatical patterns which occur before and/or after the node word.

Because concordance lines can provide many examples of patterns of use, they have application to the language classroom and are now being used in ELT materials. For example, here is an extract from the entry on ***there*** in ***Natural Grammar*** (Thornbury 2004), where concordance lines have been adapted for an inductive grammar task:

Exercises

1 Look at these concordance lines, and identify the meaning of *there* in each case. Is it a pronoun (showing that something exists) or is it an adverb (saying where something is)?

a **There**'s a bar and a lecture room for guests' use.
b **There**'d been another quake at 4am, a 6.5 shock.
c It was only in my third year that I really felt happy **there**.
d You say **there**'s a certain amount of risk. How much?
e I was **there** for her birth and it was the most exciting thing.
f But **there**'ll be no alcohol on sale.
g He was standing **there** with Mrs Kasmin as she tried to give him tea.
h He had been **there** since he left the Pit a year earlier.
i He was confident **there**'d be no problem. So was I.

<Extract from *Natural Grammar* (Thornbury 2004)>

Another example is found in McCarthy and O'Dell (2002), where students are invited to look at an extract from a concordance for the word *eye* and to decide which of the occurrences are idiomatic/metaphorical.

50.4 Here are some random examples from a computer database containing lines from real conversations. The figures in diamond brackets, e.g. <s1>, <s2>, mean 'first speaker', 'second speaker', etc. How many of the examples use *eye* as an idiom, and how many use the word *eye* in its literal sense as 'the organ we see with'? Use a dictionary if necessary.

1	go into town and get erm an **eye** test. <s1> Mm. <s2> In town.
2	you er keep an **eye** out for tramps, do you then?
3	In your mind's **eye** how are you going to do that?
4	<s1> So I'll keep a general **eye** on it. And er <s3> Yeah
5	<s1> There's something in my **eye**. There's that thing floating
6	difficult to put that to your **eye**. You also have to have one eye
7	good offer? <s2> Yeah it caught my **eye** <s1> Yeah it's
8	I'm casting my **eye** over this form and I think
9	this year. <s4> Just keep an **eye** out for it. <s4> Yeah.
10	<s2> You'll have to keep an **eye** on her. <s1> Yeah. <s2> Oh my
11	so you're about **eye** level with the monitor.
12	saw her out of the corner of my **eye**. <s3> Her lipstick is all over

<Extract from *English Idioms in Use* (McCarthy and O'Dell 2002)>

(E) Computer Adaptive Testing

| Computer Adaptive Testing | computer-based tests that adapt to the examinee's ability level |

최시원 **전공영어 영어교육학 PRACTICAL**

Chapter 15 Mind Map

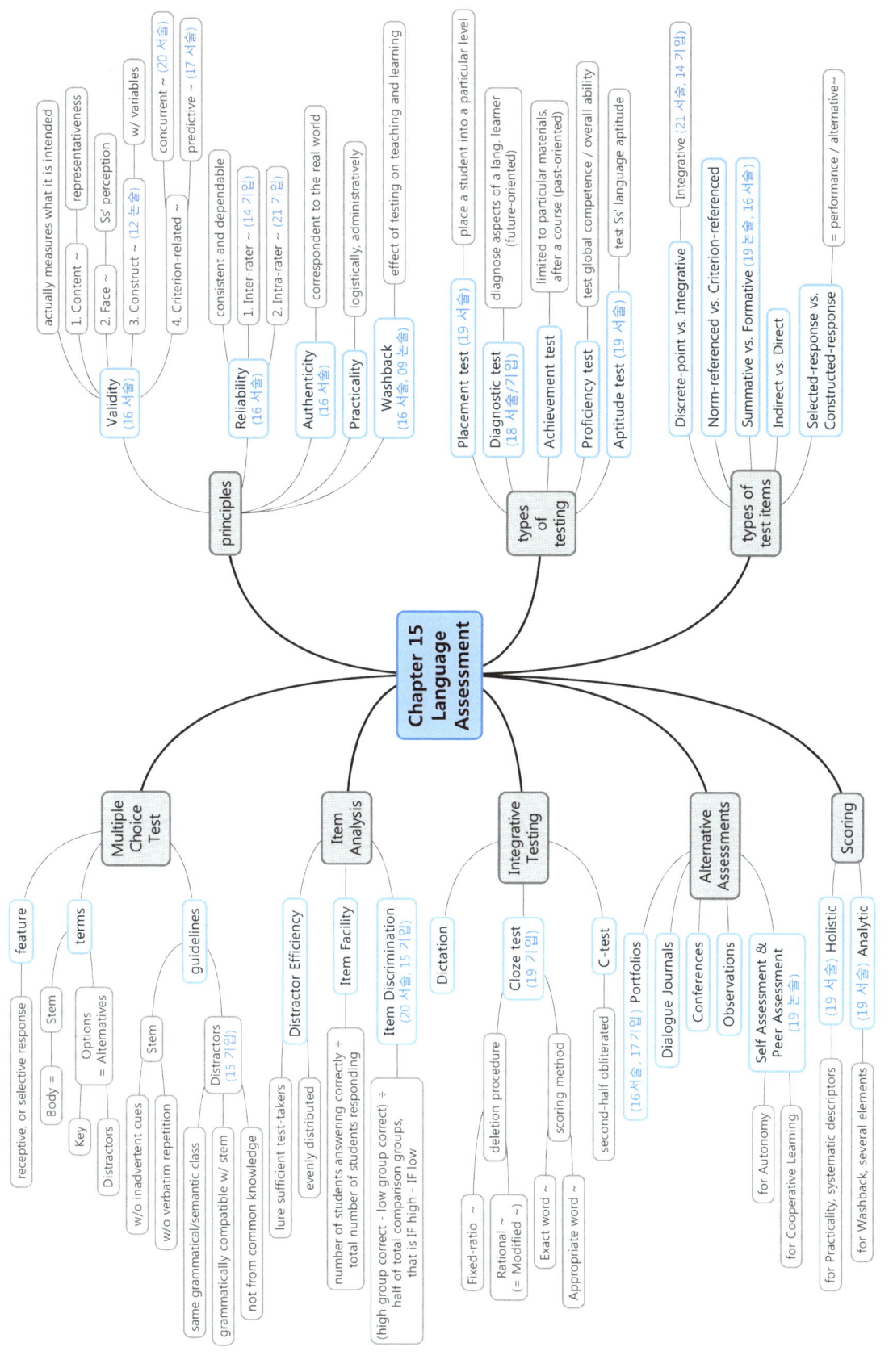

Chapter 15   Language Assessment

(A) Principles of Language Tests

	Validity	actually measuring what it is intended
	Reliability	consistent and dependable
	Authenticity	correspondent to the real world
	Practicality	logistically, administratively
	Washback	the effect of testing on teaching and learning

Content validity		the representativeness of the test
Face validity		the participants' perceptions of the test
Construct validity		measuring the underlying construct, the higher level concepts
Criterion-related validity	Concurrent ~	supported by other concurrent performance beyond the test
	Predictive ~	assessing a test-taker's likelihood of future success

Inter-rater reliability	Two or more scorers yield consistent scores of the same test.
Intra-rater reliability	One scorer yields consistent scores in different situations.

⟨The framework of test usefulness⟩

According to Bachman and Palmer (1996), a model of test usefulness should include such qualities as reliability, construct validity, authenticity, interactiveness, impact and practicality.

> Usefulness = Reliability + Construct validity + Authenticity + Interactiveness + Impact + Practicality

1) Test reliability

Test **reliability** refers to the consistency of scores on a test despite the varied occasions in which the test is administered. Bachman and Palmer (1996) highlight that reliability can be considered as a function of the consistency of scores from one set of tests and test tasks to another.

An important reason to be concerned with reliability is that it is a forerunner to test validity. That is, if test scores cannot be assigned consistently, it is impossible to conclude that the scores accurately measure the domain of interest. Ultimately, validity is the aspect about which we are most concerned. However, formally assessing the validity of a specific use of a test can be a laborious and time-consuming process. Therefore, reliability analysis is often viewed as a first-step in the test validation process. If the test is unreliable, one need not spend the time investigating whether it is valid — it will not be. If the test has adequate reliability, however, then a validation study would be worthwhile.

2) Test validity

Test validity pertains to the degree to which the test actually measures what it claims to measure. It is also the extent to which interpretations made on the basis of test scores are appropriate and meaningful. According to Hughes (2003), a test is considered to be valid if it measures accurately what it is intended to measure. If test scores are affected by other abilities rather than the one we want to measure, they will not be the satisfactory interpretation of the particular ability.

Language tests are created in order to measure a specific ability, such as 'reading ability', or 'fluency in speaking', which is referred to as a **construct**, on which a given test or test task is based which is used for interpreting scores. The term construct validity is therefore used to refer to the general notion of validity, and the extent to which we can interpret a given test score as an indicator of the ability(ies), or construct(s) that we want to measure.

2.1) Content validity

Content validity is one type of evidence which demonstrates that a particular interpretation of test scores is justified. A test is said to have content validity if its content constitutes a representative sample of the language skills, structures and so on, with which it is meant to be concerned. Moreover, the sample is expected to be representative so that it appeals to the purpose of the test. Therefore, a specification of the skills or structures, etc., which the test is meant to cover is needed for the purpose. The specification will provide the test constructor with the basis for making a principled selection of elements for inclusion in the test (Hughes 2003). A comparison of test specification and test content is the basis for judgments as to content validity. Thus, whenever feasible, use direct testing. If for some reason it is decided that indirect testing is necessary, reference should be made to the research literature to confirm that measurement of the relevant underlying constructs has been demonstrated using the testing techniques that are to be employed.

2.2) The relationship of reliability and validity

The primary purpose of a language test is to provide a measure that we can interpret as an indicator of an individual's language ability. The two measurement qualities, reliability and construct validity, are thus essential to the usefulness of any language test. Reliability is a necessary condition for construct validity, and hence for usefulness. However, reliability is not a sufficient condition for either construct validity or usefulness. Suppose, for example, that we needed a test for placing individuals into different levels in an academic writing course. A multiple-choice test of grammatical knowledge might yield very consistent or reliable scores, but this would not be sufficient to justify using this test as a placement test for a writing course. This is because grammatical knowledge is only one aspect of the ability to use language to perform academic writing tasks. In this case, defining the construct to include only one area of language knowledge is inappropriately narrow, since the construct involved in the TLU domain — ability to perform academic writing tasks — involves other areas of language knowledge, as well as metacognitive strategies, and may involve topical knowledge and affective responses as well.

3) Test authenticity and interactiveness

Two elements that are crucial but often neglected by research in the test usefulness framework are authenticity and interactiveness.

3.1) Authenticity

A key element in the test usefulness framework is the concept of **target language use (TLU) domain**, which is defined as 'a set of specific language use tasks that the test taker is likely to encounter outside of the test itself, and to which we want our inferences about language ability to generalize'. A TLU task is an activity that an individual is engaged in by using the target language, so as to achieve a particular goal or objective in a particular situation (Bachman & Palmer 1996).

Authenticity is defined as 'the degree of correspondence of the characteristics of a given language test task to the features of a TLU task' (Bachman & Palmer 1996). It is considered as a critical quality because it relates the test quality to the domain of the TLU task and provides a measure of the correspondence between the test task and the TLU task. Authenticity 'provides a means for investigating the extent to which score interpretations generalize beyond performance on the test to language use' (Bachman & Palmer 1996).

For example, in tests which examine communicative ability, the test construct must facilitate communication tasks which closely resemble the situations a test-taker would face in the TLU domain, so that they are more authentic. In a language test, authenticity is sometimes distantly related with real communicative tasks by carrying out a series of linguistic skills rather than genuine operational ones for reliability and economy (Carroll 1980). A language test is said to be authentic when it mirrors as exactly as possible the real life non-test language tasks.

3.2) Interactiveness

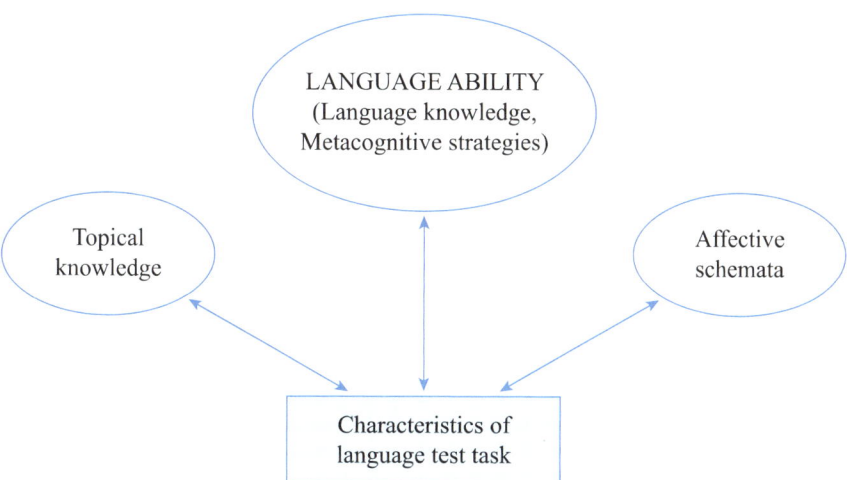

Interactiveness refers to 'the extent and type of involvement of the test taker's individual characteristics in accomplishing a test task' (Bachman & Palmer 1996). Specifically, individual characteristics, i.e. the test-taker's language ability (including language knowledge and strategic competence, or metacognitive strategies), topical knowledge and affective schemata, which are engaged in a test, may influence the candidate's performance on the test.

The double-headed arrows in the above figure represent the relationship, or interaction between an individual's language ability, topical knowledge, affective schemata and the characteristics of a test task. Due to these individual differences, the question is always how we could give each test-taker a fair chance. Bachman and Palmer (1996) further highlight that for a test task to show a high level of interactiveness depends on its degree of correspondence with construct validity. Thus the importance of well-defined test-taker characteristics and the construct is clear and self-evident. Otherwise, it is difficult to infer language ability based on an examinee's test performance when the test task does not demand that their language knowledge is used, despite a high level of interaction.

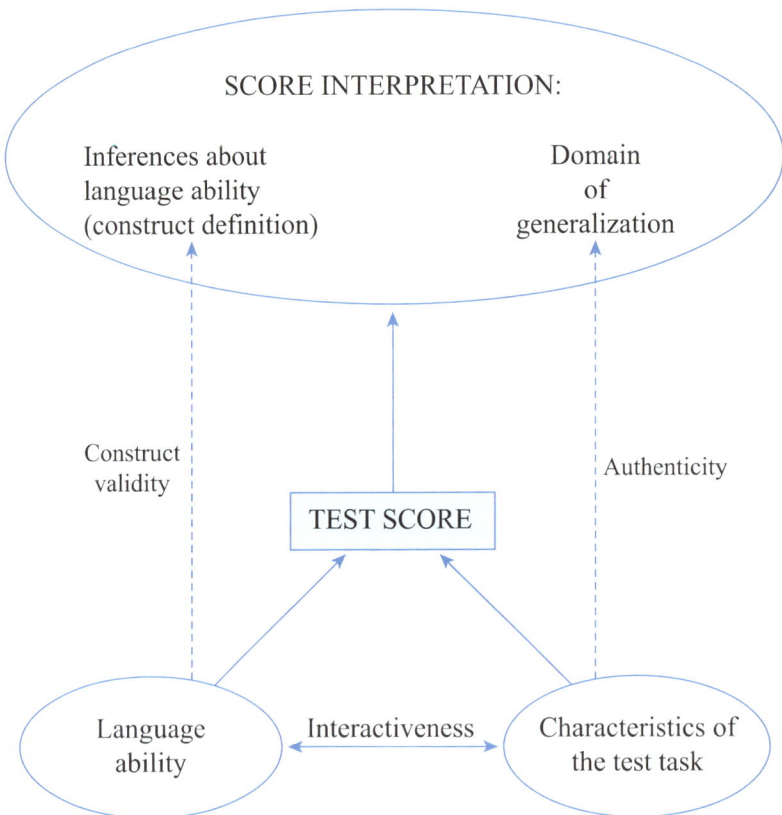

3.3) The distinction between authenticity and interactiveness and their relationship with construct validity

As is shown in the above figure, both authenticity and interactiveness are linked inextricably to construct, so validity is first required to clearly establish the distinction between the two notions. Authenticity pertains to the correspondence between the characteristics of a test task and those of the TLU task, and is thus related to the traditional notion of content validity. It is thus highly dependent on the extent to which test materials and conditions replicate the TLU situation (McNamara 2000). In the case of interactiveness, it indicates the interaction between the individual and the test task (of the test or TLU). That is, it is the degree of the test-taker's involvement when they are solving questions which assess their language competence, background knowledge, and affective schema.

4) Impact and practicality

Impact can be defined broadly in terms of the various ways in which test use affects society, an educational system at a macro level, and the individuals within these from a micro level (Bachman & Palmer 1996). Impact can be presented in the figure below.

4.1) Washback

When we deal with the notion of impact, we must first get to know an important aspect of impact referred to as the washback (Bachman & Palmer 1996) or backwash (Hughes 1989). The concept pertains to the effect of testing on teaching and learning, and can be beneficial or harmful. An example of harmful washback is if a test includes no direct spoken component, it is possible that the skill of speaking will be downplayed or ignored completely in the classroom, to the ultimate detriment of the candidate's ability in that area, while the course objective is meant to train them in the comprehensive language skills (including speaking). 'Teaching to the test' is an inevitable reality in many classrooms, and not only on those courses which aim to specifically prepare candidates for a particular exam. It is, therefore, important to ensure that the test is a good test, in order that the washback effect is a positive one.

4.2) Impact on test takers

Test takers can be affected in terms of three aspects (Bachman & Palmer 1996). First, the experiences of preparing for and taking the test have the potential for affecting those characteristics of the test takers. For example, when a high-stakes nation-wide public test is used for decision making, teaching may be focused on the specifications of the test for up to several years before the actual test, and the techniques needed in the test will be practiced in class. Secondly, the types of feedback which test-takers receive about their test performance are likely to affect them directly. Hence, there is a need to consider how to make feedback as relevant, complete and meaningful as possible. Finally, the decisions that may be made about the test takers on the basis of their test scores may directly affect them. In order for a fair test use to happen, test developers need to consider the various kinds of information, including scores from the test, which could be used in making the decisions, as well as their relative importance and the criteria that will be used.

4.3) Impact on teachers

In many occasions teaching to the test is found unavoidable. However, if a test is low in authenticity in the way that teachers feel what they teach is not relevant to the test, the test then could have harmful washback on instruction. To prevent this kind of negative impact on instruction, it, again, should be ensured that the test is a good one in order that the washback is a positive one.

4.4) Impact on society and educational system

Bachman (1990) points out that "tests [⋯] are virtually always intended to serve the needs of an educational system or of society at large". The very acts of administering and taking a test imply certain values and goals, and have consequences for society, the educational system, and the individuals in the system. This is of particular concern with high-stakes tests, which are used to make major decisions about large numbers of individuals (Bachman & Palmer 1996).

4.5) Practicality

Practicality is defined as "the relationship between the resources that will be required in the design, development, and use of the test and the resources that will be available for these activities" (Bachman & Palmer 1996). The resources required are specified as three types: human resources, material resources and time (Bachman and Palmer 1996). A practical test is one whose design, development, and use do not require more resources than are available.

<Practicality (from Bachman & Palmer 1996)>

$$\text{Practicality} = \frac{\text{Available resources}}{\text{Required resources}}$$

If practicality≥1, the test development and use is practical.
If practicality≤1, the test development and use is not practical.

Of the six qualities in Bachman and Palmer's framework of test usefulness, practicality holds a great deal of importance in high-stakes testing contexts (such as a large-scale placement test (Gennaro 2006). Of course, all six qualities are relevant for test fairness, but practicality is a particular concern if it is given a disproportionate amount of weight compared to the other five components.

⟨Checking Test Reliability⟩

There are ways of checking statistically to see if a test is reliable. They all share similar features, but they look at different aspects of reliability.

One way of checking is called **test/retest**. In this procedure the same test is given to the same people twice, usually with a gap of a week or so between the first test and the retest. A reliable test should give very similar results on the two occasions.

Another way of checking is called **split halves**. In this procedure the test is given to a group of learners and then when the test is being marked the items in the test are split into two groups. For example, if the test had 50 items, all the odd numbered items would be put into one group, and all the even numbered items would be in the other. The scores for the two groups of items are compared. For a reliable test the scores for the two groups of items would be similar.

A third way of checking is to make two **equivalent forms** of the same test. The two forms should be as similar to each other as possible without being exactly the same. When the same learners are tested with the two forms of the test, the scores for the two forms should be similar.

What is common about all of these ways of checking reliability is that they are trying to see if the test does the same job on all occasions that it is used. If performance on the test keeps changing when the same learners sit it again, it cannot be measuring what it is supposed to be measuring. A reliable test is not necessarily a valid test, but an unreliable test cannot be valid.

(B) Types of Testing: in terms of Purposes

Placement test	placing a student into a particular level
Diagnostic test	diagnosing aspects of a language learner (future-oriented)
Achievement test	limited to particular materials, after a course (past-oriented)
Proficiency test	testing global competence / overall ability
Aptitude test	predicting a person's future success in advance

(C) Types of Test items

only one skill, analytic	Discrete-point	Integrative	more than two skills, global
mean, median, standard deviation, percentile rank	Norm-referenced	Criterion-referenced	feedback on specific course or lesson objectives
at the end of a course	Summative	Formative	in the process of a course
performing a task related	Indirect	Direct	actually performing the task
select one of the alternatives	Selected-response	Constructed-response	develop S's own answer

<Selected-Response vs. Constructed-Response test>

A good deal of the assessment literature focuses on how to construct various forms of assessment tools, and it also provides numerous useful examples. One perspective on understanding the range and variety of assessment types examines how students are expected to respond when engaged in a specific type of assessment. The following figure presents such framework, along with examples of each assessment type. The typology is divided into two main divisions: tools that require students to select an answer or response and tools that require students to provide a response using language that they have learned. All the tools listed serve specific kinds of pedagogical purposes. For selected-response tools, students demonstrate learning by choosing a response from among a selection provided by the test maker. Such kinds of assessments are useful, for example, for determining what students know about a particular language structure or text; they are also useful for assessing beginning students who have a limited repertoire of language skills they can call on to interpret a test or produce a response. Multiple-choice and matching tests are the most familiar examples of this type of format.

To get a sense of how students use the language they have been studying, teachers choose assessments that require students to produce a response, ranging from short answers, such as filling in a blank or responding to a partner with words or phrases, to language performances requiring extended text, such as writing an essay or engaging in a role play.

selected-response format	constructed-response format			
	brief constructed response	performance-based assessment		
		product-focused	performance-focused	process-focused
Multiple choice	Gap filling	Essay	Oral presentation	Observation
True/false	Short answer	Story/play/poem	Dramatic reading	Reflection
Matching	Cloze	Portfolio	Role play	Journal
Same/different	Label a visual	Report	Debate	Learning log
Grammatical/ ungrammatical	Sentence completion	Video/audiotape	Interview	
	Error correction	Poster session	Online chats	
		Project		

The design of an assessment includes both the way in which a language performance is elicited — via either a selected- or constructed-response format — and a means of scoring that performance. For selected-response assessments, scoring appears fairly straightforward. Such assessments are scored via reference to an answer key that provides the predetermined correct selection for each item. Constructed-response formats require the use of a scoring guide — such as a rubric — to assist in recording and making judgments about a language performance. Because learners can generate a range of responses, it takes more time and expertise to score these assessments.

Just as each type of assessment serves specific pedagogical purposes, each format also presents specific challenges. As previously noted, selected-response formats provide opportunities for students to show what they know about language but not how effectively they can use that knowledge in communicative tasks. The format may also restrict the range of possible language areas to be tested since it is not always possible to come up with an appropriate range of options for possible answers. Given that these items provide a fixed number of answers, guessing has to be factored into how well students perform on these types of tests. Last, a good deal of time and effort is required to construct useful items. To ensure that such tests meet the teacher's intention in using them, they should be tried out beforehand, perhaps by other teachers.

When students are called on to generate language during a constructed-response type assessment, they provide evidence of how they can use that language. Tests that engage learners in producing extended oral and written texts also often engage students in demonstrating higher-order thinking skills. However, this format presents challenges as well. Because it takes longer for students to respond to these kinds of tests, teachers must allot more time to them in the classroom, reducing the number of items that can be included in a test and thus the range of student learning. Scoring the language that students produce also require a sizable investment of time on the part of the teacher as well as careful attention to the process of providing useful feedback and arriving at a score for the language performance.

(D) Multiple-choice Tests

(D1) Principles and Terms

principles	Practicality		easy to administer
	Reliability		consistent and dependable
terms	Stem (= Prompt)		the body of the items
	Options (= Alternatives)	Key	the correct response
		Distractors	the rest

(D2) Some guidelines for designing multiple-choice items

Since there will be occasions when multiple-choice items are appropriate, consider the following four guidelines for designing multiple-choice items for both classroom-based and large-scale situations.

1) Design each item to measure a single objective.

Consider the following item from a secondary school class in English at the intermediate level. The objective is *wh*- question:

> Test-takers hear: Where did George go after the party last night?
> Test-takers read: A. Yes, he did.
> B. because he was tired
> C. to Elaine's place for another party
> D. around eleven o'clock

Distractor A is designed to ascertain that the student knows the difference between an answer to a **wh-** question and a yes/no question. Distractors B and D, as well as the key item, C, test comprehension of the meaning of **where** as opposed to **why** and **when**. The objective has been directly addressed.

On the other hand, here is an item that was designed to test recognition of the correct word order of indirect questions:

> Excuse me, do you know ___?
>   A. where is the post office
>   B. where the post office is
>   C. where post office is

Distractor A is designed to lure students who don't know how to frame indirect questions and therefore serves as an efficient distractor. But what does distractor C actually measure? In fact, the missing definite article (the) is what J. K. Brown (2005) calls an 'unintentional clue' — a flaw that could cause the test-taker to eliminate C automatically. In the process, no assessment has been made of indirect questions in this distractor.

2) State both stem and options as simply and directly as possible.

We are sometimes tempted to make multiple-choice items too wordy. A good rule of thumb is to get directly to the point. Here's a negative example:

> My eyesight has really been deteriorating lately. I wonder if I need glasses. I think I'd better go the ____ to have my eyes checked.
>   A. pediatrician
>   B. dermatologist
>   C. optometrist

You might argue that the first two sentences of this item give it some authenticity and accomplish a bit of schema setting. But if you simply want a student to identify the type of medical professional that deals with eyesight issues, those sentences are superfluous. Moreover, by lengthening the stem, you have introduced a potentially confounding lexical item, **deteriorate**, that could distract the student unnecessarily.

Another rule of succinctness is to remove needless redundancy from your options. In the following item, 'which were' is repeated in all three options. It should be placed in the stem to keep the items as succinct as possible.

> We went to visit the temples, _____ fascinating.
>
>   A. which were beautiful
>   B. which were especially
>   C. which were holy

3) Make certain that the intended answer is clearly the only correct one.

In the test item described earlier, which turned out to be suitable, a draft of the item appeared as follows:

> Test-takers hear: Where did George go after the party last night?
> Test-takers read: A. Yes, he did.
>   B. because he was tired
>   C. to Elaine's place for another party
>   D. He went home around eleven o'clock

A quick consideration of distractor D reveals that it is a plausible answer (because of the mention of 'home'), along with the intended key, C. Eliminating unintended possible answers is often the most difficult problem of designing multiple-choice items. With only a minimum of context in each stem, a wide variety of responses may be perceived as correct.

> **Suggestions for revising your test:**
>
> 1. Are the directions to each section absolutely clear?
> 2. Is there an example item for each section? If not, are the directions and format so familiar to students that they will clearly understand the tasks they are being asked to perform?
> 3. Does each item measure a specified objective?
> 4. Is there a single correct answer for each question?
> 5. Is each item stated in clear, simple language?
> 6. Does each multiple-choice item have appropriate distractors; that is, are the wrong items clearly wrong and yet sufficiently "alluring" that they aren't ridiculously easy?
> 7. Is the difficulty of each item appropriate for your students?
> 8. Is the language of each item sufficiently authentic?
> 9. Is there a balance between easy and difficult items?
> 10. Do the sum of the items and the test as a whole adequately reflect the learning objectives?

(D3) Item Analysis

Distractor Efficiency	luring a sufficient number of test-takers & evenly distributed
Item Facility	(= Item Difficulty) easy or difficult for the group of test-takers
Item Discrimination	differentiating between high- and low-ability test-takers

‹Item Facility›

Item facility (**IF**) is the extent to which an item is easy or difficult for the proposed group of test-takers.

$$IF = \frac{\text{\# of students answering the item correctly}}{\text{Total \# of students responding to that item}}$$

‹Item Discrimination›

Item discrimination (**ID**) is the extent to which an item differentiates between high- and low-ability test-takers. For example:

$$ID = \frac{\text{High group no. correct - low group no. correct}}{\frac{1}{2} \times \text{total of your two comparison groups}}$$

(E) Integrative Testing

Dictation	listening + writing
Cloze test	closing the gap with a calculated guess (the table below)
C-test	some variations on standard cloze testing, the second half of every other word is obliterated

‹Cloze test›

Fixed-ratio	deletion procedure	every seventh word (± two)
Rational		all words according to grammatical or discourse functions
Exact	word scoring method	only the exact word in the origin
Appropriate		any word grammatically correct and making good sense

(E4) Pragmatic Language Testing

At about the same time as the ***direct approach*** was being promoted, but essentially independently of this, Oller was conducting a program of factor analytic research that led to his unitary competence hypothesis. This hypothesis stated that language proficiency is essentially a single unitary ability, rather than separate skills and components. In the most extensive discussion of this research and the theory that underlay it, Oller (1979) identified the general factor from his empirical research as 'pragmatic expectancy grammar', which he defined as 'the psychologically real system that governs the use of a language in an individual who knows that language'.

Having defined the ability to be tested, Oller then discussed Carroll's earlier notion of 'critical performance' and described a 'pragmatic test', which he distinguished from both discrete-point and integrative test, as 'any procedure or task that causes the learner to process sequences of elements in a language that conform to the normal contextual constraints of that language, and which requires the learner to relate sequences of linguistic elements via pragmatic mappings to extralinguistic context'. Examples of pragmatic tests were the cloze, dictation, the oral interview, and composition writing.

Oller's conceptualization of the ability to be tested as a single, global ability, was, in my (Bachman's) view, both simple and sophisticated. The notion of a single unitary ability meant that language testers did not need to concern themselves about testing the bits and pieces of language, while the notion of pragmatic expectancy drew upon current theory in both linguistics and pragmatics. Similarly, the types of tasks Oller proposed, such as the cloze and the dictation, were appealing to practitioners, since they promised to be both valid and easy to construct. The research upon which Oller's claims for a unitary competence were based was eventually rejected, and Oller himself (1983) admitted that the unitary competence hypothesis was wrong. Nevertheless, Oller's work has had a major and lasting impact on the field. In terms of language testing practice, his work was instrumental in reviving the use of the dictation and cloze as acceptable methods for testing language ability. His conceptualization of language ability as pragmatic expectancy grammar also foreshadowed later notions of strategic competence.

(F) Alternative Assessments

Portfolios	a purposeful collection of students' work
Dialogue Journals	an interaction between T and S thru dialogues or responses
Conferences	a conversation between T and S about a draft
Observations	assessing students without their awareness for authenticity
Self- and Peer-Assessment	for autonomy and for cooperative learning

⟨Dialogue Journals⟩

Journals are written conversations between students and teachers. Dialogue journals have a number of important benefits as in the following table.

[Table 1] Benefits of dialogue journals

1. They provide useful information for individualizing instruction, for example: writing skills, writing strategies, students' experiences in and outside of school, learning processes, attitudes and feeling about themselves, their teachers, schooling, their interest, expectations, and goals.
2. They increase opportunities for functional communication between students and teachers.
3. They give students opportunities to use language for genuine communication and personalized reading.
4. They permit teachers to individualize language teaching by modeling writing skills in their responses to student journals.
5. They promote the development of certain writing skills.
6. They enhance student involvement in and ownership of learning.

Journals can also be used to gain insights about students' writing skills in the second language and the strategies they use when writing, if their entries are spontaneous and free flowing, including any or all errors, correction, and editing. Students should not feel that their language must be correct or perfect. If they feel they lack certain methods of written expression, they should be encouraged to ask for help from their teachers or fellow students and to use whatever means of expression they have, even pictures. Evidence in students' journals of recurrent or specific writing difficulties can be used to plan writing activities or lessons of a more formal nature at another time. If regular entries are made, journals can provide a continuous record of students' writing development.

Because of their personal, student-centered nature, journals have the added advantage that they allow students opportunities to express themselves personally about their interests, goals, and desires using the second language. Table 2 identifies certain writing skills whose development can be promoted by dialogue journal conversations; these are particularly relevant to second language learners in the elementary and secondary grades. Journals provide teachers with opportunities to assess their students' ability to express themselves personally in writing using the second language without the pressures that students may feel during whole class activities.

[Table 2] Literacy skills promoted by journal conversations

Topic initiation	Awareness and use of print
Topic variety	Creativity and independence in writing
Elaboration of topics	Grammar
Metacommunication about reading and writing	Language functions
Audience awareness	

An Example of Dialogue Journal

Journal Entry:

Yesterday at about eight o'clock I was sitting in front of my table holding a fork and eating tasteless noodles which I usually really like to eat but I lost my taste yesterday because I didn't feel well. I had a headache and a fever. My head seemed to be broken. I sometimes felt cold, sometimes hot. I didn't feel comfortable standing up and I didn't feel comfortable sitting down. I hated everything around me. It seemed to me that I got a great pressure from the atmosphere and I could not breath. I was so sleepy since I had taken some medicine which functioned as an antibiotic.

The room was so quiet. I was there by myself and felt very solitary. This dinner reminded me of my mother. Whenever I was sick in China, my mother always took care of me and cooked rice gruel, which has to cook more than three hours and is very delicious, I think. I would be better very soon under the care of my mother. But yesterday, I had to cook by myself even though I was sick, The more I thought, the less I wanted to eat, Half an hour passed. The noodles were cold, but I was still sitting there and thinking about my mother, Finally I threw out the noodles and went to bed.

MingLing

Teacher's Response:

This is a powerful piece of writing because you really communicate what you were feeling. You used vivid details, like "… eating tasteless noodles …", "my head seemed to be broken …" and "… rice gruel, which has to cook more than three hours and is very delicious." These make it easy for the reader to picture exactly what you were going through. The other strong point about this piece is that you bring the reader full circle by beginning and ending with "the noodles."

Being alone when you are sick is difficult. Now, I know why you were so quiet in class.

If you want to do another entry related to this one, you could have a dialogue with your "sick" self. What would your "healthy" self say to the "sick" self? Is there some advice that could be exchanged about how to prevent illness or how to take care of yourself better when you do get sick? Start the dialogue with your "sick" self speaking first.

(Brown 2015)

(G) Holistic vs. Analytic Scoring

Holistic scoring	a systematic set of descriptors, for Practicality
Analytic scoring	descriptors on several elements, for Washback

최시원 전공영어 영어교육학 Practical　　　ISBN 979-11-91391-20-6

- 발행일 · 2021년 2月 19日　초판 1쇄
- 발행인 · 이용중
- 저　자 · 최시원
- 발행처 · 도서출판 배움
- 주　소 · 서울시 영등포구 영등포로 400 신성빌딩 2층 (신길동)
- 주문 및 배본처 · Tel : 02) 813-5334　Fax : 02) 814-5334

| 저자와의 협의하에 인지생략 |

본서의 無斷轉載·複製를 禁함. 본서의 무단 전재·복제행위는 저작권법 제136조에 의거 5년 이하의 징역 또는 5,000만 원 이하의 벌금에 처하거나 이를 병과할 수 있습니다. 파본은 구입처에서 교환하시기 바랍니다.

정가 21,000 원